# BENEATH

## THE

# METROPOLIS

# BENEATH THE METROPOLIS

## THE SECRET LIVES OF CITIES

# ALEX MARSHALL

EDITOR, DAVID EMBLIDGE

CARROLL & GRAF PUBLISHERS
NEW YORK

BENEATH THE METROPOLIS:
*The Secret Lives of Cities*

Carroll & Graf Publishers
An Imprint of Avalon Publishing Group, Inc.
245 West 17<sup>th</sup> Street
11<sup>th</sup> Floor
New York, NY 10011

AVALON
publishing group incorporated

ISBN-10: 0-7867-2026-3
ISBN-13: 978-0-78672-026-2

9 8 7 6 5 4 3 2 1

Printed in China
Distributed by Publishers Group West

*To Kristi Barlow, for her love, support and eagle-eye editing.*

# TABLE OF CONTENTS

# BENEATH

## THE

# METROPOLIS

### THE SECRET LIVES OF CITIES

# INTRODUCTION

THE HEART OF NEW YORK CITY'S NEW THIRD WATER TUNNEL IS THE valve chamber: a control center in the Bronx as long as three football fields and 250 feet underground. There, water rushes in from huge pipes and, through a series of computer-controlled valves, is redirected out to the boroughs of Queens, Brooklyn, and Manhattan. This hidden, and by and large unknown, machinery makes it possible to turn on a faucet and get pure, clean water without a thought. Clearly, to say that water comes from a faucet is only the beginning.

This book tells the rest of the story.

From the lost secret chambers of a first-century religious cult under the streets of Rome to the steel and glass trains that whisper through the Paris Métro, and the murky rivers and streams that run under London—these subterranean regions reveal a city's character— its purpose, its past, and perhaps its future. Life below the street tells us how cities survive, grow, and change; of engineering brilliance, political upheaval, and hidden history—a DNA imprint of what goes on aboveground.

Yet when most people walk down the street in a big city, they don't think much about the labyrinth beneath, which may hold anything from deep water tunnels to secret command posts to forgotten cemeteries. Hidden from plain view, and sometimes containing history that people would like to forget, these underground realms avail themselves only to the curious.

Welcome to the world beneath the metropolis.

If you were to arrive in a city from underneath, and if you knew what to look for, you could assemble at least some idea of what to expect up above. Under Manhattan, for example, you would see row after row of steel girders set in rectangular frames. Some compose the walls of subway tunnels. Others support the high skyscrapers that the subways serve. You could surmise just from seeing that world of steel that a dense, mighty city lay overhead. Similarly, if you looked beneath Cairo, located on the banks of the Nile, you would see polluted water rotting away the foundations of ancient brick buildings. You would also notice a relative absence of advanced infrastructure—except for some major subway and sewer projects actively under construction. From such evidence, you could intuit that Cairo is a modernizing, third-world city with a very long history. While the underground of a city does not give us an exact map of what sits above, it does give us a good idea of it.

To decode and understand what's beneath the metropolis, it is helpful to organize the various elements into three distinct realms:

- Archeology is the study of the physical remains of the past—the graves of our ancestors, and their temples, streets, buildings, and monuments.
- Infrastructure (as we use the term in this book) is the vital framework of machinery and equipment that carries people, electricity, waste, water, voices, and digital bytes beneath the earth.

Fitting somewhere between archeology and infrastructure are the inert spaces—the iron and concrete foundations of skyscrapers, the hushed basements of libraries, and the cold spaces of parking garages . . . or bomb shelters. There is not much activity in these hidden places, but they are still essential to a functioning city.

All of these realms are found below the streets of any great city: an underground world that is a ghostly mirror image of the space above. Even a lowly sewer pipe or electrical cable is laid out in a fashion that reflects its ground-level counterpart. The sewers of Paris, for instance, laid in clean, efficient lines, reveal the French expertise in both technology and its government's inclination for comprehensive state planning. To study an urban underground is to study a less volatile version of the corresponding world above, because the underground systems change at a slower rate than the visible world at the surface.

## GEOLOGY

Great cities are almost always built near water—rivers or the harbors of oceans and large lakes. The urban need for transportation and shipping services is the prevailing motivation but waterside locations prove a constant challenge because the land is often marshy, and the soil unstable. Thus most large cities have at one point or another been forced to drain away water, to create usable land from what was mostly muck. For some cities, such as New Orleans or Venice, this is a constant challenge. Such difficulties are overcome because the city's location is ideal in other ways, generally for commerce or defense.

Case in point: Chicago is built on soil that is virtually quicksand. Yet the city led the way in the construction of the steel-frame skyscraper, inspired by Louis Sullivan and other architects in Chicago in the late nineteenth century. To deal with the unstable soil, the architects and developers invented a new type of foundation, essentially a latticework of logs and concrete on which the buildings "floated." New York's geology is very different. Its soaring skyscrapers in downtown Manhattan, and the even bigger buildings in midtown, are  built on giant slabs of Manhattan Schist, an extremely hard rock that generally rises closer to the surface in both downtown and midtown, as if magically preparing the way for skyscraper districts. This has led some commentators to conclude that the presence of these great slabs of rock was the principal reason for the location of these skyscraper districts. But a review of historical evidence shows that companies and developers constructed these tall buildings principally to be near central transportation hubs, which then as now were magnets for commerce and business. The presence of good rock for strong foundations was simply an added benefit.

A variety of natural forces shaped the landscapes that lie underneath and around the great cities. Where New York sits today, tens of thousands of years ago, great glaciers swept across the plain, leaving jagged rock outcroppings in their wake. The Dutch, who first saw Manhattan in the early 1600s, described it as an island of hills. Today the gently undulating slopes remain, save for one steep hill at the north end of the island, inside Inwood Hill Park. If you stand in the middle of Fifth Avenue by Rockefeller Center and look south, you can detect the curve  of the hills as the street rolls downtown toward Washington Square. Broadway, meandering diagonally across Manhattan, in contrast to the city's rational grid, follows the path of an old watercourse, now invisible to anyone above ground. In London, a dozen or so rivers and streams once fed into the Thames; they are now covered over, and many form part of the central sewer system. In Cairo and Rome, the Nile and the Tiber rivers, respectively, used to flood their banks annually, fertilizing the surrounding soil but making construction difficult. Both were tamed in the late nineteenth century with dams, canals, and other devices, making more monumental city building possible.

Because the seacoast is often the edge of a continental tectonic plate, many of the world's great cities are also built on or near fault lines that periodically move, toppling much of the city above them. Earthquakes have repeatedly destroyed substantial parts or nearly all of San Francisco, Mexico City, and Tokyo, to name just a few such casualties.

But earthquakes are unusual events, and geologic safety is generally trumped by convenience of location. San Francisco has a stunning natural harbor that allowed it to become a commercial center of the American West. Tokyo has an extraordinary harbor as well. Mexico City is built on top of Tenochtitlán, an ancient Aztec city that the Spanish, for political reasons, wanted to raze and build anew as a Spanish colonial capital.

## UNDER THE WEATHER—MONTREAL'S VILLE SOUTERRAINE

Extremes of heat and cold can push people underground. It's no accident then that Montreal and Moscow, each with severe winters, have built some of their prime shopping space underground. Montreal, in Canada's Québec Province, is another city we might well have featured in this book. Its famous Underground City, or Ville Souterraine, opened in the 1960s and for decades was one of the city's top tourist attractions. Much of Ville Souterraine was developed in anticipation of Expo '67, Montreal's successful world's fair. At the time, the underground shopping spaces had the air of novelty and modernity. These underground "streets" were given chic French names like "Champs-Élysées" and "rue de Versailles." The system includes passageways under the city's prominent cathedral and Montreal University, as well as the central business district. By some estimates there are more than twenty-six hundred stores under this French-Canadian city.

An estimated half-million people still use Montreal's Underground City every day in wintertime. One reason it functions so effectively is that it was built in concert with the city's admirable Metro (the subway, running quietly on rubber wheels, an engineering idea imported from Paris). Place Ville-Marie, a skyscraper and civic plaza above the underground shopping and cultural center, was designed by I. M. Pei and opened in 1962. The first Metro line opened in 1966. The "streets" of Montreal's underground are laid out as constellations around individual subway stations; they don't all connect with each other. These constellations have separate names, such as Place Bonaventure, and they also connect to high-rise office buildings, which typically have three to four levels beneath them. In all, there are approximately twenty miles of underground passages beneath Montreal.

Most of Montreal's underground shopping world is privately owned. Private companies are sometimes (although not always) more efficient than public agencies at building underground facilities, but they may be less comprehensive in their planning or coordination. In Montreal's Underground City, for example, it has been difficult to find a map that shows all the underground districts because so many are owned by separate private companies.

 ## ARCHEOLOGY

Beneath every large metropolis are forgotten streets, buildings, tunnels, graves, chambers, and other detritus that serve little active purpose today. But beneath the millennium cities—those that have lasted thousands of years—are entire ancient worlds.

A thriving, inhabited city rises over time, as streets are paved and repaved, new buildings are built atop old buildings, and dust itself gradually settles into layers. Over a century, a growing city will increase in elevation by inches or sometimes feet; over centuries, that adds up to many feet, and what is above ground gradually becomes the substrata. Rome, which is one of the longest continually inhabited cities in the Western world, has risen as much as fifty feet in the last 2,000 years.

As with a palimpsest (a medieval parchment that was repeatedly erased and written on), cities are continually built and rebuilt in layers that are visible over time. Old streets and buildings are erased but leave traces of their former lives. In Paris, today's Boulevard St. Michel, a central thoroughfare across the island that was the original city (Île de la Cité, in the River Seine), follows the same path as the major Roman thoroughfare in Lutetia, the ancient city predating Paris. Notre Dame Cathedral is built on top of the site of an old pagan temple, a building strategy common to churches in many cities. In Rome, some of the ancient sewers not only still exist but are still used as central components of the contemporary waste removal system. Under Moscow, there are secret chambers built by the city's Communist leaders in the twentieth century near other secret chambers built by Czars in the fifteenth. Underneath the fabled 172-acre Forbidden City in Beijing, lies the body of Mao Tse-tung within chambers built by the country's emperors in previous centuries.

Over time, the process of building and rebuilding a city can blur the boundaries between above- and belowground. In Chicago, engineers raised the streets in the nineteenth century, then built multiple boulevards above them in the twentieth. Consequently, when you are standing on Wacker Drive, on what may appear to be a surface street, you are actually several stories above older streets and even farther above the historic level of the ground. New York's Park Avenue, with its elegant apartment buildings and flower-decked median, is in fact a platform of steel, concrete, and macadam over railroad tracks feeding into midtown's Grand Central Station.

The underground of a city also acts as its unconscious, storing away bits of itself that the present city might like to forget. In colonial New York, everyone knew that slaves and other African Americans were buried at the African Burial Ground in what is now Lower Manhattan. The site was used for two centuries. But after slavery was made illegal in 1827, the city and its leaders forgot about the cemetery, as they began to repress or deny the memory that slavery was ever an integral part of the economy of a city that eventually boasted about the Statue of Liberty in its harbor. It took the rediscovery of that African Burial Ground, inadvertently exposed when the foundations of a new office building were being dug, to bring all that disquieting history back to light.

Before 1800, with a few exceptions like Rome, underground realms were inert spaces, rarely used. They held the bones of dead citizens, as in Paris, or books in the Czar's library under Moscow, or chambers to torture dissidents in other cities. But starting with the Industrial Revolution in the 1800s, cities grew dramatically in population and wealth, requiring the creation of active systems of management. The huge water pipes of New York and the sewers of Paris were manifestations of modernity. Other pipes brought in natural gas to fuel the factories, light the streets, and warm the ovens of domestic stoves. New York and Paris had innovative pneumatic tube systems to shoot mail and messages around town faster than a man could deliver them on foot. The great age of subways began when cities burrowed beneath the earth to create tunnels for trains that would carry millions of people. Cities became gigantic, containing not just a few hundred thousand people, but a few million, or tens of millions of people. The modern metropolis was born.

Along with modernity came less praiseworthy aspects of the subterranean regions. Homeless people—the sick, the poor, and occasionally criminals—learned how to survive in the unclaimed or less supervised underground spaces of every city. They carved out illegal spaces that are sometimes ingenious, even relatively comfortable, in subway tunnels, steam vents, crypts, and other obscure domains. New York City had thousands of people living beneath Grand Central Terminal in half-used or abandoned tunnels before the station was renovated in the 1990s.

Underground spaces have their own allure to others as well. In most major cities, there are unofficial groups whose sole purpose is to delve, often illegally, into the hidden stories of that city's underworld. Paris has its "Cataphiles" who investigate the city's catacombs and are pursued by "Catacops." Sydney has its "Cave Clan" who explore, and hold parties, in the city's many tunnels, and underground London receives close scrutiny from an organization called "Subterranean Britannica," which surveys and documents the city's lightless depths.

## INFRASTRUCTURE

Cities are often thought of as self-operating organisms; they seem to have just happened. In fact, the complex water, sewer, and transportation systems that public officials control and operate (and that in turn help determine how a city grows) are always the result of specific choices, usually by government. Some of these choices, such as constructing a regional water system, are deliberate. Other underground patterns reflect historical events, and in a sense are not choices but indirect consequences. Take Boston, a medium-sized American city not featured in this book, which has a less extensive subway system compared to New York's. One explanation is that Boston is more fragmented politically than New York. In 1898, New York City (then just the island of Manhattan) merged with neighboring Brooklyn, the Bronx, Staten Island, and Queens, to form one sprawling metropolis. This made the challenge of building subway lines in the early twentieth century under the water and across these jurisdictional lines much easier politically.

Boston, by contrast, was torn by intense political battles in the late nineteenth century between native Protestants and immigrant Irish Catholics. Protestant towns such as Cambridge and Brookline, fearful of being consumed by Catholic-majority Boston, incorporated themselves as cities to stave off annexation. This made building subways across these city lines much more difficult in the following decades. Although Boston built the first subway in the United States, opening in 1896, key subway lines into some of these separate "cities" were not constructed until the 1970s. Boston today is still isolated politically in its metropolitan area, compared to New York, with about 1.5 million people inside Manhattan alone, compared to 8 million in the five boroughs of New York.

Underground infrastructure is so important that many cities actually fill in waterways to create more land—under which they can then place more systems. Substantial sections of San Francisco, New York, Tokyo, and many other seaports are made by dumping stone and earth into the water, and beneath these landfills lie transportation and utility networks. In Boston, the graceful Back Bay neighborhood of elegant townhouses was created next to the city in the nineteenth century by dumping garbage and debris into a shallow, swampy area (known as "the Back Bay Fens" from which baseball's Fenway Park, built in 1932, gets its name). People walking today down Boston's Newbury Street little imagine that the expensive designer boutiques are built upon the lowly castoffs of their ancestors.

Cities are unnatural creations. Those that thrive overcome major obstacles that would have defeated other places. Shortages of water, transportation hurdles, and other complications require a combination of political and commercial clout—even military effort—to ensure the future growth of a city. And it doesn't always work. Great historic cities like Troy have disappeared. A number of colonial-era American cities—from Salem to Providence to Baltimore—arguably could have emerged, at one time or another, as some of the United States' biggest and most important urban centers, only to be held back by some combination of accidents and obstacles. New York, which made some key choices correctly in the 1800s, ultimately dwarfed all other early communities.

Do market forces create the infrastructure of great cities? Commerce drives great cities, it is true. Cities survive for the most part because they generate wealth, which allows millions of people to live in them. But it is the choices made by government that allow commerce to happen.

There was no direct market force behind New York's third water tunnel, which will take a half-century to build, cost billions of dollars, and burrow up to 1,000 feet beneath the earth. Yet without such underground machinery, North America's leading city could someday lack sufficient water, a frightening prospect. The tunnel will back up two earlier water tunnels created in the early part of the twentieth century—water conduits, like the subways between Brooklyn and Manhattan, that enabled New York to reach new heights of commercial success and sustain even larger populations.

And although subway and train lines are expensive and not profit centers in and of themselves, they enable cities to grow their economies and prosper. With a subway system, an urban center can achieve an intensity of economic and cultural life that would be impossible otherwise. The rents per square foot in midtown Manhattan or the Right Bank of Paris reach $700 a square foot per month, versus $10 a square foot in many midsize American cities. These high rents are justified by commerce, which in turn generates the high tax receipts necessary to support the intensive and extensive underground infrastructure of a great city.

Building anything underground is also many times more expensive than above-ground construction. To afford it, cities usually depend not only on their own resources but, directly and indirectly, on those of people and lands around them. It's no accident that of the dozen cities featured in this book, many were or are centers of world empires of some sort. In some fashion or other, the resources to build their great subways or water systems were sucked in from their colonies or from neighboring territories the cities controlled, at least commercially. Rome, for example, was the capital of an ancient empire that spanned the Mediterranean, and in modern times became capital of unified Italy. Tokyo has been the capital of Japan since the mid-nineteenth century, as it conquered neighboring lands, militarily in the early twentieth, and then after World War II, commercially. Beijing has been the capital of China, the world's most populous country (a land of diverse ethnic and language groups, scattered over a vast region), on and off for more than a thousand years. Paris is the city from which the nation of France was created, as the city defeated and absorbed neighboring principalities in the Middle Ages and the Renaissance. London was the capital of Great Britain, on whose empire the sun famously "never set." Chicago has been, in effect, the economic capital of the American Midwest, bolstered by resources and powers transferred to it from the federal government. And New

York, although only briefly the political capital of the United States, has been the commercial and financial center of the country during the last two centuries, as America grew from a fragile colony on the East Coast, to a country that spanned a continent and dominated the world.

Only cities that can draw on great resources of wealth can sustain and construct more of these great projects underground. Buenos Aires was another city we could have featured here. This Argentinian city was poised for greatness in the early decades of the twentieth century, built South America's first subway system in 1917 (before even Chicago's) and a half century ahead of Beijing, Mexico City, or Washington had underground transportation. A cosmopolitan city of broad boulevards and sidewalk cafés, Buenos Aires is often compared to Paris. In the 1890s, during its golden era, the city built the 4,000 Teatro Colón, an opera house and theater with seven tiers of balconies. But the theater is almost as impressive below ground, where a small artistic empire spreads out beneath neighboring streets. Rehearsal spaces, studios, and set workshops reach fifteen stories underground. Thousands of costumes and stage props are stored here, and this is also where the opera's lavish sets are made. After World War II, Buenos Aires and Argentina declined into economic malaise and such underground feats are now beyond this city's capacity. A new subway line did open in 1997, but the system as a whole remains small for a city of its size.

The infrastructure for any city can be ranked in importance. At the bottom of the pyramid is water delivery, the most important public service. Citizens cannot survive without it, and great cities use huge quantities of this precious liquid. Whether ancient Rome, which tapped streams and rivers hundreds of miles away, or Mexico City, which is lifting water a mile and a half from the valleys below, cities perform Herculean tasks to quench their thirst and increase their capacity for growth. Great pipes are almost always buried beneath the earth, often at remarkable depths.

Next comes sewage. An enormous city needs to dispose of its waste efficiently to prevent disease and deterioration. And as streets became paved and impervious to water, cities needed drainage facilities for rain and rivers, which would otherwise flood roads and buildings.

After water, sewage, and waste systems, comes transportation. Train lines beneath the earth are phenomenally expensive to build and only the largest and wealthiest cities have them in any number. But they allow a city to achieve the fantastically high densities that, in turn, make the contemporary metropolis so unique. The skyscraper districts of New York, Tokyo, and Hong Kong, where millions of people work within a few dozen square blocks, could not exist without the subways beneath them, which quickly deliver huge numbers of people.

Commerce, industry and shopping have always clustered around transportation hubs, whether they be a railroad station, a great port, or a superhighway interchange.

New York's first skyscraper district arose in downtown Manhattan adjacent to the historic harbor, where ships docked from all over the world, and near the site of the present World Trade Center, where an early train station was located. The later skyscrapers of midtown Manhattan were built near Grand Central Terminal and Pennsylvania Station, the great train hubs that carried millions of people in and out of the city on underground tracks. Once these Manhattan rails were in place, the passenger stations became as immovable as the harbor itself. In 1869, financier Cornelius Vanderbilt constructed the first Grand Central Depot at Forty-second Street (then the outskirts of town) because New York still prohibited steam-driven trains from traveling below that line, due to the danger of an explosion within the heavily populated city. Later, this danger of fire subsided as railroad technology became more reliable. But by then the network of tracks was set in place, and when Grand Central Terminal was reconstructed in 1913, it spurred developers to situate the Chrysler Building and other early skyscrapers in clusters nearby in today's Midtown Manhattan. Robert Yaro, president of the urban planning group the Regional Plan Association, in New York, calls Midtown "the original 'Edge City'" because it arose around the train stations the same way that contemporary clusters of shopping malls and office parks arise around suburban highway interchanges. These suburban areas are often known now as "Edge Cities."

The transportation capacity of subways and commuter rail systems are truly astonishing. In 2003 in Portland, Oregon, for example, a new streetcar line was considered a success because it carried 4,800 trips a day (one person taking two distinct journeys, say, to and from work, is counted as two "trips.") One subway train can deliver that many people in a few minutes in Moscow, Seoul, or New York. The Lexington Avenue line in New York City (one of twenty-five lines) handles more than a million trips every weekday. Most of these major subway systems were built before World War II, when labor was cheaper and crowding in the cities was extreme enough to push the collective will to build them. It's a paradox that even as technology has progressed, building new subway lines and similar underground projects seems to have become more difficult in the industrialized world, in part because the price of labor has risen so much. More advanced nations are no longer able to deploy thousands of workers on a project. It's just too expensive. A country like China, which is undertaking an unprecedented subway development program in Beijing, Shanghai, and other cities, relies on both advanced technology and an inexhaustible supply of relatively inexpensive labor.

Finally comes an assortment of services that are increasingly vital to modern cities (and almost always housed underground), such as electric lines, gas pipes, telephone cables, and the newer fiber-optic telecommunication lines. While these systems are indispensable to a modern metropolis, just how they are built depends on the economic and political systems in each city. In New York or San Francisco, such private companies as Verizon (communications) and Con Edison (power) lay out and manage much of this infrastructure. In Beijing or Paris, the state plans and supervises the installation of such infrastructure more directly.

## THE CITIES

The worlds beneath the metropolis are so many and so varied that one could easily write a dozen books on the subject. Every major city around the globe has its own rich story that would merit a full volume. For this book, we chose twelve principal cities (each featured in its own chapter) to represent the cultural diversity of several continents. We also focus on these cities for the particular range of their stories, each of which illustrates a different aspect of the forces that shape and sustain cities in general. Venture beneath each metropolis that follows:

- *Beijing*, one of the ancient capitals of Asia, shows the whims of power in the miles of tunnels underneath its streets built with hand tools by peasants because the country's aging Communist leader, Mao Tse-tung, demanded their construction.
- *Cairo*, situated at the delta of Africa's most important river and in a strategically powerful corner of the Mediterranean world, illustrates the challenges that a third-world "megacity" must tackle in the form of sewers, subways, and trash if it is to control its destiny.
- *Chicago*, in the middle of the United States, was once a frontier wilderness village overlooking a swamp. The story of how the city built its sewers and streets, in the end like Hercules changing the path and directional flow of an entire river, demonstrates the lengths to which ambitious business leaders will go to conquer a resistant and harsh geology and geography.
- *London* is built over swamps, rivers, and many layers of history, stretching back to the Stone Age. In its diversity and richness, London's underground reveals the country's steadily evolving commercial and political systems as the city that led the Industrial Revolution in late eighteenth and early nineteenth centuries.
- *Mexico City* today, now the capital of a modern industrialized nation, was once the capital of the ancient Aztec culture and then became the focal point of Spanish colonialism in the Americas. At present, Mexico City struggles to dispose of its waste and to deliver clean water to its millions of inhabitants living high on a mountain plateau. Many of the actions of the city's initial colonial rulers ended

up planting the seeds of later disasters, which the country is now working to overcome.

- *Moscow*, capital of the now-dissolved Soviet Union, manifests a different ideology of public spaces in its fabulous subway stations. In its forgotten underground towns and subways built for protection during a potential nuclear war, it represents the history of cold war anxiety. In its Czarist secret chambers, it discloses Russia's long and often cruel history.
- *New York*, with its enormous, efficient, but unglamorous subway, its water and the rest of its underground system of infrastructure, shows how the relentless drive to make money can result in some one the highest levels of public services per square foot in the world.
- *Paris*, with its neatly crisscrossing network of sewers worthy of touring and its modern, high-tech Métro (subway), proves that a state can blend the values of beauty and efficiency, even underground.
- *Rome* has layers upon layers beneath its present surface, entire empires and eras buried with ancient streets and buildings. The city's underground shows how long and rich history can be.
- *San Francisco*, like Chicago, has struggled to beat geology, but the most serious burden is its perilous and unfortunate location above California's destructive earthquake fault lines that can shift and topple the city with little warning.
- *Sydney*, isolated "down under" in Australia, far from its industrialized brethren to the north, has quietly pursued the construction of underground roads, parking garages, and other services as a means to enhance livability and attract international business.
- *Tokyo*, the largest city on a crowded island nation, has shopping malls and subways packed beneath it in a quantity and density that amazes. They illustrate the extent to which a city can burrow beneath the earth under the pressure of many demands, but particularly that of astronomical real-estate values.

As we discuss the major cities listed above, we also detour frequently to look at special underground features of other fascinating cities scattered around the globe, such as Venice, Boston, and Montreal.

## THE FUTURE

Given how unpredictable history has been, can we predict how cities and their underground infrastructures will change in years to come? What is certain is that the past will serve as a foundation for the future. In Paris, workers have recently strung high-tech fiber optic cables using late-twentieth-century technology right inside the city's spacious brick sewers built with the "latest technology"—in the mid-nineteenth century.

Certainly the rise of telecommunications and the Internet will reshape cities, as they have already. But just how, is fiercely debated. Some experts say that the ease of telecommunications will allow people to disperse and that dense concentrations of people in cities will no longer be necessary. In 1995, the U.S. Office of Technology Assessment released a report called "The Technological Reshaping of Metropolitan America," which pointed to how telecommunications had allowed once-centralized jobs like check processing and insurance adjusting to leave expensive center cities. "The new technology system is creating an ever more spatially dispersed and foot-loose economy, which in turn is causing metropolitan areas to be larger, more dispersed and less densely populated," the report says.

But there are conflicting indicators. In a global economy, it may be more valuable than ever for many people to work together in a small area of dense concentration, which would mean the fortunes of old-fashioned tightly packed cities could soar as well. The 2000 U.S. Census showed that New York City, during the height of the Internet boom in the previous decade, had actually increased in population, reversing decades of losses and matching its highest total from the 1940s at eight million people. While some of Manhattan's new growth came from poor, uneducated immigrants seeking shelter in a democratic society, other components of this new growth reflect a surge in new, high-tech jobs, or service jobs created by the high-tech economy, which needs to be centered in or near great cities to cater to the concentration of businesses there. Improved underground services, from subways to parking to fiber optic and copper-wire telephone cables are essential to such new urban economic growth. And with heavy manufacturing no longer located in city centers, living in the urban matrix is decidedly more pleasant.

If the forecast is the latter, it seems likely that the substrata of cities will become richer and more complex. In some cities, wireless networks will soon allow access to the Internet while on the subway. Fiber optic lines and massive switching systems are being buried underground. And recently new subway lines have been built in Budapest, Istanbul, Paris, London, Bombay, and other major cities, a strong indication that what lies beneath will continue to be a crucial part of our great cities' futures.

Whatever the future holds, the worlds beneath our cities will continue to be integral parts of the amazing agglomerations of wealth, power, production, culture, and lifestyles that define the great metropolises. A city's underground allows us to see much of the machinery that currently determines the shape and quality of our urbanizing world, and it serves as a lens into the past as well, perpetually revealing the roots upon which this important human habitat ever draws and depends.

**A**NDREW HOFFMAN IS AN EXECUTIVE AT New York's JP Morgan Chase & Co., the richest bank in the richest city in the richest country in the world. In his office inside Chase's sixty-story glass tower in lower Manhattan, Hoffman is far removed from the bustle on the streets below; only the muted melody of taxi horns brings an occasional reminder of the real world.

The taxis are stuck in gridlocked traffic, as usual on a weekday morning, and from Hoffman's window the streets look like endless yellow ribbons. But Hoffman doesn't concern himself with taxi troubles. Like most New Yorkers, he rides the subway to work from his apartment near Union Square.

"It's what makes New York great," Hoffman said. "Everyone rides the subway. There's everyone from construction workers to top executives, and everything in between. The full gamut."

Beneath the jammed streets, he and other commuters zip along in crowded but reasonably clean, air-conditioned trains. "New York as we know it could not exist without the subway," says Robert Olmsted, a former planning director of the city's Metropolitan Transportation Authority. "A different New York would be here without it . . . You can't have the density of New York without the subway."

Those subway and commuter trains run through a vast underground realm that weaves together New York's archipelago of five boroughs plus neighboring New Jersey, Connecticut, and Long Island. Amtrak trains carry long-distance passengers through a two-track tunnel under the Hudson and a four-track tunnel under the East River to Pennsylvania Station, itself entirely underground—right below Madison Square Garden. Cars and trucks have their own tunnels—the Holland and Lincoln tunnels burrowing under the Hudson River between Manhattan and New Jersey, the Midtown Tunnel under the East River between Manhattan and the borough of Queens, and the Brooklyn-Battery Tunnel under New York Harbor itself, connecting Manhattan and the teeming borough of Brooklyn.

The tunnels are just one part of New York's complex underworld. Also snaking under the streets are 90,000 miles of electrical cables and conduits (some drawing power from the Indian Point nuclear plant north of the city); 600 miles of gas mains; tens of thousands of miles of telephone cable, water, and sewer pipes; plus a growing network of fiber optic cables carrying their cargo of bytes into computers and telephones. Alongside the high-tech strands are considerably quainter systems: 100 miles of high-pressure steam pipes still in operation that force heat into 2,200 buildings, and 55 miles of pneumatic tubes that once delivered 200,000 letters per hour between post offices and office buildings (It worked like a vacuum cleaner). In use until 1953, the pneumatic system is now abandoned although proposals to reuse it occasionally surface. The pneumatic tubes are part of the detritus beneath the street of Manhattan, left by events and businesses from a past age.

So extensive is the city's underground world that the Chase Tower requires six floors beneath the street level just to accommodate all the subterranean services. Below those six subfloors is bedrock—the 500-million-year-old Manhattan Schist, to be precise, on which Chase and many other Manhattan skyscrapers rest—and deep within that rock is yet another underground labyrinth: tunnels as wide as a tractor trailer, which funnel water into the city from the Catskill Mountains 100 miles distant.

You won't find many postcards in a New York souvenir shop of those obscure caverns. The New York of recognition is the aboveground tiara of gleaming skyscrapers and graceful suspension bridges. But that New York would not be possible without what lies below. Although about 1.5 million people live on the island of Manhattan, some 7.6 million people stream in and out of that borough every day, mostly to work but also to attend schools, see Broadway plays, or visit museums. Moving those workers, students, and tourists around—as well as providing them with water, power, and heat while connecting them with phones and computers—is essential to the city's livelihood and indeed to the entire U.S. economy. New York's annual economic output totals about $500 billion, and the metropolitan region totals about $1 trillion. About 200 of the so-called Fortune 500 companies are based in New York. The city symbolizes to the world America's economic power and the triumph of free markets. JP Morgan Chase alone manages assets of $750 billion.

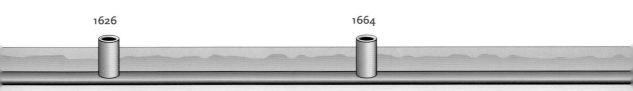

| 1626 | 1664 |
|---|---|
| Peter Minuit of the Dutch West India Company buys the "island of hills" that is Manhattan from the Native Americans and formally establishes New Amsterdam at its southern tip. | Dutch governor Peter Stuyvesant, whose leadership turned a trading post into a small prosperous city, surrenders New Amsterdam to the British without fighting. The English rename it "New York," after the Duke of York and future king of England, James II. |

**Country:** United States

**Location:** Southeastern New York State, on the Hudson River and the East River and New York Bay (an arm of the Atlantic Ocean)

**Population:** In 2003, 8,085,742; in the metropolitan area, 20,000,000

**Area:** 799.5 sq km (308.7 sq mi)

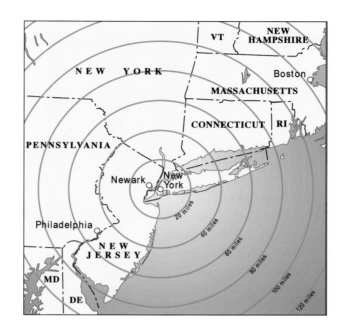

Despite the city's dependence on the underground infrastructure, its creation did not come easily. In fact, the underground has been a battleground since the early nineteenth century, when New York's population exploded as a result of immigration and industrialization. Each new component of public underground infrastructure—water, sewers, subways, phone lines, electricity—was accompanied by fierce battles over whether and how it should be built, over who would pay and who would benefit. The difficult fight to build public infrastructure reflects America's ambivalence to government. Although the city's water system, sewers, train lines, and subways were integral to the city's financial health, none was built without a chorus of businessmen complaining about a waste of government money and an unfair interference in the private market. In many cases, private companies were first allowed to build competing underground systems, often with impractical results.

**1741**

**1774**

Slaves revolt in and around New York City in an unsuccessful rebellion. Twenty-five ringleaders are hung, burned at the stake, and otherwise executed in front of City Hall. Their remains are put in the African Burial Ground, newly established by city leaders a few years previously.

New York Common Council accepts bids for public water system and approves proposal by English engineer Christopher Colles. Revolutionary war interrupts project. Citizens will wait more than a half-century for a public water system.

## SAVING SPACE UNDERGROUND

Let's say you have a complex of office buildings where 50,000 people work. If they all were to drive, you would need twenty-five lanes of freeway and a 500-acre parking lot to handle the estimated 50,000-plus cars of the commuters.

Or, you could have one subway track. No parking would be needed at all. A subway can deliver hordes of people quickly. A single subway car, at what engineers call a "crush load" of shoulder-to-shoulder users, holds 100 to 200 riders, depending on how tightly people pack together. A New York subway train usually consists of ten to twelve cars, which means one train can transport 1,000 to 2,000 people. With trains running about ninety seconds apart, a single subway track can deliver 50,000 people an hour. Thirteen separate tracks meet in midtown Manhattan at Times Square station. That's why millions of people can pack into Times Square on New Year's Eve without any logistical problems.

Compare that to auto traffic. While one subway track can deliver 50,000 people an hour, one lane of interstate highway can only handle 1,800 cars per hour, and that is in ideal conditions. Cars in America typically carry an average of 1.1 people, which adds up to around 2,000 people traveling per lane, per hour. A major highway usually has four lanes in each direction, and is thus capable of moving about 7,200 cars, holding (again on average) 8,000 people, per hour. And of course, all those thousands of cars must be parked somewhere.

One acre of surface parking can hold about 100 cars. An urban baseball stadium would be dwarfed by the parking lots or garages surrounding it—which is in fact the case with many stadiums and office complexes located in suburban areas. The twin towers of the World Trade Center, where about 50,000 people had worked, would have needed two parking garages 190 stories tall to handle the cars of people working there, if all they had had to drive.

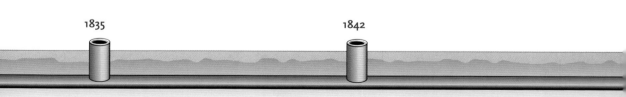

1835

Fire rages across the city and destroys seven hundred buildings because firefighters lack access to a reliable water source. Along with a cholera epidemic a few years before, the fire helps build public pressure for public water system.

1842

New York draws its first water from the new Croton Aqueduct, the linchpin of its first public water system. It will grow to eventually supply an estimated 9 million people over 2,000 square miles with 1.5 billions gallons of water daily.

A common perception is that public places—Times Square or even a shopping mall outside Atlanta—happen on their own, and we figure out how to move around them. Actually, it works just the opposite: We create ways to move around, and that creates the public places. Subways created New York City the same way America's interstate highways created suburban sprawl.

In 1900, at least a dozen separate electric and gas companies competed in New York, each laying its own lines, jockeying for control of the neighborhoods. They included the Edison Electric Illuminating Company, founded by Thomas Edison. Eventually, all these competing companies merged or were bought out and formed Consolidated Gas. The city's current electric power producer, Con Edison, is a descendant of that company, and it now operates New York's network of both gas and electric lines.

Those power lines, first installed in the late nineteenth century, crisscrossed the streets in an overhead spider's web until the blizzard of 1888 dragged them down and cut power to the city for weeks. By the next year, work had begun to put them underground.

Turf battles often delayed development. New York lacked a public water system until 1841 and sewers for all its citizens until well into the twentieth century. The city's first subway opened in 1904—forty-one years after London's, and after the subways were built in Glasgow, Budapest, Boston, Paris, and Berlin as well.

But once the subway finally arrived, it changed the way New Yorkers worked and lived, and produced a new city. W. Barclay Parsons, chief engineer of New York's Rapid Transit Commission, understood how great transportation creates its own demand. "The city is very much like the victim of the opium habit, who needs more of the drug the more he gets," he said. "By the time the railway is complete, areas that are now given over to cows and goats will be covered with houses, and there will be created for the new line, just as there has been created for each new line constructed

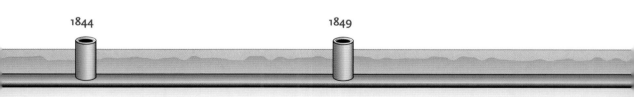

1844

Long Island Railroad completes tunnel under Brooklyn, one of the first underground train tunnels in the world. Abandoned in 1859 after the route of the train line is shifted, it is forgotten until rediscovered in 1980 by an amateur train enthusiast Robert Diamond.

1849

After years of delay, city starts constructing comprehensive network of sewer lines. Within a half-decade, the city will have laid out more than 70 miles of main-line sewers.

in the past, a special traffic of its own, independent of the normal growth of the city. The instant that this line is finished, there will arise a demand for other lines, and so on, until the northward growth of the city reaches the districts beyond the Harlem River, where a spread can be made in other directions besides one due north."

Just as Parsons predicted, sprawling neighborhoods of townhouse and apartments in Brooklyn and Queens followed the new subway lines within a few years of their opening. The growth fostered by the subway led in turn to more subway lines, and then more growth, so that today the New York subway is by far the largest in the United States and the second largest in the world in terms of passenger miles. Some five million people ride the subway every weekday—more than use the entire commercial air system in the United States. The subway has 490 stations, 6,210 train cars (with 1,700 new ones on the way), and twenty-seven different lines.

The city's first subway began, like so many big-city ventures, with a savvy entrepreneur and a corrupt politician—although in this case they were not in cahoots. The year was 1870 and the politician was William Marcy "Boss" Tweed, leader of the powerful Democratic political machine in New York. The entrepreneur was Alfred Ely Beach, inventor of the pneumatic tube, newspaper publisher, and founder of the magazine *Scientific American*, who was convinced New York needed a subway. Beach was right, but that didn't impress Tweed, who opposed a subway, probably because he and his allies earned fees and kickbacks from the operators of New York's extensive private streetcar lines. Tweed rightly assumed a subway system would put the streetcar companies out of business, and he maneuvered to thwart any subway development.

But Beach did not give up easily. Exploiting a license he had obtained to build an underground pneumatic tube to send letters, he quietly built a tube big enough to hold a train car, under Broadway near City Hall. This first "subway" was about three city blocks long, with a lavishly decorated waiting room. An enormous fan blew a car down the grooved gun barrel-like tube, then sucked it back the other way. Beach opened his underground railroad to great fanfare and

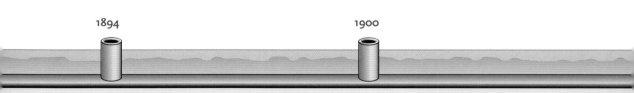

1894

1900

After decades of unsuccessful efforts, a city subway plan is begun after citizens overwhelmingly vote in a referendum for municipal ownership of subway lines. Under the plan, the city will construct the tunnels and will lease them long-term to private companies, who will supply and operate the trains.

U.S. Postmaster General Charles Emory Smith predicts that the pneumatic tube system of mail delivery common in New York would eventually be extended to every household in major cities, "thus ensuring the immediate delivery of mail as soon as it arrives."

This is a detailed cutaway drawing of Herald Square at 33rd Street, circa 1920. This imagined cutaway shows the deep tunnels of the Pennsylvania Railroad, which still bring commuters across the Hudson; the subway lines above that; street level; and then the Sixth Avenue elevated train torn down in 1939.

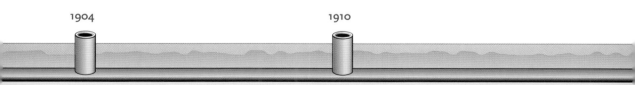

**1904**

**1910**

New York's first subway opens, extending from Wall Street in Lower Manhattan up to Grand Central Depot at 42nd Street, across to Times Square, and then up the West Side of Manhattan. It is an instant success, with passenger traffic drastically exceeding forecasts. The public demands more subways.

The grand, marble-columned Pennsylvania Station is completed at 33rd Street and Eighth Avenue. But the core of the project is deep beneath the station: two mammoth tunnels under the Hudson River and four under the East River, fully connecting the station and thus Manhattan Island by train from the east and west for the first time.

confidently stepped back, awaiting a public demand that would permit him to build a complete subway line.

It almost worked. The New York state legislature went over Tweed's head and gave Beach funding and a franchise to build a subway. But the state's governor, allied with the powerful Tweed, vetoed the bill. It was probably just as well. Vacuums worked fine for sending letters through small tubes, but they were unlikely to be powerful enough to propel hundreds of trains.

New York waited thirty-four years before its first complete subway line opened. A series of private businessmen attempted to build subways, only to be thwarted by political and financial difficulties, the biggest being the enormous sums of capital needed. In the 1890s William Steinway, president of the famous piano company, built most of a tunnel under the East River to link Manhattan and Queens (where the company's factory is still located), but had to abandon it after an explosion stopped work and panicked investors.

A well dressed gentleman prepares to take a ride in Alfred Ely Beach's lavishly adorned pneumatic-tube style subway, which pulled and pushed bulletlike cars through a cylindrical tube using air pressure and suction. Constructed in 1870, the demonstration of the system worked, but notorious mayor "Boss" Tweed, shut it down shortly thereafter.

**1913**

**1915**

Grand Central Terminal is completed on East 42nd Street. The project includes an 80-acre network of tracks, once at street level, now decked over and converted into an underground realm.

Water Tunnel Number One is completed, after four years of construction using horses to maneuver heavy pipes into place. Eighteen miles long and from 11 to 15 feet in diameter, it is part of the new Catskill Water system, which brings in fresh, pure water from mountains more than 100 miles away.

Finally in 1894, voters overwhelmingly approved a referendum to establish municipal financing and construction of a subway system. Essentially, the city and state paid to dig the tunnels, while a private company supplied the trains and tracks in return for a fifty-year lease and the right to charge a five-cent fare.

The first line, the IRT or Interborough Rapid Transit, went from City Hall in Lower Manhattan up the east side to Grand Central Terminal, then across to Times Square, and then up the west side of Manhattan. Extensions and other lines quickly followed, including ones to neighboring Brooklyn, Queens, and the Bronx. By 1930, more than 2 billion passengers a year were using the subways, substantially more than the current 1.3 billion.

But the financing of the subways remained a political hot potato. Each new line was built with a different arrangement of public and private capital. In 1940, the city bought out the private companies and took over the operations of all subway lines. Plaques for the IRT, the BMT (Brooklyn-Manhattan Transit), and the IND (Independent Subway System) can still be seen in some subway stations, the familiar initials of the subway companies before they were all unified under public management.

When designing New York's first subway in 1900, engineers debated whether to skim the surface as in Boston, a style that engineers still call "cut and cover," or to burrow deep underground as in London. Going deep would be easier because builders could bypass all the wires, pipes, and basements that already existed. But deeper would be less convenient for passengers because they would have to take elevators to these lower depths. New York's engineers for the most part went shallow—and their decision has meant a quicker, more convenient journey each day for millions of New Yorkers.

They also went wide. Noteworthy is the city's unusual four-track tunnels, which allow lines to have both local and express service. A morning commuter can travel on the A train from 125th Street to 59th Street without a stop, while another passenger can take the C train on a parallel train track to local stations in between.

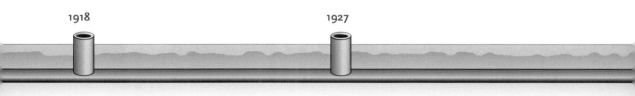

**1918**

**1927**

A subway accident kills 102 people after an untrained driver, hired during a strike by the subway's regular employees, takes a train too fast around a curve and derails it. Officials of the private company BRT are acquitted in criminal trial.

The Holland Tunnel under the Hudson River between New Jersey and New York is completed. About a mile and a half in length, it costs $48 million and is the longest underwater tunnel in the world and one of the first built for automobiles. Instantly popular, traffic congestion quickly becomes a problem.

One of the shallowest train lines is just inches below Park Avenue. Although it is among the most fashionable addresses in the world, Park Avenue exists largely because of the commuter train lines beneath it. Those tracks bring 150,000 passengers daily into Grand Central Terminal from New York's northern suburbs. But until 1913 when the current Grand Central Terminal opened and replaced Grand Central Depot, Park Avenue was not the leafy, flower-decked promenade of today. Noisy steam trains ran down the center of the street (then known more prosaically as Fourth Avenue), obscuring buildings with soot. As they approached the station, the trains fanned out into a smoky railyard dozens of tracks wide on the north side of the station. New York Central railroad, run by the Vanderbilt family in partnership with the city, built Grand Central Terminal, which included putting all the tracks underground in two levels. This made Park Avenue a desirable address, and not incidentally led to construction of the new station complex. Soon large, luxurious apartment buildings and hotels sprouted. (The tracks emerge from the ground around Ninety-sixth Street, where Park Avenue again becomes considerably grittier.)

The underground lines make for some unusual arrangements in Park Avenue's tonier buildings. With its underground storage area usurped by tracks, the Waldorf-Astoria Hotel, which takes up a full block at Park Avenue between Forty-ninth and Fiftieth Street has its wine "cellar" on the fifth floor. But the hotel does have its own dedicated track and private elevator for private railcars, once used by visiting presidents and other dignitaries. Today, however, leaders arrive at the hotel by motorcade.

Except New York's billionaire mayor Michael Bloomberg, who often rides the subway because, as a savvy citizen, he knows it's the fastest way to get around. Someday it may even be possible for a New York mayor to catch a subway near Gracie Mansion, the official mayoral residence, on the Upper East Side. The east side of Manhattan is underserved by the subway, with only one crowded line under Lexington Avenue. A new line under Second Avenue has long been planned—and in fact is already partially built. In the early 1950s, voters approved the subway in a referendum,

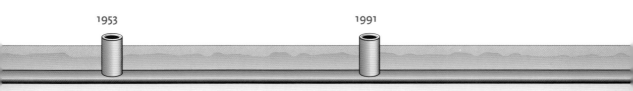

**1953**

The Goodyear Tire Company constructs model of a conveyor belt system that would move people under Midtown Manhattan. The president of the New York City Transit Authority, Col. Sydney H. Bingham, backs the idea, but it is never tried.

**1991**

During construction of a major office tower, workers find the remains of the African Burial Ground. Many New Yorkers are surprised to learn that slavery had once been common in the city.

but the money was diverted to maintenance. Then in the late 1960s, several tunnel sections were built, but work stopped during the city's fiscal crisis in the 1970s. In recent years, New York City Transit has gone back to the drawing board on the Second Avenue line. It's still not clear who will pay for the estimated fifteen-billion-dollar project.

If the subway gave New Yorkers mobility, the city's underground water system gave them basic sanitation and good health. New York lacked a public water system for its first two and a quarter centuries—and suffered greatly for it. When the link between poor water and disease was only dimly understood, if at all, epidemics of cholera, yellow fever, and other diseases swept across New York, spread by bad water and the lack of sewers.

Even so, there was a sense that cleaner, clearer water had some link to health and prosperity. In its first centuries of exsistence, the city's inhabitants relied on wells, cisterns, and city's "tea water men," who sold marginally better water from casks carted into the city. Manhattan became famous for its bad water, which even visiting horses wouldn't drink.

In the 1770s, the colonial city (then with a population of about 20,000) started to build its own water system, but the Revolutionary War intervened. After the war, the state legislature made ready to pass a bill authorizing construction of a public water system for New York City. It would seem the city's water troubles were to be solved.

Aaron Burr, vice president of The United States and the killer of Alexander Hamilton, impeded the development of a public water system in 1798 when he used political influence to start a shoddy private water system. New York would have to wait another four decades, and suffer multiple epidemics, before getting a true public water system in 1842.

**2003**

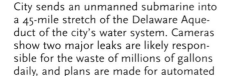

City sends an unmanned submarine into a 45-mile stretch of the Delaware Aqueduct of the city's water system. Cameras show two major leaks are likely responsible for the waste of millions of gallons daily, and plans are made for automated repairs.

## SECRETS OF THE NEW YORK SUBWAY

New York's underground is full of secrets, and rich in American history. Here are a few of the more surprising finds:

- Across from the Chase Tower, under the streets of Lower Manhattan, billions of dollars worth of gold bullion—40 percent of the world's gold, are held in safe-keeping for foreign countries. The treasure is stored in the vaults of the white-columned Federal Reserve Bank of New York.
- Farther uptown, stacks of priceless paintings and sculptures are stored in an abandoned water tunnel under the Metropolitan Museum of Art. The tunnel, 1,000 feet long and 32 feet in diameter, was acquired by the museum in 1917, after the city closed the tube when Water Tunnel Number One opened.
- In a locked basement at Columbia University are the remains of the cyclotron used to split the first atom in 1939, forming the basis for building the world's first atomic bomb. The cyclotron, which includes a forty-ton magnet, is too radioactive to move.
- Under Atlantic Avenue in Brooklyn is an ancient train tunnel used from 1844 to 1861, then sealed and forgotten. Rediscovered in 1980, artists held an exhibit under its vaulted brick ceilings in 2002.
- In May 1991, workers digging the foundations for a new office tower on Duane Street in Lower Manhattan came across skeletons wrapped in shrouds, with copper coins over their eyes, and shells and jewelry nearby. The site was an African burial ground, until the early 1800s a familiar part of the city's land-scape. Slave ownership was common in New York during the city's first two centuries and was not outlawed until 1827. The city's economy was tightly linked to slave economies in the West Indies. Slaves worked on the wharves, as servants in upper-class homes, and on farms outside the cities. Historians believe that some of the bones interred at the African Burial Ground are from slaves that were executed in 1712 and 1741, when two major slave rebellions occurred. The bones were removed to Howard University for study. An office building now stands on the site.

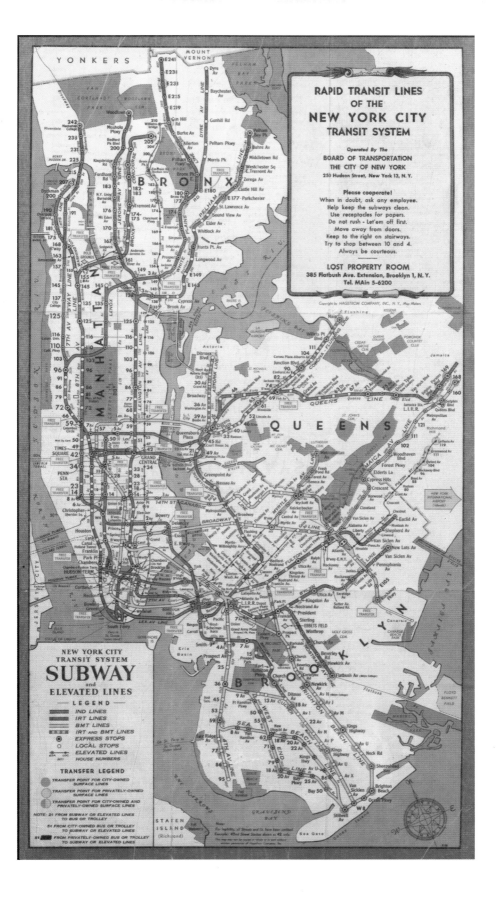

Enter Aaron Burr, one of the more notorious figures in American history. Burr, who traced his ancestry to the Puritan founders of the American colony, was a brilliant attorney (he graduated from Princeton at age sixteen) and a hero in the Revolutionary War. In the new nation he used his connections to rise quickly, serving as New York's attorney general before being elected to the U.S. Senate in 1791. He was known for his lavish lifestyle, residing in a mansion in Manhattan with a staff of slaves.

In 1798, when the city's Common Council contemplated construction of a public water system, Burr persuaded the state legislature to overrule the motion and instead grant his Manhattan Company a franchise to build a private water system, and, not incidentally, to start a bank with the leftover funds. The proposal for a water system was essentially a ruse to gain permission to start a bank. In those times, the state limited the number of banks. Primarily focused on bank building, Burr and company installed a leaky, inadequate water system of hollowed-out logs buried a few feet underground, serving (badly) only the wealthiest homes. Starting a public water system was made even more difficult, because the state had granted the Manhattan Company an exclusive contract.

Burr went on to become vice president under Thomas Jefferson, and later became famous for killing his political arch rival Alexander Hamilton (the nation's first Secretary of the Treasury) in a duel. After fleeing to the unsettled West, Burr was charged with treason for allegedly attempting to start a revolution against the new country. But his shoddy water legacy lived on for decades.

Once again, crisis was the final catalyst. It took the cholera epidemic of 1832 for New York politicians to finally approve the massive public works project of constructing an aqueduct and reservoir system. In 1842 the city, then with a population of 401,612 people, finished construction of the Croton Aqueduct to the Croton Lakes, forty miles north of Manhattan in Westchester County. When the first water came through, the citizens celebrated with fireworks and street parties. The magnificent stone High Bridge, which still exists with its Roman arches, carried the water over the East River into the city. A central reservoir in Manhattan, occupying the block at Forty-second Street and Fifth Avenue (now the site of the New York Public Library and Bryant Park), stored the water.

A decade later, the city began construction of its first public sewer system, but even that served only about a quarter of New York's inhabitants. Until the early twentieth century, substantial portions of the city lived with privies, pit toilets, and outhouses. The city's sewage now flows into a network of fourteen sewage treatment plants, but until World War II, most of it was dumped untreated directly into the harbor and the East and Hudson rivers. Only by the 1990s did the city complete enough plants to treat all of its waste.

The Croton Aqueduct supplied what at first seemed inexhaustible quantities of clean, healthy water to New York City. But the growing city quickly outgrew its

The magnificent High Bridge, reminiscent of the ancient Roman aqueducts with its stonework and high arches, brought clean fresh water over the East River into the city as part of the city's first public water system.

capacity. In the late nineteenth century, city leaders imagined a link to virtually unlimited sources of pure, fresh water—sparkling lakes in the pristine Catskill Mountains, a wilderness area 100 miles north of the city that had been celebrated in paintings by the famous Hudson River School of artists.

To get that water, city and state leaders initiated one of the largest public works projects ever undertaken. In a display of political muscle that would probably be impossible today, entire towns were condemned to make way for the system of tunnels and reservoirs. Constructed between 1907 and 1927, the Catskill system now meets 40 percent of the city's water needs. Another pipeline opened in 1944, drawing water more than 125 miles from the Delaware River along the New York State–Pennsylvania border. This Delaware system, as it is known, includes one of the world's longest tunnels, 85 miles long.

Both Catskill and Delaware aqueducts flow into the Kensico Reservoir north of New York City, where the water is chlorinated and fluoridated but, significantly, not filtered. The water is so clean it does not need it. From there, the water travels down to a new valve chamber facility in the Bronx. In this high-tech distribution center— a 600-foot-long room, 250 feet under Van Cortlandt Park—the flow is directed into massive city water tunnels to the boroughs.

Water Tunnel Number One travels down Manhattan and then crosses the East River at a depth of 1,114 feet beneath the layer of bedrock—almost as deep as the Empire

State Building is tall. Water Tunnel Number Two travels from the Bronx across Queens and to Brooklyn. Neither of these tunnels, each eighteen feet in diameter, has ever been shut down, although both are thought to have numerous leaks; engineers fear that if they closed the old valves to perform tunnel maintenence, they might never be able to open them again.

This photo from the early twentieth century shows the bewildering assortment of pipes and tubes that lies underneath most Manhattan streets. Photo courtesy of Con Edison.

For that reason, the city has embarked on the construction of Water Tunnel Number Three, which will add flexibility and redundancy to the current system. Once operational, Water Tunnel Number Three will allow engineers to turn off tunnels One and Two (although not both at once) to inspect and repair them. The third Tunnel is sixty miles long and twenty-four feet in diameter. Much of the work is being done by automated tunnel-boring machines, developed in Europe, that dig up to seventy feet a day and eliminate the need for dangerous explosives.

Despite the high-tech equipment, Water Tunnel Three has been under construction since 1970 and is not scheduled for completion until 2010. Gone are the days when the city could simply condemn vast swaths of land; today the work is often slowed when neighborhoods mobilize to protest the siting of a tunnel shaft, a device that allows workers to access the cavernous depths.

New York's water system is probably its single most valuable asset. The city and state make every effort to closely guard facilities, such as the Kensico reservoir and the Bronx valve chamber, from terrorist attacks or sabotage, as well as to monitor and regulate suburban construction in the upstate watershed.

Once all this water enters the city, it runs through 6,200 miles of mains and pipes. Then much of it is pumped upward to fill an estimated 10,000 to 15,000 wooden water tanks that sit atop almost any building taller than six stories. The tanks are necessary because what remains of the water system's internal pressure, from its journey from the Catskills and other mountains, is only sufficient to carry water up to the sixth floor. Higher than that, and it must be pumped.

Those quaint-looking rooftop water barrels have become as symbolic of New York as yellow taxicabs. Most are still built in Brooklyn by the family-owned Rosenwach Tank Company, where workers still make them by hand out of rot-resistant cedar planks.

As New York gradually solved its water problems, the bank that Aaron Burr founded grew and prospered. In 1955, the Bank of the Manhattan Company became Chase Manhattan Bank, then the largest in the country. In 2002 it merged with another legendary financial institution, J. P. Morgan, and became JP Morgan Chase & Co. The building where Andrew Hoffman works opened in 1961 as its flagship edifice, although it is now eclipsed by the bank's skyscraper in midtown Manhattan near Times Square. But into the late nineteenth century, the Bank of the Manhattan Company still occupied a building in Lower Manhattan at Reade and Centre streets that maintained a working water well in its basement—because its charter was legitimate only so long as the bank could claim to be a distributor of water.

## THE WORLD TRADE CENTER ATTACK

When two jet planes smashed into the World Trade Center on September 11, 2001, they also destroyed the vast subterranean realm under the buildings. Several subway and commuter lines ran directly beneath the towers or immediately adjacent to them. Damage from the attacks forced the city to close and reroute at least a dozen lines in and around the city, disrupting the commute of hundreds of thousands of people for years. Hardest hit were 80,000 daily commuters from New Jersey, who took the PATH commuter train that ran directly underneath the center.

Almost as serious was the damage to utility lines; telephone service for more than 100,000 people was immediately knocked out when the towers collapsed.

Buried under the rubble were several levels of parking garages and the Trade Center's underground shopping mall. Although not much loved by New Yorkers because of its bland design, the mall had a virtually captive market, betweeen the 50,000 workers in the World Trade Center and the thousands more who walked by its stores every day to and from the trains. The mall grossed one of the highest revenue rates among shopping centers anywhere in the United States.

The rebuilding process will ultimately replace and arguably improve what was the World Trade Center. The underground shopping mall may be scrapped for traditional street-level stores. A new one-billion-dollar transportation hub, designed by Spanish architect Santiago Calatrava, is scheduled to be constructed, with a moving walkway to connect subway and PATH lines, and additional easy access to ferries and buses above ground. The new station might be disorienting to New Yorkers accustomed to dimly lit subway stations: plans call for skylights to flood corridors with natural light from the city above.

# Chicago

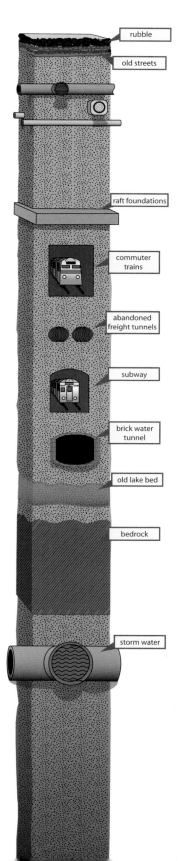

rubble

old streets

raft foundations

commuter trains

abandoned freight tunnels

subway

brick water tunnel

old lake bed

bedrock

storm water

LTHOUGH AMERICA'S SECOND CITY HAS actually slipped to third in size (now lagging behind both New York and Los Angeles in population, it's easy to see why Chicagoans bow their head to no other metropolis. Here on the windy shore of sparkling Lake Michigan, amid elegant century-old department stores and stately townhouses, lies the birthplace of modernity, the proving ground for the skyscraper. Although Chicago still boasts the tallest building in America (the Sears Tower) as well as many of the greatest architectural landmarks of the twentieth century. Call it "The City That Works," or like Carl Sandburg said "The City of the Big Shoulders"—either way, Chicagoans pride themselves on getting things done.

It's a reputation well earned, for no other city in the world has struggled harder to lift itself out of the muck. It took 150 years of engineering feats, most of them underground, to tame this swamp at the foot of Lake Michigan and free the city from filth and disease. The task, which involved the rerouting of a river, raising the entire city a story higher, and then completely rebuilding the town after a cataclysmic fire, was Herculean. You can appreciate these labors from the observation deck of the Sears Tower, but the story begins deep underneath State Street, one of the city's principal thoroughfares that cuts through the heart of downtown. Parallel to Lake Michigan, below the lakefront boulevards and gleaming architecture of downtown Chicago, are the remnants of a lost city, an automobile thoroughfare, an abandoned system of freight tunnels, and the underground shopping arcades of the Illinois Center, designed by noted architect Mies van der Rohe in the late 1960s . Even the city's O'Hare Airport, one of the largest in the world, uses underground tunnels to connect different terminals. Chicago's underground world exists both because and in spite of its incommodious setting. Chicago is not only built on a swamp, but a nondraining swamp at that. In the early nineteenth century, when just a few thousand people occupied this city, it was already starting to rot. Solving the drainage problem would occupy Chicago for almost 100 years to come.

A swamp might seem a poor location for a settlement, but in every other way, Chicago (derived from an Indian word meaning "smelly place") was perfectly sited. Since 1637, when the French explorer Louis Joliet and the missionary Father Jacques Marquette discovered the slow, meandering 100-mile Chicago river that linked the Mississippi to the Great Lakes, national leaders assumed that a city would one day rise on this spot. Joliet reported back to the governor of New France that if the sluggish, barely navigable Chicago River was supplemented by a more navigable canal from the Great Lake over to the Mississippi River, and if a fort or town was situated at the lake, then France could control most of North America through this key spot. Joliet was right, but it was another two centuries before work began in the mid-nineteenth century on what was called the Illinois and Michigan Canal, and before Chicago grew from trading post to real city.

During that time, Chicago passed from the French to the British, and then remained a small postcolonial outpost until the opening of the Erie Canal across New York State in 1825. By shortening the distance from the Great Lakes to the busy ports of the Northeast, the Erie Canal transformed commerce between the Midwest and the Atlantic states. The success of the Erie Canal provided an incentive for Chicago backers to go ahead and construct a canal between Chicago and the Mississippi River, which had been repeatedly attempted unsuccessfully. But in 1848, the Illinois and Michigan Canal finally opened. By the 1850s, a cargo of furs from Nebraska or grain from Kansas could make its way over to Chicago via the Illinois and Michigan Canal, then across the Erie Canal to New York City, and from there across the Atlantic to London or other parts of the world.

But the Illinois and Michigan Canal was never as successful as anticipated, because by the time it was completed, another system of transportation was already starting to replace canals—railroads. As trains replaced canals in the mid-nineteenth century, however, Chicago made out well. It became the rail hub for the entire country, and consequently a city of industry, particularly for the slaughtering and packaging of

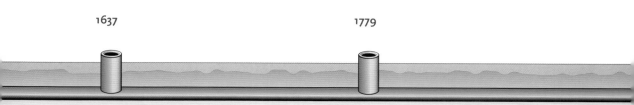

1637

Explorer Louis Joliet and missionary
Father Jacques Marquette, both of France,
are the first Europeans to see the Chicago
River connecting the Great Lakes to the
Mississippi River.

1779

Jean Baptiste Point du Sable, a Haitian
trader, sets up the first permanent house
where the Chicago River empties into
Lake Michigan.

**Country:** United States

**Location:** In the central Midwest, on Lake Michigan

**Population:** The City, 2,869,121; In the metropolitan area, 9,000,000

**Area:** 600 square km (230 square miles)

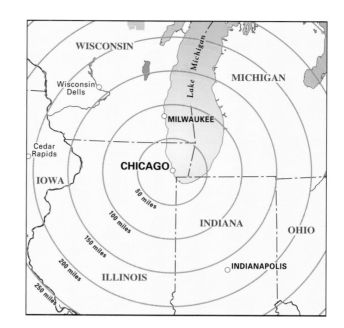

pigs, cows, and lambs for consumption. Live cattle, for example, were transported to Chicago by train from Kansas City and other points west. There, the steers were transformed into steaks and chops, and then sent out again by rail to destinations all over the country.

The meatpacking industry helped make Chicago a mighty industrial center, but it also fouled the waters—dumping the carcasses and other waste directly into the Chicago River, which in turn emptied into Lake Michigan, the source of the city's drinking water. Compounding the problem was that the city was just a few feet above lake level, and so any sewer pipes had little if any gravity to "feed" the waste into the river and lake. Not surprisingly, disease spread quickly. In 1854, a cholera and typhoid epidemic killed 6 percent of the city's population.

1803                                        1825

The U.S. Army constructs Fort Dearborn to defend the Chicago River, recognized now as important to commerce.

New York State opens the Erie Canal, a shipping route from the Atlantic seaboard to Lake Erie and the West. Chicago, which is accessible by the canal because of its position on Lake Michigan, begins to boom.

So Chicago essentially had two problems. One, the city lacked the elevation for a sewer system to function; and two, the sewage all emptied into the lake, which fouled the city's drinking water. Town fathers tackled the first problem for several decades, but did not address the second until the dawn of the twentieth century. But even the first problem, a lack of elevation, was tremendously challenging. Sewer systems usually work by gravity being sufficient to carry water and waste away from a city. In Chicago, any sewer pipes installed in the flat, swampy land were at or below the level of the polluted river and the lake that authorities wanted the sewage to drain into. So authorities had to figure out some way to enlist the help of gravity.

In desperation, the group of speculators that ran the young city agreed to an audacious scheme dreamed up by a visionary engineer—Ellis S. Chesbrough—brought in to solve the problem: raise the streets.

Chesbrough theorized that if the entire city was raised ten to twelve feet, the city could install sewer pipes that would then have enough *fall*, or gravity, for their contents to flow away from the city and into the river. And if the Chicago river were dredged a little, then the waste would flow sufficiently away, and typhoid, cholera, and other diseases would cease to infect the city. Chicago would be clean. At least, that was the theory. (Authorities thought at first that if they could only create a functioning sewer system, it wouldn't matter that all the waste went into Lake Michigan. There, it would be away from the city itself. But, as they would learn, that would not be enough. What's hard to imagine is that initially, the city had no functioning sewer system at all. Human waste from privies simply backed up into the streets themselves, and into the quickly polluted Chicago River.)

In 1858, Chicagoans watched the six-story Tremont Hotel, the city's finest, being raised by thousands of workers standing at jackscrews while the hotel guests were still in it. (A man named George Pullman did this and many other raising jobs. He used the money he earned to found the Pullman Car Company, which developed and

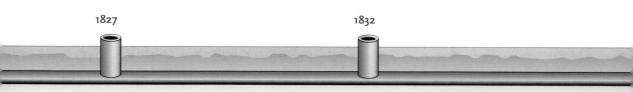

1827

Backed with land and money from the federal government, work begins on the Illinois and Michigan Canal, a long-dreamed-of shipping link between the Mississippi River and the Great Lakes.

1832

Anticipating the canal, real estate speculation seizes the city. In three years, the price of a small downtown lot goes from $100 to $15,000.

Chicago's twenty-eight-mile-long Sanitary and Ship Canal was built in 1900. Reversing the flow of the Chicago river, the canal was instrumental in providing the swampy city with proper drainage, which led to a spectacular drop in the city's disease rate.

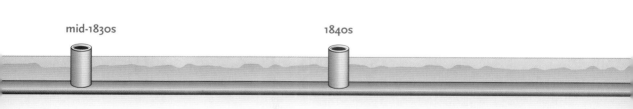

mid-1830s

1840s

Native Americans are forced away from the bustling town of Chicago.

The city expands rapidly and confronts lack of clean water and adequate sewage disposal. Typhoid, cholera, and other diseases become common.

The Great Fire of 1871 destroyed over 17,000 buildings, the rubble and debris of which actually formed the foundation for the city's new streets.

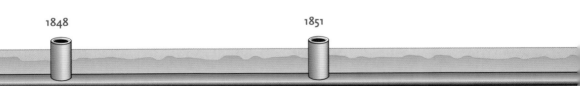

1848

1851

Delayed for decades by financial panics, Indian attacks, and other calamities, the Illinois and Michigan Canal opens. But the economic impact is less than expected because of the competition with an emerging new technology: railroads.

The city constructs a 600-foot cast-iron tunnel into the lake to gain access to clean water. But the effort doesn't help much because the water is still too polluted that close to shore.

dominated the business of sleeper cars attached to passenger trains.) The Tremont Hotel was essentially put on wooden stilts. Other less fancy buildings simply converted their first floors into their basements. Still others ignored the edict, so for a while the city was a mix of different levels.

Evidence of the citywide raising can still be seen today. In older Chicago neighborhoods like Bridgeport, where sewers were not installed until the late nineteenth century, the streets and sidewalks are above the level of the houses, which were built before the sewers were put in. "You'll see old frame houses with the sidewalks essentially leading to the second floor," says Fred Deters, a planner with the Chicago Planning Department. "The yard and first floor are down. The streets are built on fill, and the sidewalks are vaulted. People will store stuff under them."

There was one problem with the newly raised city: it didn't solve the sewage predicament. Although having a functioning sewer system at least carried the sewage away from the houses and business that produced it, the waste still drained into the river and thus into the lake. People first thought that Lake Michigan, which was, after all, the size of a small sea, was big enough to digest all the city's waste without any ill effect. They found out that was not the case. It would take the city until the turn of the next century to admit this.

In 1861, however, the city did reluctantly turn to one of Chesbrough's more expensive proposals. The engineer supervised legions of laborers, mostly Irish immigrants, who built a two-mile-long tunnel under Lake Michigan. The brick-lined 5-foot-in-diameter tunnel went under the lake bed, and there sucked in what was hopefully clean, fresh water for drinking. When completed in 1867 it was one of the longest tunnels ever built and an engineering marvel. Unfortunately, the new water intake tunnel helped only a little. The city was producing so much sewage that the water in the lake was polluted, even two miles from shore.

In 1871, the city burned to the ground in the Great Chicago Fire. Thanks to the previous raising task, much of the city was sitting on wooden streets and sidewalks.

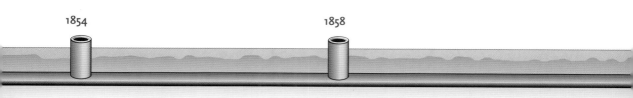

**1854**

Chicago loses 6 percent of its population to a typhoid and cholera epidemic, traced to sewage and bad water. Ellis S. Chesbrough, the city's visionary engineer, proposes raising streets to give sewer pipes better gravity drainage.

**1858**

Chicago raises its downtown streets an entire level, converting first floors into basements. The plan eases public health problems but not enough, because the new sewer system still drains into Lake Michigan, on the edge of the city.

Chicago's unique system of freight tunnels served as a delivery route for businesses in "the loop" in Downtown Chicago. Used during the first half of the twentieth century, the system was eventually closed down and forgotten about until it flooded in the early 1990s.

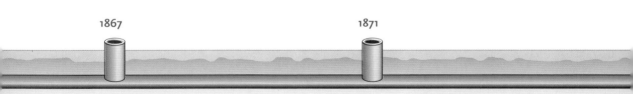

1867

1871

Gangs of Irish immigrants complete construction of a 5-foot-diameter, brick-lined, 2-mile-long water tunnel stretching beneath Lake Michigan to an intake valve beneath the lake. But the new water supply does not help much because the lake has become polluted even that far from the shoreline.

A massive fire from October 8–10 kills an estimated 250 people, leaves 90,000 homeless, and levels about 4 square miles (10 square kilometers) in the city center, almost a third of Chicago.

# FREIGHT TUNNELS BECOME
# WATER TUNNELS

On the morning of April 13, 1992, employees at Chicago's famous Marshall Field's department store noticed that fish were swimming in their basement. People all over downtown were discovering that everything below ground level was flooded. A worker driving a pile underneath the Kinzie Street Bridge had accidentally broken into one of the city's old freight tunnels, allowing Lake Michigan to pour into basements all over the city center. Within a day, more than 200 million gallons of water flowed from the lake and river into the city's underground. The city lost electric power, and its downtown was shut for a week.

The accident was the first time many Chicagoans had even heard of their city's extensive but abandoned system of freight tunnels, built 40 feet underground in the early twentieth century. The tunnels connected almost every public and private building in central Chicago built before 1950.

As Chicago's streets grew more congested in the automobile era, the city that was built on train commerce naturally thought to add freight lines under buildings, as a way of securing fast and reliable delivery of goods. A succession of private companies built and owned the tunnels, starting with the Illinois Telephone and Telegraph Company, and ending a half-century later with the Chicago Tunnel Company. With only shaky legal authority, companies built a small-scale underground railroad, nearly sixty-two miles with two-foot wide tracks. Miniature engines pulled open cars filled with freight inside the seven-foot-high tunnels, similar to narrow-gauge rail systems used in mines. Train engineers straddled the electric locomotives like drivers of toy trains.

Although the trains looked cute, they did useful work. A department store like Marshall Field's would receive coal for its furnaces as well as new supplies of shirts

*continued on p. 44*

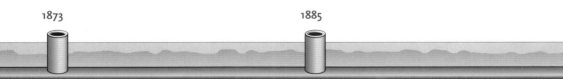

**1873**

Another cholera epidemic strikes the city.

**1885**

Louis Sullivan, Daniel Burnham, John Root, and other Chicago architects construct some of the world's first steel-frame skyscrapers. They pioneer the use of "raft foundations" to support the tall buildings on the city's spongy soil.

*continued from p. 43*

and shoes for its shelves. Most buildings had elevators that connected to the tunnels. The trains went to the Chicago Board of Trade, the *Chicago Tribune* newspaper, the train stations, warehouses, and major office buildings. The freight tunnels helped curtail truck traffic on city streets, and provided a redundancy that most cities did not have. In its heyday, the system had 3,300 cars that delivered more than 600,000 tons of freight a day. Movie theaters even cooled their auditoriums by piping in air from the fifty-five-degree tunnels.

Unfortunately, the companies that built and managed the freight system could not make money. Transportation is historically a low-margin industry without public subsidies. Faced with competition from trucks, which paid nothing to use the city-owned streets, the Chicago Tunnel Company abandoned the system in 1952.

After the system was shut down, company employees ripped out the tracks and anything else valuable. Crucially, they even removed the steel doors that acted as emergency gates on the eleven tunnels that went under the lake and river. When a pile driver slammed through a tunnel in 1992, there were no doors to cut off the water.

With the exception of that flood, the freight tunnels have proved useful in recent years. The city has leased them out to more than a dozen companies to lay telecommunication lines, including more than 600,000 feet of fiber optic cable.

The fire quickly spread beneath buildings, and the city burned from below. Hundreds of people were killed and thousands left homeless. More than 17,000 homes, offices, and factories were destroyed. The city rebuilt itself quickly, with better streets, and buildings of stone and brick to replace those of wood. Much of the rubble remaing after the fire was used to raise the city even higher and more solidly. But its intractable sewage problems remained.

**1893**

The World's Columbian Exposition opens in Chicago, marking the 400th anniversary of European "discovery" of America. Chicago pipes in clean water from Wisconsin for tourists, not residents.

**1889**

Chicago has become a sprawling city, a cross-continental railroad junction, and industrial center, filled with immigrants. Jane Addams and Ellen Gates Starr found Hull House in Chicago to meet immigrants' health and assimilation needs, initiating the social welfare reform movement in the United States.

As the nineteenth century neared its end, the spread of disease resulting from the lack of a decent water and sewer system earned Chicago the nickname "Typhoid Fever City." When the World's Columbian Exposition opened in the city in 1893, city officials piped in water from Wisconsin to assure visitors of a clean water supply. In fact, before the fair began, the city had started work on a project of enormous complexity and expense. It had been recommended in the past, but only now were Chicago's leaders able to muster the financial and political will to attempt it.

The solution was to actually reverse the flow of the Chicago River so that rather than drain into Lake Michigan, its mouth, it would drain into the Mississippi. To accomplish this seemingly impossible task, engineers planned to dig a deep, twenty-eight-mile-long canal to allow the Chicago and several other rivers to flow backward into the Mississippi River. The Sanitary and Ship Canal, as it would be named, would move water the way other canals moved ships: by using a series of locks, which would take water (and ships, for the canal was also used for commerce) from one elevation to another. It meant moving millions of tons of earth, and employing thousands of laborers. The Sanitary and Ship Canal would be bigger than the French-built Suez Canal, completed in 1869. Techniques pioneered on the Chicago Sanitary and Ship Canal would be used in constructing the fifty-mile Panama Canal, completed in 1914, which connected the Atlantic and Pacific oceans.

Just as difficult as the engineering were the political hurdles, because the river cut through so many different political boundaries. To make the canal project possible, the state of Illinois created the Sanitary District of Chicago, which covered hundreds of square miles and was given unprecedented powers of condemnation and taxation. Voters in the affected areas approved the new political jurisdiction in 1889 by a whopping 79,958 to 252, a measure of the desire for clean water.

The canal took ten years to build. On January 2, 1900, workers dynamited the last temporary lock holding back the water. This potentially ceremonious event was in fact carried out in secret at midnight, because the state of Missouri had threatened to

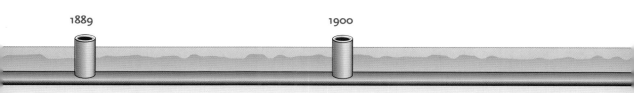

1889

1900

Voters overwhelming approve political changes necessary to construct the Sanitary and Ship Canal, which will reverse the flow of the Chicago River and allow sewage to drain into the Mississippi River, away from the city.

Government officials blow up the last temporary lock to open the Sanitary and Ship Canal, allowing water to flow in the new east-to-west direction. The new canal, coming at the end of a half century of failed efforts, finally solves the city's sewage problems.

The LaSalle Street Tunnel was completed in 1867. As one of the largest tunnels ever built at the time, it was considered a marvel of engineering.

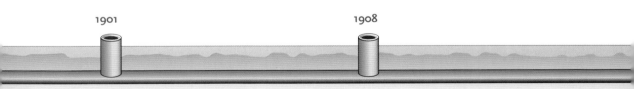

**1901**

The Illinois Telephone and Telegraph Company began construction of what will become a 50-mile underground network of freight tunnels for delivery of merchandise and supplies to businesses.

**1908**

Public health statistics show Chicago's typhoid rate has fallen to one of America's lowest.

sue Illinois to stop the great canal. Missouri, which was downstream on the Mississippi, was concerned about receiving Chicago's waste. Although the interstate lawsuits continued for a decade before fizzling out, the new canal was up and running. And it worked. By 1908, the city's rate of typhoid deaths had dropped 91 percent. The Metropolitan Sanitary District of Greater Chicago built two more canals in the next few decades to improve the flow of sewage and drainage in the city. The state of Missouri's worries about being inundated with Chicago's waste were unfounded. The Mississippi River, while hardly very clean, was far more able to handle the waste pumped into it, because the mighty river flowed down to New Orleans and out into the Gulf of Mexico.

Since then, the canal and related systems have been steadily improved, including the addition of sewage treatment facilities that clean most of the waste water before pumping it into the Sanitary and Ship Canal. In 1972, as suburban sprawl began to add more waste to the system, the Chicago Sanitation District, renamed the Metropolitan Water Reclamation District of Greater Chicago, began constructing the so-called Deep Tunnel to carry storm water and sewage away from the city when the regular system exceeds its capacity. The extra flow is delivered to giant abandoned stone quarries, which can hold the extra water until it can be released into the regular sewage system and treated. Burrowing at depths of as much as 360 feet, the Deep Tunnel will be 130 miles long and up to 30 feet in diameter. Still only partially finished, the Deep Tunnel system will ultimately cost at least three billion dollars and is scheduled for completion in 2017.

After winning its long battle for a functioning sewer system, Chicago began to think about putting other services underground. Daniel Burnham, the great Chicago architect and urban designer, was a key figure in those plans. Burnham had organized the World's Columbian Exposition, which brought millions of visitors to Chicago to marvel at the fair's centerpiece, the Great White City. This model city of the future, designed by Burnham, featured sweeping boulevards fronted by clean white,

**1926**                                                **1943**

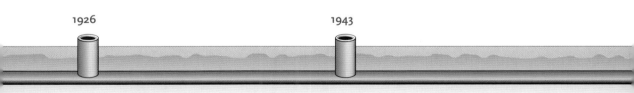

The city opens Wacker Drive, a center-piece of the Plan of Chicago developed by architect Daniel Burnham and partner Edward Bennett. The raised waterfront boulevard contains two levels that allow basic movement of deliveries and other commercial traffic on underground streets, creating wide avenues for shopping and business.

More than a generation behind New York and Boston, Chicago opens its first subway line.

monumental buildings that emulated Classical Roman or Greek architecture. Its pop-
ularity helped spawn the City Beautiful movement around the country, and it was a
major influence on a young Chicagoan named Walt Disney.

To Burnham, a key component of a beautiful modern city was efficient use of the
underground, the logical realm for all the necessary but inelegant aspects of industrial life. Cities at that time—and particularly Chicago—were becoming gritty waste-
lands of belching factories, dingy warehouses, and noisy trains. The riverfronts were
aquatic highways, crammed with ships and boats unloading supplies and carrying
away finished goods.

In 1909, Burnham and his partner Edward Bennett proposed elevating Chicago
(once again) above its waterfront, so that the city could look out on the lake, while
many of the waterfront industrial activities went on as usual beneath it. The plan also
proposed putting train lines and through streets underground. "Make no little plans,"
Burnham said famously, in a much-quoted passage. "They have no magic to stir men's
blood and probably themselves will not be realized. Make big plans; aim high in hope
and work, remembering that a noble, logical diagram once recorded will not die."

Indeed, Burnham's plans did not die. Business leaders distributed the plan to
schoolchildren, building momentum for the necessary work. In the first decades of
the twentieth century much of it was carried out.

A centerpiece of the waterfront plan was the creation of the double-decker Wacker
Drive, which runs along the lakeshore and was recently renovated at a cost of some
$200 million. The bottom level of Wacker Drive provides a system for the delivery of
goods and the removal of garbage. The upper level is more of a promenade for regular traffic. But both levels look out on the lake, and the top level constructed in the
more picturesque, ornamental style typical of early-twentieth-century architecture
makes the roadway rise above the mere utilitarian.

"Essentially, he took a river that was lined with warehouses and docks and a
produce market, and turned it into a riverside boulevard with brand new office

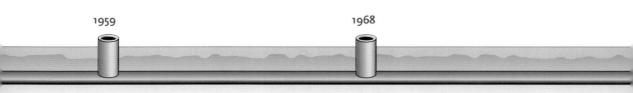

**1959**

The Chicago Tunnel Company closes
down the freight tunnel system. The tunnels revert to ownership by the city.

**1968**

Demonstrators disrupt the Democratic
National Convention. Chicago police
crack heads and consider putting arrested
demonstrators in the abandoned freight
tunnels.

buildings," says Fred Deters, from the Chicago Department of Planning and Development. "He opened up the river. Before Wacker Drive, these functional buildings backed up to the river. You had no public access. With Wacker Drive, the river became the front door."

Functional but beautiful—that was Burnham's legacy, and perhaps the ultimate tribute to Chicago, a city that owes as much to the underground engineers who raised it from the swamp as to the world-famous architects who shaped its soaring skyline.

The ongoing Deep Tunnel project, designed to provide the city with extra drainage during floods, will ultimately cost the city three billion dollars and is not scheduled to be completed until 2017.

**1972**

Chicago's water managers began work on the Deep Tunnel system to flush away storm water and sewage that the city's old systems can't handle. At the time, this is one of the most extensive city-based public-works project in U.S. history.

**1980s**

Chicago's downtown skyline has become world famous for the number, height, and beauty of its skyscrapers, boasting three of the six tallest buildings anywhere: the John Hancock Center, the Amoco Building, and the Sears Tower, that, at 110 stories, was, for a time, the tallest building in the world.

# BUILDING SKYSCRAPERS ON MUCK

The advent of steel-frame construction allowed Chicago architects like Louis Sullivan and others to design taller buildings, because the exterior wall, or *skin* of the building, no longer had to support the weight of the structure. That also meant windows could be larger, and the skin or *curtain wall* thinner and less evident.

Even so, skyscrapers require deep, strong foundations. And in Chicago, which was famous for its swampy, mucky soil, this was a challenge. Architects and engineers spent as much of their time developing new foundations as they did designing the buildings themselves.

Sullivan, Daniel Burnham, and such structural engineers, as Frederick Baumann came up with a number of innovations to help spread the load of a building across the weak soil. Burnham wrote a pamphlet called *The Art of Preparing Foundations for all Kinds of Buildings with particular Illustrations of the 'Method of Isolated Piers' as Followed in Chicago.* Sullivan and his structural engineer partner Dankmar Adler developed methods of reinforcing concrete under the walls of the seventeen-story Auditorium, a significant historic edifice in downtown Chicago. Under the Auditorium and other buildings, Sullivan and Adler used what were called "raft foundations." In essence, they floated the foundations of a building on crisscrossed layer of timber and steel rails, so the weight would spread out over the spongy soil.

Eighty years later in 1970, when it came time to build a modern skyscraper that would be the tallest building in the world, the Sears Tower, the structural engineer Fazlur Kahn used a modern foundation building technique that had similarities to Sullivan's raft foundation.

The Sears Tower is composed of nine vertical modules, similar to a handful of cigarettes, which help distribute the load of the building evenly. The tower is one of the largest buildings in the world, with 4.5 million square feet of office space, as much as the entire downtown of a mid-sized city.  By some standards, it is still the

1992

On April 13, the city's abandoned freight tunnels flood after a construction worker mistakenly drives a pile through an old tunnel and allows water from Lake Michigan to rush into basements throughout downtown. The city center loses power and closes down for a week.

tallest building in the world because the top floor of this 110-story building is higher than any other *floor* in the world.  That means it has the highest space that can be occupied, as opposed to a spire or communication tower.

But how could such a massive building, reported to weigh 222,500 tons, be supported on Chicago's mushy soil? Here's how they did it.

First, construction crews dug a ten-story, 100-foot hole in the ground down to bedrock, well below Chicago's infamously wet surface  level. This depth of excavation was something impossible to achieve when Sullivan and Burnham were constructing the first, far smaller skyscrapers. Then, crews sunk 200 circular caissons—open cylinders made of steel and anchored in the bedrock—and then filled them with concrete. These caissons formed a reliably solid foundation, improving on Sullivan's rafts of timbers and rails. The caissons and their concrete are what support the mammoth Sears Tower, including three basement- level floors.

The smooth glass and steel façade of the Sears Tower is very different from the ornate surfaces of Sullivan's buildings, such as the Carson, Pirie, Scott department store in Chicago. But some things in construction techniques haven't changed. Builders a century ago on the early skyscrapers used steel frame construction and so did the builders of the Sears Tower. As always, the architects and engineers used their intellect and imagination to work around environmental circumstances that initially might have appeared insurmountable.

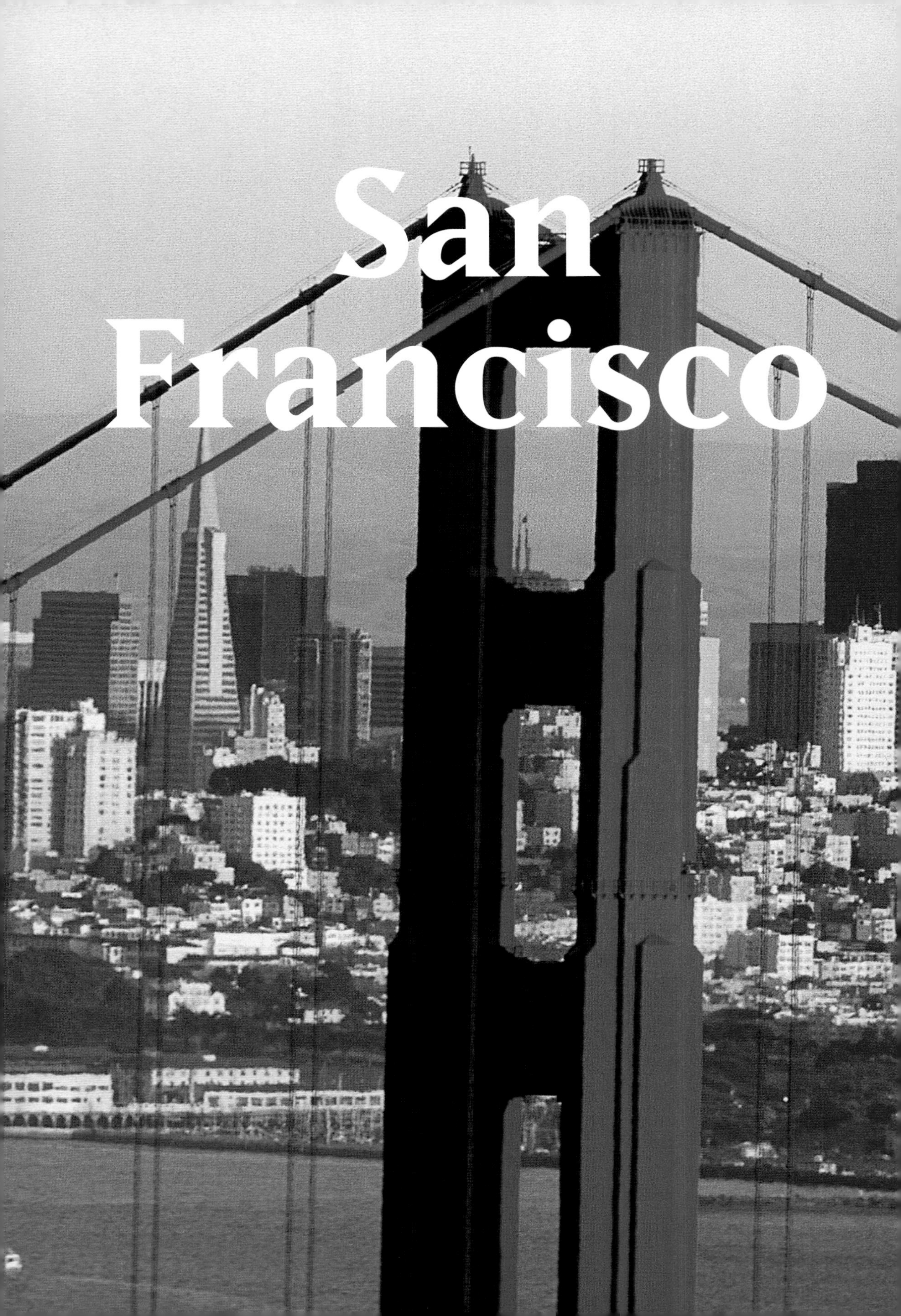

# San Francisco

I F THE EARTH WERE A TENNIS BALL, THE seam would run down the coast of California from Alaska, on through Central America, down the Andes Mountains of Peru, and then down the western coast of Chile. From there, the seam would make a U-turn at Antarctica and come back up on the other side of the Pacific Ocean, running through Indonesia and Japan. This seam, called the Circum-Pacific Belt, or the "ring of fire" is the edge of a massive tectonic plate, one of several that demarcate the world's major geological partitions. These plates bump and collide into each other, causing the earth to quake or erupt with volcanic activity

One of the many cities that lie along this seam is San Francisco, which rests between two branches of the Circum-Pacific Belt—the San Andreas fault to the west, and the Hayward fault to east. San Francisco is famous for its steep hills, historic cable cars, and colorful Victorian homes overlooking a glittering bay. And it is arguably the most beautiful city in America—a delicate porcelain tea set ready to be knocked from its shelf.

San Francisco's underground realm faces a challenge most cities do not: What happens when the earth moves? Seismologists estimate that in the next thirty years, there is a two-to-one chance of a major earthquake destroying much of the city, as happened in 1906. Such a quake would shatter buildings and roads as well as subway lines, water pipes, and other underground systems. Consequently, determining how to safeguard these structures has been a persistent preoccupation of city planners and engineers for more than a century.

Technically small in both size and population, San Francisco is the historic, cultural, and financial center of the entire Bay Area, a sprawling metropolis that extends around the San Francisco Bay and into the foothills of the Coast Ranges. Like most major cities, San Francisco is the Queen Bee of its region, using various underground systems to draw in resources from the much larger suburban lands that surround it. Its underground water pipes snake out hundreds of miles to tap lakes and rivers and its underground train lines bring in

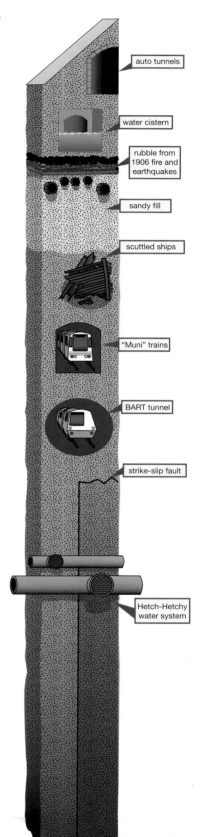

auto tunnels

water cistern

rubble from 1906 fire and earthquakes

sandy fill

scuttled ships

"Muni" trains

BART tunnel

strike-slip fault

Hetch-Hetchy water system

people from the Silicon Valley, Berkeley, and Oakland—home, respectively, to some of the world's leading computer industries, one of the region's top universities, and a working-class city.

The region has been inhabited for 10,000 to 20,000 years by various Native American peoples, including the Oholone tribe, whom Spanish missionaries encountered when they established a small settlement at the harbor in the late eighteenth century. But the small town did not become a city until the gold rush of 1849, when thousands of fortune-seekers (forty-niners) made their way west to pan for nuggets in the California mountain streams east of San Francisco. The discovery of gold made the city a major banking center and other industries soon developed around the excellent natural harbor.

In other ways, however, the location of this new coastal city was less than ideal. Its topography of rolling, uneven hills, with virtually no flat land, made development difficult. Back then, the city had huge sand dunes—including one, located in what is now the "South of Market" or SoMa district, soaring eighty feet high. To facilitate development, the dunes were removed and used to fill in gaps between the hills and the water's edge. During an earthquake, such areas are particularly vulnerable because the sand shifts, or *liquefies*, readily. *Liquefaction*, considered one of worst things to happen to a piece of terrain in an earthquake, occurs when sandy or waterlogged soil shakes to the point of behaving like a liquid. Film footage of earth that is liquefying during an earthquake shows the ground jostling and sloshing, with ripples just like those in a body of water. A building on such soil will sink or fall to pieces during a quake, because the structural support beneath it vanishes. During the 1989 Loma Prieta earthquake in California, San Francisco's waterfront areas suffered the worst damage because the earth beneath the buildings, most of it infill that is most vulnerable to liquefaction, did indeed liquefy. This also occurred in the poorer South of Market neighborhood that once was a swampy area called "Sullivan's Marsh."

The young city experienced major quakes in 1868, 1898, and 1900, but none

**10,000 BC**                                    **1776 AD**

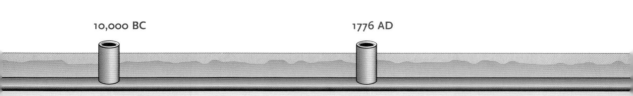

Various tribes of indigenous people, believed to have come across the Bering Strait from Asia into North America, populate the land around the fine natural harbor on the Pacific Ocean.

Spanish missionaries and troops found the fort and mission of San Francisco on top of a high hill overlooking the harbor. A village called Yerba Buena is established in a cove closer to the water.

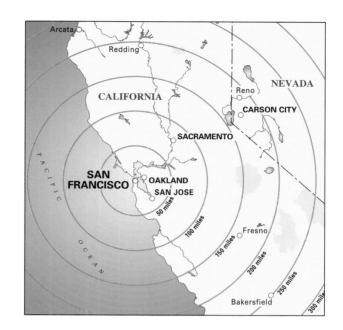

**Country:** United States

**Location:** A peninsula in northern California between the Pacific Ocean and San Francisco Bay

**Population:** 746,000; in the metropolitan area, 7,000,000

**Area:** 46 square miles

caused as much damage as the trembler and subsequent fire in 1906, which destroyed 28,000 buildings in 512 square blocks—then most of the city. More than 3,000 people died. Every April 18, on the anniversary, the handful of elderly survivors (and descendants of the victims) gather at Lotta's Fountain downtown, although the group has dwindled.

Those survivors lived to witness the rebirth of their city, and gained an increasing awareness about the dangers of earthquakes. The science of seismology in the first decades of the twentieth century was relatively new. German meteorologist and geologist Alfred Wegener's theory that shifting tectonic plates caused earthquakes was ridiculed when it was first published in 1915, and not fully accepted until the 1960s. Today, continental drift is an accepted principle and researchers in California have

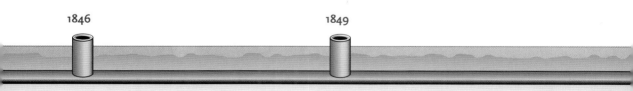

1846

The fort and village pass from Mexican to American control, and the name of the small village is changed from Yerba Buena to San Francisco.

1849

The California gold rush begins as thousands of people from all over the world make their way by boat or over land to the area. The village of San Francisco quickly becomes a city.

identified ten major and six minor faults running under and around San Francisco. Fault maps of the region look like a shattered piece of glass, with the fracture zones running vertically north and south, up and down the state. The faults underneath the Bay Area are known as *strike faults*, also called *strike-slip faults*, because the edges of the tectonic plates slip past each other in a lateral movement. Farther south around Los Angeles are "thrust faults," where one plate pushes the other downward at the point of convergence. Regions atop strike faults are considered more vulnerable because strike faults seem to produce earthquakes more readily. Many of the world's areas renowned for earthquakes, such as Japan or Central America, have strike faults underneath them. But some scientists say that earthquakes in a thrust-fault region, when they do occur, tend to be larger because the pressure builds to more destructive proportions.

Despite the presence of these faults, San Francisco (as well as the nation) has suffered no city-leveling earthquakes since 1906. The lack of extensive damage is due in part to the extensive building code modifications and other preparations taken by San Francisco and other Bay Area municipalities. But that's not all. Earthquakes come in cycles that are often separated by decades or even centuries. The 1906 and the 1989 Loma Prieta earthquakes in San Francisco marked the end of one period of seismic activity, and the probable start of another, experts say. With time, the danger looms all the greater. "We are entering a new period of seismic activity," says Mary Comerio, author of *Disaster Hits Home,* a study of the effect of large disasters on cities, and a professor of architecture at the University of California at Berkeley.

The 1989 Loma Prieta earthquake hit 7.1 on the Richter scale. It killed sixty-three people, toppled a freeway, left 16,000 buildings uninhabitable, and caused $5.9 billion in property damage. Yet seismologists rated the quake as moderate in size—the ground shook for only fifteen seconds, compared to more than a minute in 1906. In the 1923 Tokyo earthquake that killed almost 150,000 people, the ground shook for a full five minutes. A quake of this magnitude would almost certainly topple every

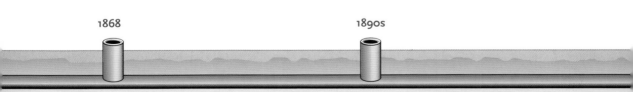

1868

An earthquake rocks the city. Others follow in coming decades.

1890s

Large sand dunes, once common in the city, are leveled and used as fill for lower areas such as Sullivan's Marsh, (now called South of Market Street). In later years, earthquakes will do extensive damage in these areas because the loose sand under the streets and buildings is particularly prone to shifting.

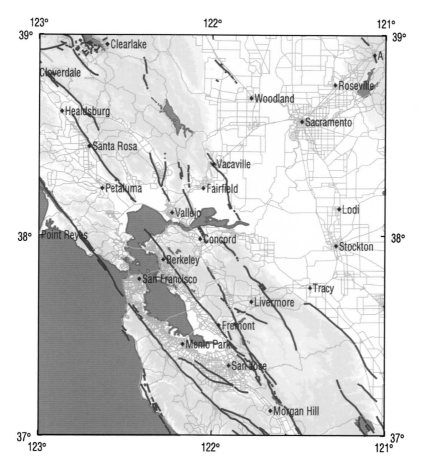

This map, showing the major faults crisscrossing the San Francisco region does not make for sound sleeping at nights.

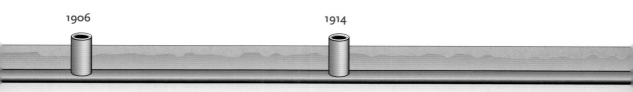

**1906**

**1914**

A massive earthquake and subsequent fire leave a smoking, wrecked city atop the hills and valleys. More than 3,000 people are killed. This natural disaster will become emblematic to the city and nation of the damage a great earthquake can do. Despite the damage, the city rebuilds rapidly.

State leaders begin construction of Hetch-Hetchy water system that will draw from lakes in Yosemite National Park, 160 miles away. It will take twenty years to build and require a special authorization by Congress to overcome legal challenges by opponents. The system will eventually provide 260 million gallons a day to 2.4 million people in the region.

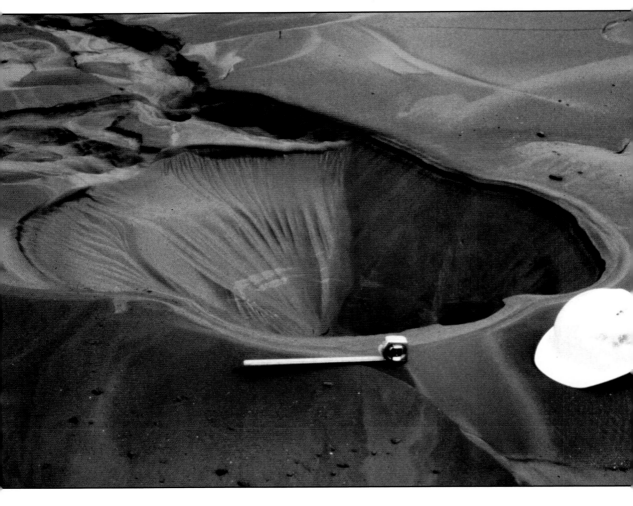

This *'sandbowl'* shows an example of *liquification* that occurred in the 1989 Loma Prieta earthquake.

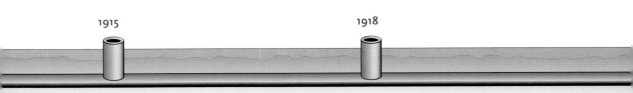

1915

1918

The new San Francisco City Hall opens in a large park in the middle of the city, replacing one destroyed in the 1906 quake. With a grand white dome, the new building more resembles a state capitol than a utilitarian municipal center. It is designed with a novel system of seismic protection that will be put to the test three generations later.

The Twin Peaks tunnel, more than 2 miles long, opens. Originally used for trolleys, it sparks a development boom in the western suburbs, now connected to downtown via the tunnel. Eventually San Francisco will have five major tunnels within its limits: Twin Peaks, Sunset, Stockton Street, Broadway, and Geary.

skyscraper in San Francisco's Central Business District, including the famous Transamerica Tower, and would destroy or extensively damage every major piece of infrastructure in the region, from water, to electricity, to train lines, bridges, and tunnels.

There is no precise definition of "major" when it comes to earthquakes. Where a city is concerned, it depends not only on how large the earthquake is but how close the city is to the fault lines. In general, seismologists refer to any earthquake lasting more than thirty seconds in length or measured as 7.0 or over on the Richter scale or IX and up on the Mercalli scale (but two among several different methods for measuring the intensity of earthquakes) as a "severe" earthquake. Although the Richter scale, one of the oldest, is the most familiar to the general public, more scientists use *the Modified Mercalli Intensity* scale. The difference in measurement systems can be partly attributed to how vibrations are calibrated in relation to the distance from an earthquake's epicenter.

One of the most vulnerable elements of the San Francisco infrastructure is what is known as the Hetch-Hetchy Aqueduct, which carries drinking water from a reservoir in Yosemite National Park, 160 miles to the east. The system, built from 1914 to 1934, provides 260 million gallons a day to 2.4 million people in the Bay Area. The pipeline runs through three major faults, the Hayward, the Calaveras, and the San Andreas, and is extremely susceptible to damage during an earthquake. The aging concrete pipes would easily shatter and tear in a big quake. A study by the San Francisco Public Utilities Commission judged that a major earthquake could leave the region without its principal source of water for up to two months, while the city's fourteen storage reservoirs and nine water tanks have only a five-day supply of water. Perhaps because of this nightmarish scenario, in 2002 the region's voters, famously reluctant to approve tax increases, supported a $1.6 billion bond measure to reinforce the Hetch-Hetchy water system against earthquake damage. (A few weeks after the vote, a broken six-inch pin cut off half the city's water supply—proof that the system

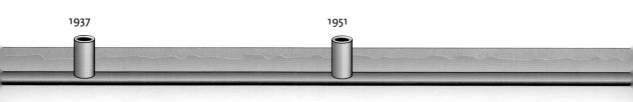

1937

The Golden Gate Bridge is finished across the harbor to Marin County.

1951

The California state legislature creates the San Francisco Bay Area Rapid Transit Commission, which studies the idea of a regional mass transit system.

needed repairs.) The money will not only reinforce key dams, it will also build alternative conduits, such as the $249 million pipeline around the southern tip of the San Francisco bay, which would give the region's water system needed redundancy in the event that an earthquake damages or destroys parts of the Hetch-Hetchy Aqueduct.

Another weak point is the Bay Area's extensive commuter rail network, much of which is underground—and underwater. The Bay Area Rapid Transit (BART) system includes the 3.6-mile *Transbay Tube*, which is 24 feet high by 48 feet wide and runs under the floor of the Bay at a maximum depth of up to 135 feet. Riding along in a sleek, quiet BART car, you may be disconcerted to notice a large sign that explains what do if the train is stranded under the bay. The word "earthquake" is not mentioned, but the implication is clear. Despite the risk, in 2002 BART was not able to secure the required two-thirds majority vote necessary to approve a one-billion-dollar earthquake protection program. (Under California law, most tax increases require not just a majority but a super-majority of two-thirds of those voting. This makes raising taxes very difficult.) Yet without additional protection, experts believe the BART system, particularly the elevated portions of the system and the Transbay tunnel, would be quite vulnerable in a major earthquake.

Just how vulnerable was a subject of some debate preceding the 2002 referendum. The BART system was constructed with reinforced steel and other materials that were judged as "earthquake ready" when work for BART was underway in the 1970s. But the 1989 Loma Prieta earthquakes prompted a reevaluation of what survives a quake. A study preceding the 2002 referendum said the pylons that bear the elevated tracks and the bolts that hold the Transbay tunnel together and in place would bend or come apart. The one-billion-dollar  protection program would essentially have paid to reinforce the pylons that held up elevated tracks, reinforce the "tie-downs" that hold the underwater tunnel in position under the bay, and in general strengthen thousands of individual weak points along the route. According to a recent study, a

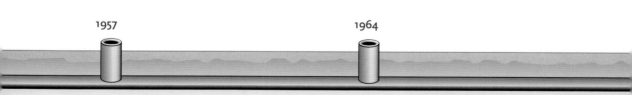

1957

A medium-size earthquake rocks the city, the worst since 1906. Many buildings are damaged but no lives lost.

1964

President Lyndon Johnson presides over a groundbreaking ceremony for Bay Area Rapid Transit or BART, a regional mass transit system that includes a tunnel under the bay to connect Oakland and San Francisco. During construction over the coming decade, crews unearth remnants of buried ships and other lost artifacts of the city's Gold Rush history.

major earthquake could shut down all or parts of the present system for up to two years. Without the money from the referendum, BART leaders are working to come up with another plan to safeguard the commuter railway .

"It's hard to imagine that after a major earthquake we will have any major systems left," Comerio says. "We have this antiquated infrastructure sitting in a seismic hot zone. And it may happen sooner rather than later."

The Embarcadero Freeway was destroyed in the 1989 Loma Prieta earthquake and was never rebuilt, which led to a revival of this district once the ugly freeway was dismantled.

1972                                          1989

The first phase of BART, including the 3.8-mile Transbay Tube under the bay, opens for business. Equipped with specially designed seismic protection measures, the tunnel and system will later be judged insufficiently safe, and experts will ask for money to do additional work.

A few minutes before the third game of the baseball World Series begins in Candlestick Park, the Loma Prieta earthquake, the biggest since 1906, hits the city. It topples a freeway, kills sixty-three people, leaves the city without power, and causes small fires around the region. But the BART system is relatively undamaged.

The city is making some progress in preparing for disaster. At key street intersections downtown, giant cisterns of water are in place under the street to be used in case the city's water system fails. This cisterns, which are intended not for drinking but to put out fires, actually date back prior to the 1906, but the city had allowed them to fall into disrepair. After the 1989 Loma Prieta quake, the city began maintaining the cistern system and checking it regularly. The city has other new precautions in place now, such as pipes leading into the bay that will fill an auxiliary water system with sea water to be used in case of a fire.

But it isn't enough. Lucien Canton, director of the city's Office of Emergency Services, is concerned that in a major earthquake, broken water lines would undermine the foundations of buildings and turn streets into rivers. But what worries him most is the subsequent lack of drinking water and potential outbreaks of disease caused by poor sanitation. "People can last seven days without food, and you can solve a lot of problems in seven days," he says. "But people can't last more than a few days without water."

People flee the fires that have erupted after the 1906 earthquake. The quake and the fires would destroy much of the city.

**2002**

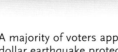

A majority of voters approve a one-billion-dollar earthquake protection program for BART—but not the two-thirds required by state law. The measure fails. Transportation officials scramble to come up with other ways to pay for improvements.

# FLOATING CITY HALL

Every year, some 3,000 couples marry at the top of the grand staircase in San Francisco's historic City Hall. There, under a dome that is larger than the one over the U.S. Capitol, brides in long white dresses and grooms in their tuxedos feel as if they're floating on air.

In reality, they're floating on rubber. Deep beneath this 1915 edifice, which in its classical monumentality and location on a stately lawn is often mistaken for the state capitol, is  a state-of-the-art subbasement foundation: 520 cylinders, each thirty-seven inches in diameter, made of alternating plates of rubber and steel. They're called base isolators, and are designed to gradually absorb and release an earthquake's energy. This massive building of brick and marble literally does not touch the ground.

City Hall did not always float on rubber and steel bumpers. When the building opened, less than a decade after the 1906 earthquake, architects equipped it with a more primitive, but still effective, means of earthquake protection. A weaker first-story floor was built to support four stronger upper stories. The idea was to prevent what usually happens in an earthquake: vibrations traveling up to the weakest point in a building—which in this case would have been the 306-foot-high dome—and causing a disaster. The hope was that by making the first floor the weakest part of the building, it would absorb the brunt of an earthquake, and spare the elaborate dome. This makes sense if you think of a multistory building as a house of cards built on a placemat. If you glue the lower levels of cards together, and then shake the placemat, then the top floors of cards will fall down and leave the lower story intact. But if you glue the upper stories together, and shake the placemat, then the bottom stories will fall down and leave the upper stories intact. With the San Francisco City Hall, they made the lower stories weaker so that any eartquake would more likely damage those floors than the upper floors and dome.

When the Loma Prieta earthquake hit, the plan worked brilliantly. The quake cracked the walls and the joints of the supporting columns throughout the first floor, but left the rest of the building relatively unharmed. Nevertheless, enough vibrations traveled up the building to rotate the dome six inches. The same solution could not work twice.

It took another decade and $300 million to retrofit City Hall with the new base isolation system. Workers jacked up each of the hundreds of columns that supported the buildings, millimeters at a time, until they could cut out a section of each column and insert the rubber base isolators. When the next earthquake hits, City Hall should be able to move up to twenty-seven inches in any direction with no damage. In fact, the building is now surrounded by a grassy moat of the same width to allow for shifting in the future. In San Francisco, only a handful of buildings are base-isolated. They include the new San Francisco Public Library, the U.S. Court House, and the Emergency Operations Center. The method is too expensive to use on anything but the most important public buildings and is not a common technique.

Just how much the city needs to prepare for an earthquake is disputed, even among the experts. "The problem is, the big earthquakes that cause severe damage are very, very rare," says Chris Arnold, an architect who has worked to help cities prepare for earthquakes. "So the question is how many preparations do you want to make when the earthquake might not happen for one hundred and fifty years? A fair amount of public money goes into all this. A lot of people feel San Francisco is not that well prepared, but it is probably as prepared, or perhaps even better prepared, than any other city. Preparation is so costly and expensive. So it's a question of how much you want to do. Then when a quake happens, there are all these recriminations. It's a pattern."

The preparations break down into two main initiatives, which are roughly equivalent to the medical principles of preventive care and emergency care. The first initiative involves precautionary engineering measures, such as retrofitting houses, office buildings, highways, bridges, and train and water tunnels to withstand seismic shifts. The second entails setting up emergency plans to supply people with food and water, care for the wounded, and rebuild after a quake.

Designing buildings to withstand massive earthquake damage is expensive, but it is possible to reinforce buildings and homes so they remain standing long enough for people to get out alive. "The goal of reinforcement is to get people out, not to leave the buildings usable," said Eric Elsesser, a structural engineer in San Francisco, and a world-renowned leader in the field of designing collapse-resistant buildings. Elsesser's firm, Forell/Elsesser Engineers, Inc., designed and installed several elaborate seismic protection systems underneath San Francisco, including City Hall (see sidebar).

Their work usually involves stiffening the walls to prevent lateral movement, and the use of specially designed fasteners that prevent floors, walls, and foundations from separating. Current city and state building codes mandate such measures in new construction, and owners of older buildings are encouraged by insurance companies and banks to retrofit their structures for seismic protection. Walking around the hilly streets of San Francisco, you can often spot bolts protruding from the sides of buildings that will hold the floor joists in place when the earth shakes.

Still, throughout the Bay Area, less than half of all homes—most of which  were built before the mandatory codes—have been retrofitted or reinforced. Authorities have found they cannot scare people into action. "You can only convince people to plan if it's fun, rather than planning their own funeral," says Jeanne Perkins from her

The Transbay tube is the linchpin of the BART (Bay Area Rapid Transit) system. Lying deep underwater, it was designed in the 1960s to withstand a major earthquake. Voters in 2002 failed to approve a billion-dollar renovation that would have made it even more secure.

# SUNKEN SHIPS, FAR FROM THE OCEAN

In 1994, workers digging a new subway tunnel in San Francisco found their way blocked by a wooden ship hull sheathed in copper. The story made the news, but nobody was too surprised. It was not the first boat to be found under the streets of San Francisco. With the gold rush came a wave of immigration, much of it by sea. In 1849, when the epic quest began, official records show that 695 ships docked in San Francisco, compared with just four the previous year. Most of these vessels were teeming with adventurers eager to stake their claim.

Ships' crews were no less eager to get rich quick, and many simply abandoned their boats. Soon the harbor was lined with hundreds of empty ships. In the ensuing decades, the ghost ships became part of the urban landscape, as the spaces between them were filled in and made into streets. Occasionally the ships themselves were turned into shops, homes, and businesses.

In the 1920s, an aging San Franciscan, Amelia Ransome Neville, remembered those days in *The Fantastic City: Memoirs of the Social and Romantic Life of Old San Francisco:*

> We went, one day, down to Long Wharf, now in 1856 part of the filled-in land that extended the city's waterfront eastward from Montgomery Street. It was strange to see old ships built into the city streets; derelicts that had been left where they lay in the mud flats when the land was filled in, waves and lapping waters forever lost to them.

As time passed and the city filled in more of the bay, the ships gradually disappeared beneath the rising land. Many are still there.

As for the hull sheathed in copper that the subway workers discovered, historians eventually determined that it was the *Roma*, a Russian-built ship abandoned around 1850. A decade previously, remains of the *William Gray* were found when the city constructed a new plaza. A few years before, workers unearthed the *Niantic*, an old whaler, while digging the foundations for a new office building. Although a few pieces of timber, tools, bottles, coins, and other artifacts of these ships have been placed in the city's Maritime Museum, such finds have become relatively common and most of these ships still rest where they were left, a busy port now hidden beneath downtown San Francisco.

office in Oakland, where she is the earthquake program manager for the Association of Bay Area Governments. "The latter is like telling people to get a root canal when their tooth doesn't hurt."

Ask your average San Franciscan if they ever think about earthquakes, and the answer is likely to be "No." For most residents, optimism is a way of dealing with the unknown, especially with the unpredictable and uncontrollable underground. Relatively speaking, San Francisco has done a tremendous amount of earthquake preparation, but experts continue to say the city is not sufficient.

"If things are not too badly damaged, we're okay," Elsesser said. "But if it is significant, we're in trouble. People are not willing to face it."

Following the 1849 Gold Rush, ships abandoned in the city's harbor eventually were turned into shops and homes as infill replaced water. Eventually many ships would end up deep underground as the city rose around them.

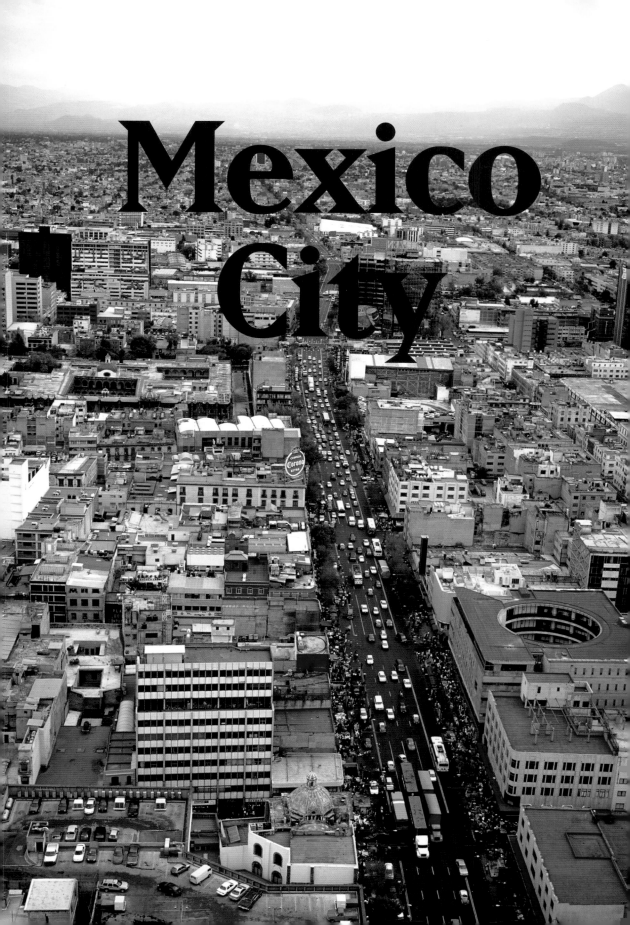

# Mexico City

Aztec ruins

Subway

Water

Sewer

Aquifer

Z ÓCALO SQUARE, AT THE HISTORIC AND geographic center of Mexico City, is an enormous ceremonial space in which everyone from demonstrators to flower sellers gathers. It is the focal point of this sprawling, polluted, problem-ridden but lively city, where a fifth of the country's roughly 100 million people live. A visitor could pass days wandering the square, visiting monuments, and exploring the lively atmosphere of the streets, buying tacos and roasted corn from vendors.

Zócalo Square, also known as Plaza de la Constitution, invites comparison to Red Square in Moscow, another vast open space surrounded by the institutions that govern a nation. On the north side is the 425-year-old National Cathedral, which Spanish conquistadors forced native Indians to build with stones taken from their own Aztec monuments. On the east side is the National Palace, where the country's president once had offices, but which now houses the National Archives, the Federal Treasury and other functions. The murals of Diego Rivera, gracing its second floor, with brilliantly colored images of Mexican history, are particularly striking. On the other side of the square, a quarter of a mile away to the west, is the Supreme Court, bracketed by important federal departments and major hotels.

Despite the stately buildings—meant to give Zócalo Square an air of grandeur and formality—you might feel off balance, maybe even a little seasick, standing in this open plaza. Why? Because the National Cathedral lists badly to the left. The National Palace, on the other hand, leans to the right. In fact, all the major buildings are askew, and the square itself slopes and slants in odd ways.

The dizzying effect is evidence not merely of bad soil or an aging city, but stems from something far more grave. Mexico City, the capital of the country, is sinking—and fast. It has sunk thirty feet in the last century alone. By comparison, Venice, Italy—a similarly unstable city whose problems have been much more widely publicized—has sunk less than a foot in the last century. In fact, Venice has sunk less in its 1,600-year history than Mexico City has in a few decades. In Zócalo

Square, random alterations to its monuments testify to this creeping submergence. For example, a water pipe, originally flush to the ground when installed before World War II, now juts out *three stories* into the air, like a straw protruding from a drink, because the city around it has fallen.

Historians believe the Aztecs founded Tenochtitlán, Mexico City's predecessor, in the early fourteenth century. It is said they picked the spot after seeing an eagle with a serpent in its mouth, which they took to be a sign from the gods. Unfortunately, the chosen location was an island in a huge body of water: Lake Texcoco. "The city was actually founded on the worst possible site," says Jose Castillo, an architect and urban planner in Mexico City. "The Aztecs were more interested in mythical aspects than good city planning. But even though they lived in swamps and lakes, they managed to build a great city."

"Great" culturally, economically, and architecturally, but *not* in consideration of what lies below. Mexico City is perched 7,250 feet above sea level—almost a mile and a half up—between Sierra Nevada and the Sierra de las Cruces mountains atop a giant aquifer—a sponge of water, silt, clay, volcanic rock, and other porous substances. Early on, even the Aztecs noticed that their pyramids and monuments tended to crack on the soggy soil. Making the situation worse is the modern city's thirst: Mexico City draws millions of gallons of water from this aquifer—water that is not being replaced fast enough to maintain an underground equilibrium. The aquifer replenishes itself with about 700 million cubic meters annually, but the city uses close to twice that amount of water per year. The result is that the "sponge" is drying up, and collapsing. Measures have been taken to slow the decline, but it is too little too late. Mexico City continues to sink.

Its submergence cannot be divorced from its bloody past. Here in the ancient capital of a mighty empire, Aztec priests once ripped the hearts out of live sacrificial victims on top of a pyramid near Zócalo Square. And this city on the lake has yet to reveal all of its secrets. Archaeologists and contractors digging beneath the metropolis

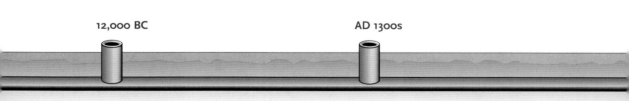

**12,000 BC**

A woolly mammoth wanders into a lake atop a high mountain plateau and drowns. Fourteen thousand years later, its bones will be discovered during construction of a subway line for Mexico City.

**AD 1300s**

The Aztecs establish a city on an island between two mountain lakes. According to tradition, they select the site after spotting an eagle perched on a cactus eating a serpent—a favorable omen.

**Country:** Mexico

**Location:** Northern Central America

**Population:** City, 8,591,309; federal district, 8,605,239; (2001 est.) metro. area, 18,268,000.

**Area:** Federal district, 571 square miles (1,479 square km)

continue to discover artifacts, monuments and temples. Traveling even further back in time, construction of the subway unearthed the fossilized remains of woolly mammoths, long extinct creatures that wandered into the lake and drowned around 12,000 BC. So to keep the water from swallowing Tenochtitlán, the Aztecs built dikes and canals to channel and contain the annual floods caused by heavy rainfall. But while Tenochtitlán was easy to defend and had a ready supply of drinking water, as with Venice and its lagoon, life in the Aztec capital meant a constant struggle against nature.

It was not, however, invincible. After the Spanish conquistador Hernándo Cortéz conquered Tenochtitlán with a handful of troops and killed the Aztec leader Montezuma

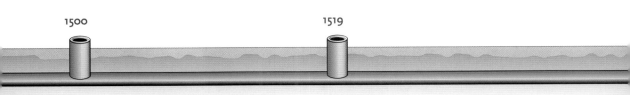

1500

1519

As the Aztecs conquer neighboring tribes, Tenochtitlán becomes their capital and grows to an estimated 100,000 inhabitants. They build dikes, canals, and bridges to channel the water and keep their temples and homes dry.

Spanish military leader Hernán Cortés and a few hundred soldiers conquer Tenochtitlán and kill its king, Montezuma.

in 1520, he razed the capital and built a new city on top of the old one. The Spanish brought in European engineers who drained most of the surrounding lakes in order to create more usable land. But the draining and subsequent construction depleted the ground's storage capacity for rain and runoff. That in turn left the new Mexico City resting on even less stable foundation, and condemned the modern metropolis to a shortage of clean water.

If there is a focal point to the city's gradual collapse, it is the National Cathedral, the oldest cathedral in the New World and one of the most significant works of architecture in North America. The Spanish architect Claudio de Arciniega designed and began construction of the twin-spired cathedral in 1573, on the site of a smaller church that had been built immediately after the conquest. Both the cathedral and the previous church were built directly on top of a major Aztec pyramid dedicated to the sun god Tonatiuh. Remnants of this and other Aztec monuments can be seen today in subway stations and the city's numerous museums. The cathedral took two and a half *centuries* to finish. One of the largest in the world, it measures 200 feet wide by 400 feet long.

Unfortunately, it also weighs about 127,000 tons. Experts estimate that, in the last century, the crushing mass of National Cathedral has settled twenty-three feet into the soft soil. From a structural point of view, the problem is not that the cathedral is sinking but that its parts are sinking at different rates. The base of the tower is now about eight feet lower than the base of the apse. To counter this uneven shifting, authorities have rebuilt foundations and put in pilings, without much effect. There were, however, monetary rewards from this work. During one foundation rebuilding, workers constructed thousands of crypts underneath the church, which they then sold to patrons to store the remains of loved ones in this holiest of spots.

The latest attempt to put the cathedral on better footing is a complex technique called "under-excavation" in which workers selectively remove even more soil from under the church, in order to let the higher points settle to the same level as the low

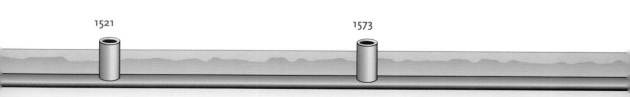

1521

1573

After establishing full control over the city and the Aztec Empire, the Spanish raze Tenochtitlán and establish Mexico City. Soon after, engineers begin draining the lakes to create more solid ground for streets and buildings.

Spanish architect Claudio de Arciniega designs and begins construction of the National Cathedral on the site of an Aztec temple. Still standing, it is the oldest existing cathedral in the New World.

Mexico City's massive Zocalo Square is sinking in the city's problematic soil, as is the National Cathedral on the left of photo.

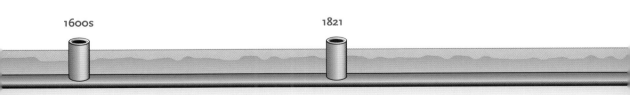

**1600s**

**1821**

Mexico City is the capital of "New Spain," a global empire that stretches from deep in South America into the present-day United States.

Mexico establishes its independence from Spain with the Treaty of Cordoba.

A model of the great temple at Tenochtitlán that was at the center of the Aztec City and that the Spanish destroyed.

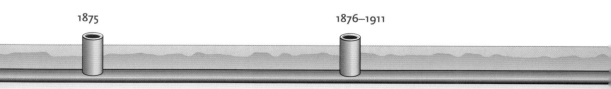

**1875**

**1876–1911**

The National Cathedral, now three centuries old, has sunk several feet, leading to numerous unsuccessful efforts over the next century to stabilize the structure.

Under the reign of President Porfirio Díaz, the city constructs first water, sewer, and drainage systems underneath the city, including the Grand Drainage Canal.

points. Rather than actually dig under the church, workers have bored more than thirty cylinders, each four inches in diameter, through the floor of the cathedral. Then machines suck up small quantities of soil from these tubes, as through a straw. Most of the soil has been extracted from beneath the north end of the church, to help it settle to the same level as the south end. Since the project started in 1993, a plumb line that hangs 139 feet down from the ceiling of the central nave shows the tilt of the church is gradually being corrected.

But Mexico City is not just tackling one church. It has initiated a variety of measures to stop the entire city itself from sinking, to clean up the polluted underground water supply, to stop flooding, and to find a safer, more dependable source of potable water. This is a vital and indispensable set of tasks, because the city cannot go on for many more years without addressing these basic problems. Without major changes, Mexico City will run out of water, sink further into the earth, and drown in its own sewage.

The first component of the plan is to stop leakage from the city's water pipes. As the city sinks, its pipes crack and break. In 1999, 32 percent of the city's water was wasted through leaking pipes. But finding the leaks is a challenge in itself. One new method uses sound waves to detect breaks in the pipes. Similar to radar, sound waves bounce back to the emitter whenever a major crack or break is detected. Once the exact location of a break is determined, a lining can be inserted to seal the break, without tearing up the streets. Leakage is gradually being reduced.

The second challenge is to bring in more fresh, clean water from outside the city, to reduce the drain on the aquifer. Mexico City currently taps several rivers and lakes, including the Cutzamala River eighty miles to the southwest. Most major cities rely on gravity to carry water from distant mountains down to the metropolis, which often sits by a river or harbor at or near sea level. But Mexico City lies in a high mountain valley, and this water must be lifted *up* to the city's elevation of more than 7,000 feet, using a series of expensive pumping stations. Gravity is no friend to Mexico City's water system.

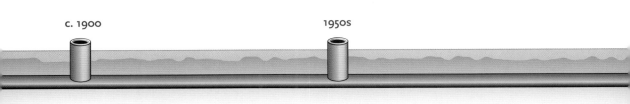

**c. 1900**

The growing city begins to sink many deep wells to supplement water from natural springs. As groundwater is depleted, the central city begins to sink.

**1950s**

The city's downtown has sunk several dozen feet. Studies are begun to consider ways to stop using ground water, and thus stop the city from sinking farther.

Another initiative seeks to charge more citizens for water use. Strange as it may seem, hundreds of thousands of people and businesses in Mexico City use its precious water at no cost. Many ancient meters have broken, and the poor condition of the system makes it difficult to keep track of usage, usage that is already outpacing nature's ability to replenish this resource. But in recent years, thousands of new electronic meters have been installed, enabling the city to earn much-needed cash while reducing free water consumption.

At the same time, Mexico City is building more wastewater treatment facilities. Currently, the city discharges millions of gallons of untreated sewage into fields around the city—mostly in the Tula Irrigation District to the north in the state of Hidalgo, where the dangerous waste pollutes the groundwater, causing rampant intestinal disease among the local population. The International Development Bank, helping to fund construction of better treatment plants, estimated in the year 2000 that more than 400,000 Mexicans were made sick by this untreated wastewater.

Paralleling improvements to sewage treatment is a plan to upgrade Mexico City's outdated and crumbling sewer pipes. Unlike its water, which has to be pumped into the city from deep below the earth and from reservoirs outside the city, its sewage moves not through a pressurized system but is expected to flow out of the city by gravity. The average home brings in water uphill and discharges sewage downhill. Given that the city sits on a mountain, you would think that sending the sewage down toward the sea would be an easy task. Yet because the city has sunk, many of the central sewage and drainage pipes now actually run uphill—an unanticipated but now obvious problem. A chief challenge is fashioning a replacement for the city's Grand Drainage Canal, a massive piece of infrastructure more than a century old. Constructed over several decades in the late nineteenth century and inaugurated under President Porfirio Díaz in 1900, this canal dropped a mere foot per mile along its route to the Gulf of Mexico. The canal travels out of the north end of the city through the seven-mile Tequisquiac Tunnel, a monumental project when constructed

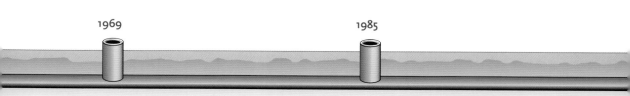

**1969**

The first line of Mexico City's subway opens.

**1985**

A major earthquake rocks the city and kills an estimated 7,000 people. Built to withstand seismic activity, the city's subway system suffers little damage and its rubber-wheeled trains are back in service within six hours of the quake. Other utilities, however, are badly damaged.

These Aztec figures perch beside the great temple that excavations beneath Zocalo Square have revealed.

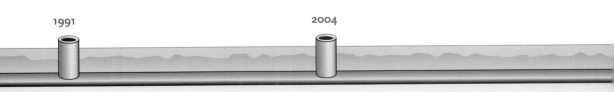

**1991**

**2004**

The federal government initiates an expensive project to stabilize National Cathedral, parts of which have sunk an estimated 23 feet.

With the cooperation of the national government, the city initiates a package of ambitious plans to patch up its leaky water system, improve drainage, and find ways to better integrate the city with its difficult high mountain environment. One plan would restore one of the lakes that the Aztecs depended on half a millennium before.

in the late nineteeenth century, and then into the Moctezuma River. From there, the water and waste travels out to the Gulf of Mexico. By 1970, the drop had been reduced to 6 inches per mile, and by 2000 there was scarcely any slope at all. A new, deep tunnel system is now necessary for sanitation but also to prevent the flooding that the summer rainy season brings. The city is using deep tunnel-boring technology to construct a new 124-mile network of underground sewers.

If Mexico City can succeed—if the leaks are plugged, water consumption reduced, new drainage systems built, wastewater treatment improved, more clean water brought in—it may stop its sinking, ease pollution, and restore its water program to something manageable. But it will take decades of steady effort and funding, something particularly difficult in this largely poor and very rapidly growing metropolis. Municipal officials have contracted with multinational engineering firms, such as the French giant Vivendi, to carry out most of these tasks. And there has been talk of completely privatizing the city's water and sewer systems and supplies, which many development experts say could threaten Mexico's sovereignty and long-term growth potential.

However, not everything under Mexico City is crumbling. Its innovative subway network, built largely by the French, is one of the best and busiest on Earth, despite operating on compromised subsoil in an underground cluttered with the remnants of a lost civilization. The pioneering system was the first in the world to employ rubber tires on concrete tracks—quieter

The Santa Cruz church in Mexico City, like so many historic buildings, is sinking because of groundwater depletion and now lists badly.

# A SINKING SISTER CITY

In Venice, Italy, sinking buildings are also a way of life. But while Mexico City descends into the soil, Venice sinks into the sea. Built on a series of islands in a marshy lagoon of the Adriatic Sea, Venice is surrounded by water. As a result, losing as little as an inch of terra firma can mean the difference between wet and dry streets. San Marco Square, where tourists sip pricey cappuccinos and feed the famous flocks of pigeons, is now flooded for about 100 days every year.

Venice, however, has successfully slowed its rate of descent by doing something Mexico City has yet to manage: In 1969 the city and surrounding region stopped using its underground aquifers. Particularly damaging were factories in nearby Port Marghera that had also been sucking water from the aquifers, dramatically accelerating the rate of Venice's descent. When the use of these underground aquifers stopped, the sinking of the city slowed as well. A new aqueduct was built to bring in water from the Alps for the factories and the city as a whole.

Like Mexico City, Venice also struggles to build a comprehensive sewage treatment system. Most waste is still dumped directly into the canals, compromising public health and contributing to the slow but steady rotting of Venice's stone and brick buildings.

Unfortunately, Venice is also threatened by a steadily rising sea. Some historians and hydrologists believe the Adriatic has risen six feet since Venice was founded in the fifth century AD. The latest plan to hold back the sea calls for a series of seventy-nine massive retractable underwater gates that would block high tides from swamping the city. The hollow steel gates would be positioned across three key straits in the Venetian lagoon; during periods of normal tidal activity they would be filled with water and submerged, allowing the currents to flow freely and cleanse the lagoon. At dangerously high tides, the water would be released, air would flow into the hollow gates, and they would rise and cut off more water from flowing into the lagoon—functioning like a floating dike. Although many engineers and environmentalists endorse this approach, some oppose it as an excessively large intervention. Work has been underway on the planning for this billion-dollar project for many years, and the construction of the project is still not a certainty.

than conventional steel rail systems and more forgiving of shifts in the soil. A ride on one of these trains feels at times like a roller-coaster as the cars bob up and down on concrete tracks that once were level, but now have sunk to varying depths.

Most of today's major subway systems—in large Western cities like Paris, New York, London, and Boston—were built in the early twentieth century. Later subways, like those in Washington, DC, Cairo, or Los Angeles, are limited networks that generally supplement automobile-oriented transportation. But Mexico City is an exception—its subway system originated in 1969 yet is one of the largest and busiest in the world. It carries the bulk of the city's traffic; without it, the capital would almost certainly shut down. The Mexico City subway system has more than 175 stations and 200 kilometers of track. Its ridership of 4.2 million passengers per day is comparable to that of Paris, New York, London, Tokyo, or Moscow. And it is cheap, costing just two pesos, or less than twenty-five cents per ride.

Perhaps even more impressive in this chaotic and sometime struggling city, the subway is clean and efficient. Similar to Cairo, Mexico has identified most stations with color schemes or distinctive artwork, in part so that a large illiterate population can find their way around. The Copilco station has reproductions of old masterpiece paintings, such as the *Mona Lisa*. The Insurgentes station, in a disorienting fashion, has a mural that shows a metro station in Paris. The Tacubaya station has painted murals showing Spanish conquistadors confronting Aztecs armed with spears and shields and Estación Guerrero has intricate tile work. At the Pino Suárez station,

an entire Aztec pyramid sits in the passageway between Line One and Line Two (the result of a fortuitous accident after the pyramid was uncovered during subway construction). While building Line Eight, the city's newest line whose first section opened in 1994, thousands of historic objects large and small were uncovered, including an entire Aztec neighborhood and a colonial-era Spanish

The Copilco subway station shows a rubber-tired train entering this French built system.

The Pino Suarez pyramid, shown here in 1970, was uncovered during construction of the city's subway.

hospital dating to the 1500s. Not surprisingly, these archeological finds delayed construction of the subway line and fueled battles between the National Institute of Anthropology and History and the Commission for Traffic and Urban Transportation. As is common in disputes over urban priorities, at issue was the path the metro would ultimately take and how long it was reasonable to delay construction so that more care could be taken with archeological excavations.

## THE SEWER DIVERS OF MEXICO CITY

Professional divers often find themselves in cold, dark, and inhospitable domains, but few environments are colder, blacker, and less inviting than the sewers of Mexico City. Like an intrepid hero in a fairy tale sent on perilous missions to save their societies from ruin, these well-equipped divers enter the dark domains of the sewers to keep a rickety system working. And their task is no less serious. They must succeed in order to keep some twenty million people from drowning in their own waste.

"Too many people and too much waste," one of the divers, "Cu," told a *Los Angeles Times* reporter in 2003 about why it was necessary to do what he did. "I still have fear," said Cu, who has been completing dives for more than two decades. "We never know what we're going to encounter below."

With the human body, medical science has developed ways to explore the bowels of a man or woman, and sometimes to make repairs or remove cancerous objects, without invasive surgery. Cu performs a similar operation on the bowels of a city—the hundreds of miles of antiquated pipes and conduits that carry away the waste and storm water of the populace, but are always on the verge of collapsing.

Before diving, Cu and three teammates each don a rubber "dry" suit that includes boots and a helmet, and is designed to completely encase them from any contact with the germ- and disease-ridden water which is their workplace. The divers wear waterproof gloves, which they wrap with duct tape at the sleeves to keep the sewage out. The steel-titanium helmet fits snugly over the dry suit, with a rubber collar at the intersection with the dry suit for a watertight seal. Like deep-sea divers, they do not wear tanks on their backs but are supplied air through a hose that runs back to a pump operated by another colleague above ground.

Their principal tasks are to remove obstructions and to make minor repairs. The obstructions can include everything from a plastic soda bottle lodged in the wrong place, to human cadavers, pieces of furniture, and the remains of almost every type of animal imaginable. Once half a Volkswagen car was found. Cu and his three other divers must operate completely in the dark and have memorized the design of pumps and motors, and can repair them by touch and feel alone. For more serious problems, they remove the devices and bring them out to be repaired above ground.

It is very dangerous work. A rip in their suit would expose them to all sorts of diseases. And an accident in such a murky labyrinth can mean instant death. In 2000, for example, a diver was killed after he dislodged an obstruction and was pulled deeper into the sewer by a sudden rush of water, severing his air connection. His body was found a mile downstream. Until Mexico City manages to design and build a modern, well-functioning sewer system, this ever-expanding metropolis will have to depend on heroic deeds performed out of sight and underground by Cu's small team of divers.

If bureaucratic wrangling is Mexico's intellectual sport, religious devotion is its soul. In 1997, a wet stain appeared on the floor of a subway station. Officials said it was simply a watermark, caused by rising water in the rainy season seeping upward into the floor. But an onlooker said it was in the shape of the Virgin Mary. Quickly dubbed by the press as the "Virgin of the Metro," the stain attracted thousands of visitors. Yet not all women in Mexico are so venerated. In 2000, the city designated separate subway cars for women so they could avoid the groping hands of its less saintly ridership.

Mexico City's subway stations are marked with distinctive color schemes or artwork so that illiterate citizens can find their way without reading lettered signs.

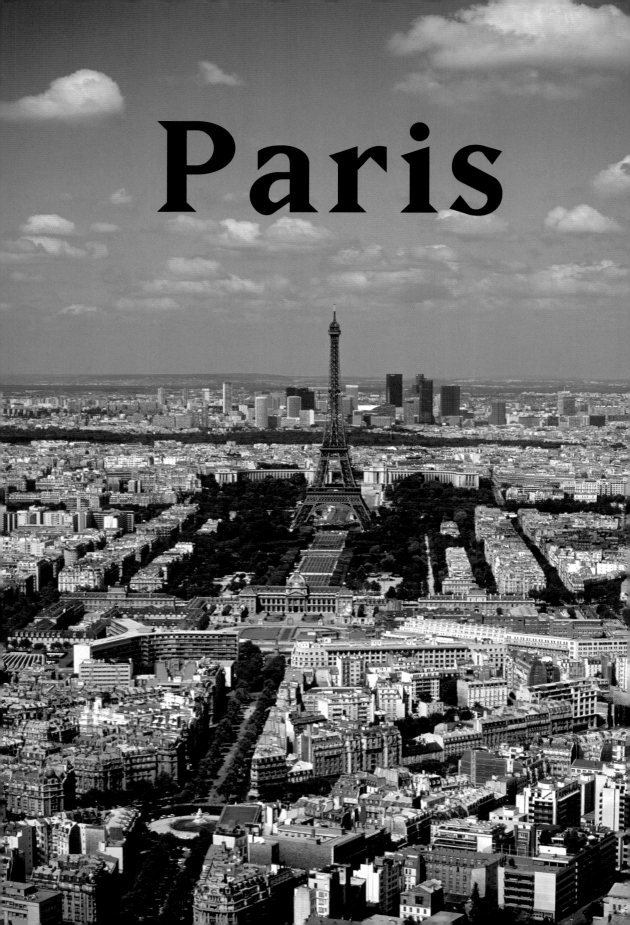

# Paris

P ARIS'S NEW NUMBER FOURTEEN SUBWAY line, the Météor, is completely automated; with no engineer's compartment, passengers can stand in the glass nose-cone of the first car and watch the light of the approaching station come closer and closer until it envelops them. The stations and the trains, which run down the Right Bank of the Seine before crossing underneath the river to terminate below the tall glass towers of the new French National Library, are marvels of engineering and design. Instead of a series of separate cars linked by the usual swinging or sliding steel doors, the Météor is one long, continuous tube lined with seats, the connections between individual cars scarcely noticeable. On the platforms, passengers wait behind a wall of glass, which opens when a train enters the station. On the platforms of the Gare de Lyon station, passengers wait next to a greenhouse, where plants bloom behind thick glass, bathed in electric growing lights. Each of the eight new Métro stations is strikingly unique architecturally.

The Météor is one of many ambitious projects underneath Paris, some very successful, others less so. There is France's new national library at the end of the Météor line—the Bibliothèque Nationale François-Mitterrand, a billion-dollar complex completed in 1998 that has eleven stories *underneath* a vast street-level plaza. There is the underground train and bus center at La Défense, the skyscraper district on the western edge of the city. Near the Louvre art museum is a fading underground shopping complex at the Forum des Halles, constructed on the site after the historic Les Halles market was torn down in 1969. In 2005 Paris began to entertain proposals to replace the unpopular Forum des Halles with yet another largely underground extravaganza. Two much older examples are the city's fabled catacombs and sewers, both of which can be visited today.

Tunnels full of bones, cavernous sewers, high-tech subways, and underground shopping malls—all were built by the various guises of the French state, whether led by Charles V in the 1300s, Napoleon Bonaparte in the 1800s, or one of the technocratic presidents in the 1900s. All have sponsored

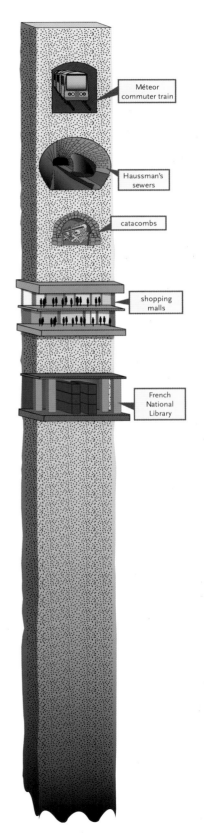

Météor commuter train

Haussman's sewers

catacombs

shopping malls

French National Library

public works that are technologically advanced, comprehensive in scope, and aesthetically ambitious. In France, bureaucratic nurturing begins early. Elite engineers—who go on to build high-speed trains, nuclear power plants, telephone systems, and subways—train at French Polytechnic University, a state-run school founded by Napoleon. Public works administrators are educated at the École Nationale d'Administration, the alma mater of numerous French presidents. Tuition there, as at the Polytechnic, is free, but admission is highly competitive.

The French capital's orderly underground realm contradicts the conventional wisdom that government is less efficient than private enterprise. In London and New York, where major public works were parceled out to private companies, the underground world is a jumble of competing systems, making it difficult to determine exactly what is under a given patch of asphalt. Beneath the streets of Paris, rational order reigns. The city's efficient infrastructure is the envy of the world and one reason Paris is still economically dynamic.

More than other major cities, Paris is one that works. More than a few of its visitors have been known to leave with a case of city-envy. "Paris is the most beautiful and well-organized big city in the world, and often insufferably smug about it," wrote staff correspondent Stuart Jeffries in the UK's *Guardian* newspaper in 2001. "Paris seems to be enjoying the best of times, London the worst of times. One is the city of light; the other a city of darkness, fog and vile things done in its forgotten corners."

The Paris Métro (subway), which Jeffries called "a gleaming affront to the [London] Tube," may be the best-functioning subway system in the world. Opened in 1900, four years before New York's and thirty-three years after London's, the Métro's sixteen lines snake to virtually every corner of the city. Usually one or more of its 380 stations is no more than a block away when you step out of a shop or apartment. The complete transit system includes the deeper express trains that are run by a separate agency, Réseau Express Régional (RER), as well as buses, suburban light rail and the high-speed trains run by La Société Nationale des Chemins Fer (SNCF). The Métro alone

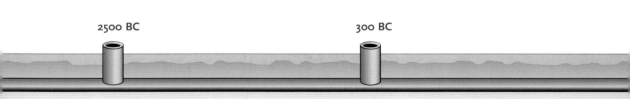

**2500 BC**

Tribes live and fish on the banks of the Seine River using hollowed-out logs as boats. The remnants will be discovered 20 to 30 feet under the earth during construction of the Météore subway, 4,500 years later.

**300 BC**

The Parisii, a branch of the Gauls, live on Îsle de la Cité and construct a small city there. Later, a greater city takes its name from the people.

**Country:** France
Location: Northern central plain, on the Seine River

**Population:** Paris, city: 2,125,000; metropolitan area: 9,645,000.

**Area:** Paris, city: 41 square miles (105 square kilometers); metropolitan area: 890 square miles (2,300 square kilometers)

carries 4.5 million people daily, a figure comparable to the ridership of New York, a much bigger city.

In the 1970s and '80s, the Métro was often named as the world's top subway, even if it occasionally had its share of trash and New York–style graffiti. But while always presentable, in recent years authorities have taken on a major renovation and rebuilding campaign, and the Métro positively gleams. Stations have been scrubbed and their platforms lined with art and exhibits, so that these areas almost become mini-museums. The pristine Louvre station features Egyptian mummies and other pieces of art—models of what a viewer will see inside the famous museum. And on the Météor line, authorities pay attention to every detail—even experimenting with

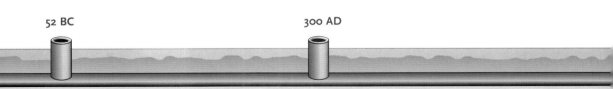

**52 BC**

**300 AD**

Julius Caesar conquers the city for Rome and drives out the Parisii. Romans establish the city of Lutetia on the Île de la Cité and the Right Bank of the Seine. Along with aqueduct for water, the Romans eventually construct a rudimentary sewer system under what is now Boulevard St. Michel, and mine the land for limestone rock.

The Roman city gradually falls into disrepair under barbarian invasions. The new town of Paris emerges on the Île de la Cité.

making the stations smell better by mixing a specially designed perfume called "Madeleine" with detergent when cleaning the stations (this is Paris, after all). Métro officials brag that the Météor line, despite its high-tech gleam and ease of use, costs less to operate than any other subway line in Paris, and cost less per mile to construct than the new Jubilee line in London, built roughly at the same time.

When French engineers were boring preliminary tunnels for the Météor line in 1990, they bumped up against a significant archeological find: several canoe-shaped boats, made of hollowed-out logs, that lay about 30 feet down in the soft mud along the banks of the Seine. The boats were carbon-dated 2800–2500 BC, making them among the earliest signs of human habitation in what would become Paris. Tribes that fished along this stretch of the river had used the boats, now housed in the Carnavalet Museum in the Marais district. Those early tribes eventually gave way to a branch of the Gauls called the Parisii, who settled on the current Île de la Cité (an island in the Seine) around 300 BC. Later, the Romans pushed out the Parisii and established their own city, Lutetia, on the island, the historic center of Paris.

Modern Paris rose from Lutetia in the fourth century CE, and began to coalesce into a capital city in the year 987, when Comte Hugh Capet proclaimed himself king. He and his successors then conquered neighboring feudal lords to establish the

The billion dollar new French National library, the bulk of which is underground, provides a cool and high-tech environment for its many users.

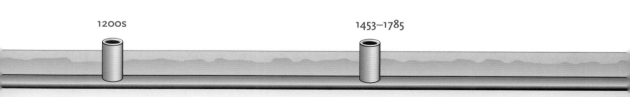

**1200S**

The Kingdom of France intensifies its underground mining for stone to build the cathedral of Notre-Dame, the Louvre, and other important state buildings. Mining continues into the nineteenth century.

**1453–1785**

The city builds a few small brick tunnels under some streets to help handle the sewage flowing there.

The cavernous sewers of Paris, laid out by Haussmann in the 1850s, not only carry waste but provide a space to put water, telephone and Internet lines.

**1780**

**1785**

Piles of human bones from an overflowing cemetery break through into the basements of elegant homes.

The minister of Louis XVI orders that the Cemetery of the Innocents and several other graveyards be cleared, and their contents packed into the unused quarries underneath Paris. Work continues for several years.

The new Météor Line fourteen, one of Paris's ultramodern new subway lines, ends at this spacious contemporary station for the French National Library.

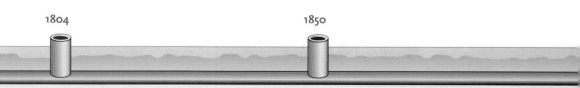

1804

1850

Napoleon I builds the first sewer system under Paris, but it is small and not comprehensive.

Baron Georges Haussmann, with his chief engineer Eugène Belgrand, build a comprehensive sewer system that becomes one of the marvels of the modern world.

nation of France. Subsequent monarchs consolidated the country's power around Paris, which grew rapidly.

By some measures the city was growing too quickly. One such measure was the mounting pile of human bones. For a thousand years, Parisians had thrown the bodies of their dead into a few mass graves in central Paris. (Individual burial was only for the wealthiest citizens.) During the reign of Louis XVI (late eighteenth century), the largest of these graveyards, not far from the city's central food market, was known as the Cemetery of the Innocents. There, the massive weight of mounting human bones forced open the foundations of adjacent buildings, spilling piles of skeletons into the basements of stately homes. City officials would periodically scoop out bones from the cemetery and bury them in an adjacent lot, but they were running out of room. Clearly, something had to be done.

In 1785, Louis XVI ordered the Cemetery of the Innocents cleaned out and the contents put into abandoned limestone quarries just outside the city. For more than a year, workers trundled cartloads of bones off to these quarries. The laborers inside the long tunnels, with priests at their side to bless their acts, stacked bones in rows with aisles in between. On either side of these narrow aisles, the bones were stacked in piles from 10 to 100 feet deep. Facing the aisles, along the walkways, the stacks of bones were held back by walls made of skulls and femurs set in decorative patterns. The skulls planted in these outer walls might form a heart, a cross, or some other design. It is a bizarre sight. The bones of approximately six million Parisians lie in these famous catacombs—more beings than in the current population of the city proper.

Visitors can see the bones of early Parisians on a tour of the Catacombs Museum, in the Montparnasse district. Take the Métro to the Denfert Rochereau stop, pay a few euros, descend a narrow, winding staircase that seems to go on forever, and soon you will be walking through more than a mile of tunnels, stacks of bones on either side. Even down here, the French bureaucracy is ever present. Chiseled into stone, next to

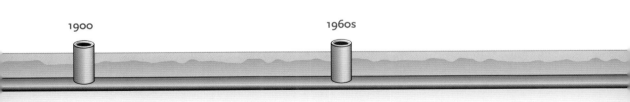

**1900**

The first Métro opens in Paris, with development continuing rapidly. Early lines include graceful art nouveau entrances designed by Hector Guimard.

**1960s**

Work begins on La Défense, a planned office district of skyscrapers that includes an underground shopping mall and transportation hub.

walls of bones, are block letters and dates, such as 65.G –1781. The date "1781" refers to when supporting pillars were placed in this section of the tunnels, and "65.G" is a number in an accounting system to keep track of all the different sections of the massive ossuary. On the bones themselves are other plaques with dates and names like "Ossements du Cimetière de St-Landry, le 18 juin 1792," which means that bones from the St. Landry cemetery were deposited here in June 1792.

More lyrical messages are also chiseled into the rock, or hung on plaques. One poem reads: "At the banquet of life, an unhappy guest, I appeared just the once, and now I die." At the entrance to the catacomb is another message: "Halt! You are entering the Empire of Death."

The abandoned quarries that served as a giant ossuary cover hundreds of miles beneath Paris, and the bones fill only a fraction of them. Much of the rock used to build the city's churches and monuments, including Notre Dame and the Louvre, came from these quarries. As the Romans had discovered, the land under Paris is limestone, excellent for construction and easy to bore through with hand tools. In addition, there are extensive deposits of gypsum which is used to make plaster. The abundance of this mineral and its association with the city produced the term *plaster of paris*. Much of it comes from the Montmartre hill that overlooks the city, where—aboveground—Pablo Picasso and other famous painters made their home.

For many centuries, mining was unregulated around the then-smaller city of Paris. Only when streets and buildings began to collapse because of the hollow spaces underneath them did the state hastily begin to regulate to construction and maintenance of the quarries. In 1774, about 1,000 feet of Rue d'Enfer collapsed, parts of it sinking to a depth of 100 feet. After this disaster, inspectors were appointed and policies drawn up. The state began inspecting the quarries and reinforcing weak points. Active mining within the old, walled city was banned in 1810, but it continued in outlying areas that are now within the city limits.

Those quarries still cause the city many problems. Constructing a new subway line

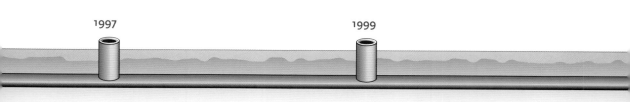

**1997**

The new National Library opens, which includes eleven stories underneath a central plaza.

**1999**

The Méteor opens, Paris's newest subway line.

is particularly difficult because engineers might be boring underneath, through, or over another large tunnel. As a result, state inspectors walk the tunnels and look for emerging holes in the ceiling, which can grow into cavities that will suck under entire streets and buildings.

Although problematic, the abandoned quarries of Paris have provided the city with an element of adventure and romance. Today, gangs of tunnel enthusiasts called Cataphiles illegally make their way into the quarries and wander for hours or days. They are pursued by the Paris police, who have earned the nickname of "Catacops" from the Cataphiles they seek to stop. In fact, these passageways have long been useful to Parisians challenging the authority of the state.

Rebellious citizens hid in the quarries throughout the nineteenth century but most memorably in 1871—when insurrectionists during the short-lived Paris Commune sought refuge from government troops amid the bones. It didn't work: soldiers entered the tunnels, hunted down the insurrectionists, and killed them. During World War II, members of the French Résistance hid in the quarries to avoid capture by the Nazis.

The Catacombs of Paris, which were originally abandoned mining tunnels, provide a resting place for millions of bones of past French citizens.

Haussmann's spacious brick-lined sewers were the envy of the world in the fifteenth century and touring the sewers in a special vehicle was a must for V.I.P. guests.

Estimates of the extent of the tunnels under Paris vary widely, and the state is constantly trying to restrict entry. "There is a map of the catacombs, but it is very complicated, and it is secret," says Alan Cayre, director of security for the Métro system. "If terrorists were to get their hands on that, it would be very bad."

But the quarries and catacombs are not the only source of mystery and legend below Paris. Perhaps even more famous are the city's nineteenth-century sewers—cavernous arched tunnels that were immortalized by Gaston Leroux in his 1911 fantastical novel, *Le Fantôme de l'Opera* (*The Phantom of the Opera.*) Almost fifty years earlier, in 1862, Victor Hugo wrote in *Les Miserables* that "the great prodigality of Paris, her marvelous fête, her Beaujon folly, her orgy, her full-handed outpouring of gold, her pageant, her luxury, her magnificence, is her sewer."

Said perhaps as only a Frenchman could, Hugo's enthusiasm for his city's great sewer (at the time a wonder of the world) is nonetheless understandable. Through the Renaissance, Paris had no sewers, relying instead on the ancient waste disposal method known as *tout à la rue*—everything to the street. (The Romans building here had at least one proper sewer beneath what is now the boulevard St. Michel in central Paris, but it was lost when Lutetia crumbled.) Hogs ate much of the garbage, leaving their own pungent excrement to mingle with the human waste, which collected in troughs running down the middle of the cobblestone streets. In rainy times, the waste might wash away; in dry times it would fester and stink, breeding insects and disease.

Making matters worse was the city's lack of a comprehensive water system. In 1700, the half-million residents of Paris relied on fifteen public water fountains, which brought in drinking water from the Seine—a river that was none too clean, given the lack of sewers. Wealthy citizens hired private water carriers—some 20,000 of them—who carried buckets balanced on bars across their shoulders.

In 1804, Napoleon constructed about eighteen miles of sewers, as well as a pipeline to draw water from outside the city. But his system was miniscule compared to the city's needs. Like New York in the same period, Paris was hit by successive cholera epidemics, caused by poor sanitation. The Seine became more and more polluted and the city's predicament worsened.

It was in 1852 that Napoleon III, nephew of the great emperor, appointed Baron Georges Haussmann as prefect of the Seine, a position akin to mayor. Haussmann was a classic French bureaucrat, having worked his way up through the government over several decades, advancing from post to post. Before being selected by Napoleon to come to Paris, Haussmann had been the administrator of the city of Bordeaux, where he acquired a fine cellar of wine and the reputation as a connoisseur of the beverage. Haussmann was an amateur student of gardening, landscape architecture, engineering, and design—all subjects that would serve him well when he came to Paris and evolved into a truly visionary civil administrator. With no formal training in city planning but with an innate sense of what worked, Haussmann immediately set out to recreate Paris. His legacy is not only the great city we now know, but also countless like-minded projects in cities around the world which took their cue from Haussmann's Paris.

Haussmann believed that modern Paris needed to be both beautiful and efficient, above- and belowground. His plan called for broad, tree-lined boulevards radiating from circular plazas and lined with identically scaled apartment buildings. Over two decades, he oversaw the construction of 125 miles of new avenues and streets, along with addition of 34,000 new buildings containing 215,000 new apartments.

To keep streets free of congestion, train lines were moved underground, and the four stations built during his tenure were grand monuments to progress. He built the Bois de Boulogne, giving the crowded city its version of New York's Central Park, under construction at the same time. Perhaps most important, the baron gave Paris sewers and a clean water system. Early-morning walkers in the historic neighborhoods of today's Paris might still see small jets of water emerging from between cobblestones for a bit of self-cleansing—a Haussmann innovation.

Napoleon III backed virtually all of Haussmann's ambitious plans, which cost huge sums of money and displaced thousands of people. The baron, who helped suppress prodemocracy revolts against his patron, preferred what he called "imperial efficiency" over "republican ineptitude." However draconian that philosophy may have been, Haussmann used his power to greatly improve the quality of life in Paris. In fact, he described his sewer and water system as if it were a living thing:

> The underground galleries, organs of the large city, would function like those of the human body. Pure and fresh water, light, and heat would circulate beneath the urban skin like the diverse fluids whose movement and maintenance support life. Secretions would take place mysteriously and would maintain public health without troubling the good order of the city and without spoiling its exterior beauty.

To accomplish his goals for a comprehensive water system, Haussmann and his chief engineer, Eugène Belgrand, designed underground canals that could accommodate both waste removal and fresh water delivery. The sewage flowed in the canal itself, while drinking water was transported through pipes attached to the brick ceilings. Walkways on either side allowed for maintenance and inspections.

His formula proved farsighted. As the machinery of the city multiplied over the

A water carrier, one of thousands who trudged back and forth between public fountains, delivers water at a home in the hilly Montmarte district of Paris.

next century and a half to include telegraphs, telephones, electricity, pneumatic tubes, fiber-optic cables, and other artifacts of modernity, the French found that much of it could simply be put in the tunnels, which were easily accessible and did not require digging up the streets.

Obtaining clean water meant bringing it in via aqueduct from the Champagne region, more than 100 miles to the southeast. For thousands of years, Parisians had drawn their water from the Seine, which doubled as a sewer, and yet many Parisians were attached to its murky water. In typical French fashion they insisted that the polluted Seine had "character," and that what had been good enough for their grandparents was good enough for them. They discounted theories that suggested dirty water caused cholera and other diseases. Haussmann complained of "the Homeric struggle against the fanatics of the Seine water."

But he eventually won the water battle, as he did most others. Once constructed, the sewer and water system sparked the pride of citizens and the imagination of

## THE FRENCH LOVE AFFAIR WITH ENGINEERING DESIGN

Alan Cayre, director of the new Météor subway line and head of security for the Paris Métro system, wears a sleek wristwatch with a gray face and minimalist black strokes to mark the hours. "Oh, this," he says when asked about the watch. "This is no big thing. It was done by one of the designers of the Météor line."

In a country where subway designers dabble in fashion accessories, it's to be expected that a bureaucrat like Cayre is attentive to matters of style. He works in the new headquarters of the French transit agency Régie Autonome des Transports Parisiens (RATP)—a striking building of steel and glass with a dramatic central atrium, part of the new Bercy district next to the Gare de Lyon train station. It's a stark contrast to the dreary warrens of cubicles that pass for transportation agencies in many other cities.

But the new office maintains the long French tradition of government projects that are both efficient and beautiful. At one point, Cayre walks to the wall of glass across from his desk and points down to an arched-steel bridge across the Seine to the Austerlitz train station, silhouetted by the setting sun and framed by the Eiffel Tower and Notre Dame Cathedral. "Even this simple bridge is well designed," he says. "It not only functions well; it is beautiful."

Just outside RATP headquarters is one of the most famous examples of the French tradition of practical beauty: an art nouveau entrance to the Métro, designed by Hector Guimard in the early 1900s. Guimard's sinuous portals still decorate many Métro stations, inviting commuters to step through a fantasy of exploding dragonfly wings holding teardrop lights, and sinuous vines wrapped around glazed

glass canopies. After World War II, as art nouveau fell out of fashion, these entrances were torn down without thought, until Parisians gradually began realizing what they were losing. The grand entrances are now symbols of both the Métro and the French love of appearances, and they are protected through historic preservation laws. Now comfortingly familiar, these entrances were once considered on the cutting edge of the avant-garde, and (like the Eiffel Tower) not immediately loved by Parisians. So—sleek Météor or nostalgic Métro? *A Chacun, son goût.*

The sinuous cast-iron portals to the Paris Métro, designed by Hector Guimard in art nouveau style, are cherished around the world and symbolize the romance of Paris.

visitors. Kings and emperors stepped into small boats that ran through the underground waterways, to marvel at the tunnels. Engineers and politicians journeyed to Paris and returned home ready to transform their own cities. The Paris water system even made some democrats yearn for an engineer-dictator of their own.

"When one hears of the marvels Napoleon has accomplished in Paris . . . it makes one wish that he, or someone like him, could be made Emperor of New York for about ten years," opined a New York newspaper in 1868. "We want a Hausmann [*sic*] who will do for New York what that great reconstructor did for Paris."

Many cities from all over the world sent their own planners to Paris for consultations with the baron. Chicago's chief engineer, Ellis Chesbrough, used Paris as a model in designing a sewer for the burgeoning American city. And when the sultan of Cairo, Khedive Isma'il, was planning to build a new Cairo alongside the old, he, too, sought advice from Haussmann.

Paris's modern sewer system, which snakes beneath the sprawling city for more than 1,000 miles, has expanded far beyond Haussmann's original canals, but his canals remain in use. The wastewater itself no longer flows into the Seine but is carried to a huge processing center at Achères, about twelve miles from Paris, one of the largest waste treatment plants in Europe. Until 1975, tourists could pay to ride in small boats through the Paris sewer canals. Today the popular tours, which begin not far from the Eiffel Tower, are limited to traversing the walkways. While most visitors are curious to see the haunts of the fictional Phantom of the Opera, they often leave the tour with a greater appreciation for Haussmann's efficient vision of underground engineering—and for the somewhat disturbing efficiency of authoritarian regimes.

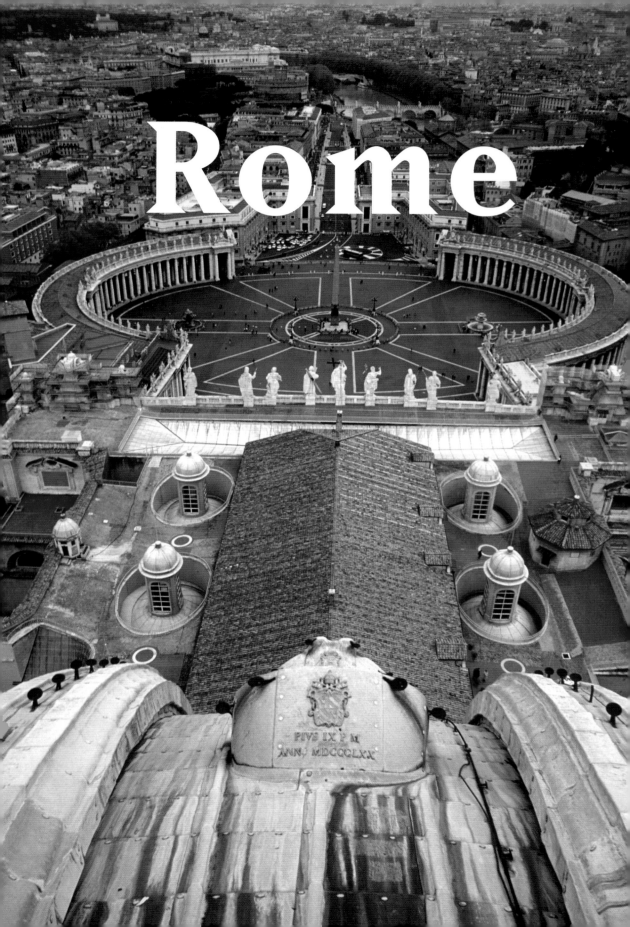

ROME, THE CAPITAL OF ITALY, IS VERY much a city of the present—frenetic, gritty, and teeming with boisterous citizens whose passion for strong coffee and cigarettes is matched only by their disdain for traffic rules. Yet the blur of Italian motor scooters is nothing compared to the head-spinning carousel of history, Roman style. In every street and plaza, under churches and fountains, behind gates and down crooked marble stairways, modern Rome merges constantly with the glorious past of the Roman Empire—from the Renaissance (the origin of the contemporary city) to the ancient territory that stretched from England to the Middle East.

Aboveground, Romans stroll past the two-thousand-year-old Coliseum, where gladiators once vied with lions for the entertainment of a bloodthirsty public. Next to a fountain by Bernini, a Baroque-period sculptor, they sip cappucinos in the Piazza Navona, site of the ancient chariot circus. And they attend outdoor concerts in the Piazza del Campidoglio, designed by Michelangelo, on the summit of Rome's most sacred hill. These monuments are on every tourist itinerary. Less well known (but in many cases accessible to the public) is Rome's underground realm of marble columns, early brick apartment buildings, and plaster walls frescoed with colorful scenes of ancient gods. The former mayor of Rome, Francesco Rutelli, says his city has many mysteries, secrets, and surprises, "but most astonishing of all is the Rome, as vast as the visible city, that lies belowground."

Just as on the busy streets above, the past and present intersect everywhere underground. In 1580, the French writer Montaigne marveled that Romans "do not seek any other foundations for their houses other than old ruined buildings or vaults, such as are seen at the bottom of all cellars." Likewise, much of the city still uses a sewer system built by the ancients. And Rome's small subway has taken half a century to build (it's still unfinished), in part because of the difficulty in avoiding underground ruins.

Indeed, it would be hard to find a place in Rome that does not have historically interesting ruins beneath it. Since

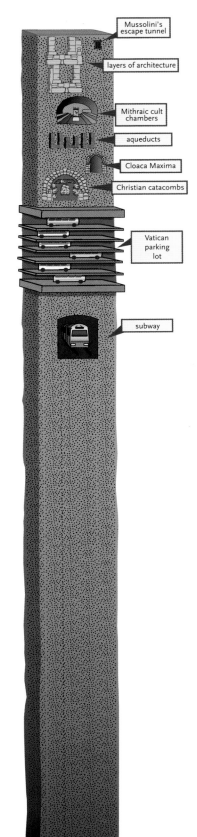

Mussolini's escape tunnel

layers of architecture

Mithraic cult chambers

aqueducts

Cloaca Maxima

Christian catacombs

Vatican parking lot

subway

the days of Julius Caesar (100–44 BC), the city has risen thirty to fifty feet, due principally to three factors: the annual flooding of the Tiber River (until the mid-nineteenth century, when the river was reengineered); rubble left from buildings destroyed in fire or war; and the general accumulation of dirt and human debris. This rise is understandable. After all, over a 3,000-year history, even a few inches per century adds up. Everything that once existed aboveground in ancient Rome—streets, latrines, fountains, stadiums, public baths, and temples—still exists beneath the current surface of the city, although much has been excavated. Lower still are even more ancient ruins that were underground to begin with, such as water and sewer lines, and burial places known as catacombs. This underground treasury, much of it in surprisingly good shape, reveals the beauty and sophistication of the earliest days of Rome.

A good place to get a sense of Rome's underground layers is the twelfth-century church of San Clemente, not far from where cars whiz around the traffic circle by the Coliseum. There, at the bottom of a small staircase, is the rectangular hall of a previous basilica, built in the fourth century. Down yet another staircase is a pagan temple from the first century. On a still lower level are the remains of a public building that was destroyed in Emperor Nero's fire of AD 64. There, the archeological excavations end, but the layers continue, with walls of tufa, one of the principal types of limestone from this region, continuing farther down. This layer awaits further excavation.

San Clemente is hardly unique. Just down the street, underneath the Esquiline Hill in the shadow of the Coliseum, are the remains of Nero's Domus Aura, his Golden House. The emperor built this lavish, sprawling villa in the heart of Rome (even then an extremely dense city) as a show of imperial power. Excavations have revealed gilded ceilings and walls decorated with elaborate drawings and frescoes. The site also contains centuries-old graffiti, from Renaissance artists who scrambled into the ruins and left their marks on the walls.

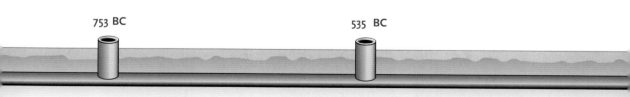

**753 BC**

According to legend, troops that survived the sacking of Troy settle near what will become the city of Rome. Soon after that, Romulus, son of the war god Mars, founds the city on the banks of the Tiber River.

**535  BC**

King Tarquinius Superbus constructs a canal to drain water from the Forum and other low-lying land. It will evolve into the Cloaca Maxima, the central trunk line sewer that will be core of the Roman sewer system.

**Country:** Italy

**Location:** On the Tiber River, about fourteen miles from the Tyrrhenian Sea (an arm of the Mediterranean Sea), between Italy's central mountains and the western coast.

**Population:** city, 2.7 million; metropolitan area, 4 million

**Area:** 582 square miles

Nero is not the only autocrat who left part of his history under Rome. In the late 1930s and early '40s, the fascist leader Benito Mussolini secretly built escape tunnels from his government offices near the Roman Forum. His labyrinth was only discovered near the end of the twentieth century.

More amusing have been excavations that reveal the leisurely side of ancient Roman life. North of the Coliseum, underneath the Via Degli Annibaldi, is a *nympheum,* one of several in the city that have been excavated and are open to the public. In ancient Rome, a *nympheum,* with its fountains and pools, was technically a shrine to water gods and goddesses, but in practice served as a recreational space in a wealthy home. Seashells embedded into the walls of this example enhance the

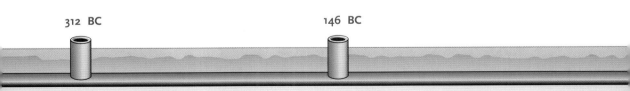

**312 BC**

Roman leader Appius Claudius Caecus constructs the Aqua Appia, a 10-mile underground channel that brings fresh water from a spring into the city. It is the first of eleven aqueducts into the growing city of Rome.

**146 BC**

The Romans conquer rival Carthage, raze the city, and expand their empire throughout the Mediterranean.

maritime theme and predate similar inlaid ornamentation by the nineteenth-century Spanish architect from Barcelona, Antonio Gaudi.

The average Roman did not enjoy such luxuries, however. In fact, the tapestry of ruins under Rome provides a surprising picture of the ancient city's dense infrastructure: its residents crammed into five- and six-story apartment buildings on tight streets. Not far from the Capitoline Hill is an almost complete set of such apartment blocks—underground.

Having a detached house was almost as rare in ancient Rome as in contemporary Manhattan. In AD 100, according to an official census, Rome had 46,602 blocks of apartments (*insulae*) and just 1,797 single-family homes (*domi*). And, as in modern-day New York City, housing was expensive. Writers in ancient times marveled at the sums people paid to live in a cramped apartment, when the same amount would buy a villa outside the city. But a country villa would not buy its occupant access to the life of the capital. Then as now, people in ancient times paid a premium to live at the epicenter of politics, commerce, and culture, rather than outside it. Demographers estimate that about 1 million people lived in ancient Rome—a metropolis whose size would not be matched again in the West until London hit that mark in AD 1800.

Despite the crowds, Rome was surprisingly clean, with a water and sewer system of impressive scope and complexity. Water flowed by gravity from springs and lakes, some more than 100 miles away, into conduits, called *aqueducts*, that were bored through rock in the countryside and then, close to the city, were carried on massive stone arches across the final distance to Rome. From the aqueducts, the water flowed into sealed holding tanks called *castellums*, then was dispersed into an underground system of lead pipes, which fed public fountains and a few private ones inside the households of the very wealthy. Contrary to popular belief, the lead pipes probably did not make Romans crazy. Many experts believe the extremely hard water would have quickly encrusted the pipes with mineral deposits that protected the flow from lead contamination.

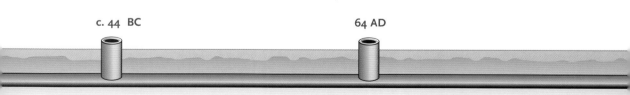

c. 44 BC

Roman dictator Julius Caesar bans chariots from city streets during daylight hours in an attempt to ease traffic congestion.

64 AD

Fire destroys two-thirds of Rome; Emperor Nero requires new buildings to be at least 10 feet apart and to have tile roofs to aid in fire prevention. Rumors circulate that Nero started the fire himself to pave the way for rebuilding, but Nero blames Christians.

Visitors stroll amid the surprisingly serene environment of the Catacombs where the bones of thousands of Christians lie.

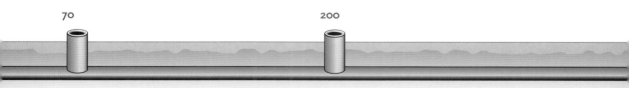

70

200

Emperor Vespasian begins construction of Rome's Coliseum for popular spectacles. Underneath the coliseum is a network of tunnels and chambers where gladiators and animals are kept before fighting.

Early Christians begin constructing what will become the extensive network of catacombs to house their dead. Scholars estimate the existence of up to 600 miles of Christian, Jewish, and Pagan catacombs in and around Rome.

The San Clemente Church sits over many layers of history dating back to ancient pagan temples on the same site.

317

476

Emperor Constantine, after defeating his rival in battle under the sign of the cross, converts to Christianity and starts construction of the new official church of the empire on the Vatican Hill.

Germanic tribes depose the last of the Roman emperors in the West, Romulus Augustus. Most of the aqueducts silt up, and the city of Rome declines in population until eventually cows graze on site of the Roman forum.

The water pipes were buried (generally at depths of ten to twenty feet) in part for security, so enemies could not cut off or contaminate the water supply. The Aqua Virgo, one of Rome's original underground aqueducts, is still in use today and delivers water to the city's famous Trevi Fountain.

Rome's sewer system was a marvel as well. The Cloaca Maxima, or Great Sewer, dates back to the sixth century BC, and parts of it are still functioning. This brick-and-stone-lined, now-underground canal cut through the center of Rome, and carried away the city's waste into the Tiber. Historians believe it was initially an open drain that in the subsequent centuries was covered over by buildings and streets. By the first century AD, the Cloaca Maxima was about 12 feet high and 10 feet wide. Smaller sewers, many of them open channels on the sides of streets, fed into the Cloaca Maxima. Because its origins are so ancient—2,600 years ago—historians still debate whether the Great Sewer was initially a natural creek that ran through the city or was entirely man made. The Cloaca Maxima was used initially to drain swampy land to make it suitable for construction.

The Great Sewer helped keep ancient Rome clean, but not all sewage flowed into it. The wealthy had private toilets, and these probably drained into cesspits. Other Romans used the extensive network of public toilets—at one time more than one hundred—sprinkled around the city. It's a feature many a modern urbanite might conceivably envy. But the toilets of ancient Rome were "public" in a way that might discomfit the average city-dweller today. Most of these "restrooms" seated a dozen or more people, who sat in rows on benches with openings cut into them. Flowing water underneath would flush the waste away into the Cloaca Maxima.

If ancient water and sewer lines demonstrate the Roman regard for cleanliness and physical comfort, religious shrines attest to the city's spiritual focus. Some of the best-preserved underground sites are mysterious shrines—many of which, in our evidence-based era, are less well understood than the empirical desire for fresh water.

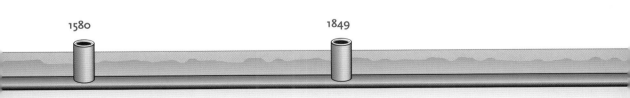

**1580**

French writer Michel de Montaigne visits Rome and describes the Renaissance city taking shape atop the ruins of the ancients.

**1849**

Italian archeologist Giovan Battista De Rossi discovers the San Callisto catacombs near the Vatican. American novelist Nathaniel Hawthorne visits them a few years later and in his novel, The Marble Faun, describes them as "intricate passages . . . hewn, in some forgotten age, out of a dark-red, crumbly stone."

Consider the cult of Mithraism, which took hold in the second and third centuries AD—just as Christianity was emerging.

Most pre-Christian Romans worshipped gods derived from the Greeks, but within this pagan spectrum were other cults and sects that gained substantial power. Mithraism, which was imported from Persia, centered on the god Mithras, who killed a sacred bull with a sword; from the bull's blood sprang wheat, grapes, and other benefits of the earth. Contemporary bullfighting may have roots in the cult of Mithras, who was often depicted wearing a cape.

Because secret initiation rites were key to the practice, Mithraic sacred sites were often hidden underground, where ceremonies, including blood initiations took place in special rooms. Such chambers were typically halls equipped with benches; on the walls were plaques or statues illustrating the story of Mithras and the bull. Once

Christianity became the official state religion of Rome in AD 317, many Christian churches were built on top of what had been pagan temples, including those of the Mithraic cults. This development ironically helped preserve the older pagan shrines, which in modern times have been discovered beneath San Clemente, Santa Prisca, San Stefano Rotondo, and several other Roman churches still in use today.

The Nymphaeum of via degli Annibaldi. The Nymphaeum served as Temples and gathering places and were usually built around fountains or natural springs.

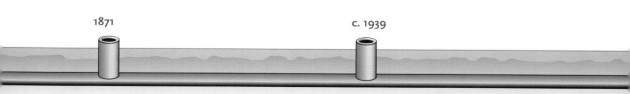

1871

Rome becomes the capital of a newly unified country of Italy.

c. 1939

Fascist dictator Benito Mussolini has a secret escape route constructed for him that leads from his offices in the Palazzo Venezia. (Excavation work in the 1980s uncovers the tunnel.)

This massive aqueduct outside Rome and others like it carried water hundreds of miles to major cities. Such systems would not be matched until the late nineteenth century.

The early Christians had some unusual rites of their own. Many involved burying the dead in special underground chambers—the Catacombs. When Christianity was still illegal or at best an unofficial religion, its followers constructed miles of tunnels to house human remains because cemeteries and above ground cremation were illegal for them. The bodies were placed in recesses beside underground corridors, a practice

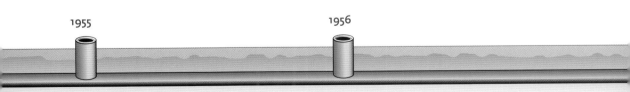

**1955**

Rome's first subway opens.

**1956**

The pastor of the San Pietro church discovers extensive archeological remains when replacing the tile floor. Ongoing archeological work reveals at least five layers beneath the building, including a basilica from the fifth century and a villa from the time of Emperor Nero.

that in fact derived from ancient Jewish custom. The Catacombs form a labyrinth underneath Rome; portions can be entered on guided tours from the Via Appia Antica.

A more recent but even stranger Christian death chamber is the underground Crypt of the Capuchins, dating from the eighteenth century. Housed beneath the Church of the Immaculate Conception, on Via Veneto, the crypt enshrines the remains of more than 4,000 Capuchin monks. The reasoning is a bit hard to understand, but the Capuchins stated that the display was meant as "an artistic representation of the

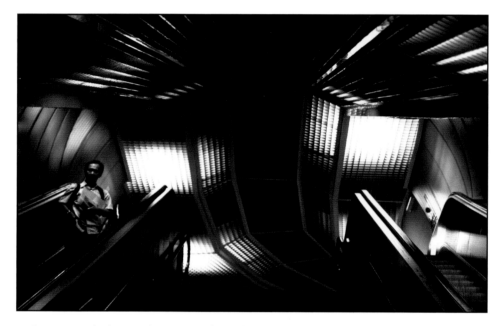

A visitor travels down to the garage underneath the Vatican that is known as "God's Parking Lot."

**2000**

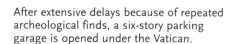

After extensive delays because of repeated archeological finds, a six-story parking garage is opened under the Vatican.

triumph of life over death." Whatever the rationale, the end result is certainly quite startling. The monks separated the bones of their brother monks into component parts— skulls, fingers, ribs, thighbones, vertebrae, scapulae—and then used them for interior decoration of four chapels underground. There are lamps made of jawbones, a clock made of vertebrae, and a hanging chandelier fashioned from vertebrae and other back-bones. These macabre chambers are both nightmarish and darkly comic—especially considering the ironic aphorisms displayed on plaques. One reads: "What you are now, we were. What we are now, you will be."

## BENEATH THE VATICAN CITY

Across the Tiber River from the heart of Rome is the Vatican City, an independent state that is the center of the Roman Catholic Church and the home of the pope. With its sacred (and priceless) masterpieces by Michelangelo, Bernini, and others, the Vatican is a pilgrimage site for Catholics and art historians alike. Yet none of its splendor would exist if not for a simple grave, long presumed to lie deep below the altar of Saint Peter's Basilica.

The grave belongs to Saint Peter himself, who was among the Christians martyred by Emperor Nero after the great fire in AD 64. The small cemetery where Peter was buried, just outside the walls of Rome, soon became a shrine to Christians. When Emperor Constantine converted to Christianity in 317, making Christianity the official religion of the entire Roman Empire, he began construction of a church atop this most sacred site.

For centuries, the exact location of Peter's grave—or even its existence—was unknown. But excavations begun by the Roman Catholic Church during World War II suggest that Peter's remains could be exactly where legend has them—directly below the main altar of the current basilica, which was built in the sixteenth century. At first the excavations revealed, as expected, the ruins of Constantine's original basilica, which was demolished by Pope Julius II in 1506 to make way for the new church. But as the digging continued, workers found a rough-hewn brick wall from AD 160. (The bricks, manufactured by a state-run union, had been stamped with the date.) On the plaster walls were a variety of religious graffiti. One line, carved out in Greek, read "PETR ENI"—Peter is here. Inside and beneath these brick walls was a human skeleton—quite possibly Saint Peter's.

"It was this modest shrine that formed the focus of the entire Constantinian complex," writes the scholar Charles B. McClendon. "The Early Christian shrine was found to lie directly below the High Altar of the present basilica of Saint Peter. The one element that never changed over the entire history of the site was the position of the tomb."

*continued on p. 112*

*continued from p. 111*

The primitive brick walls at the lowest levels give way to costly marble closer to the surface. Thus, archeology tells the story of how a beleaguered cult of the poor grew into a state-sponsored religion that would be integrated with the governing of the Roman Empire.

Intrepid visitors can view the ongoing excavations at Saint Peter's through a glass wall; appointments usually must be made six months in advance. And if you drive to your appointment at the Vatican, you'll get to experience another underground wonder—known locally as "God's Parking Lot." The six-story parking garage was built *under* the Vatican to hold 100 tour buses and as many as 800 cars. Its opening in 2000 came after extensive delays. Archeologists opposed the project as an unnecessary disruption. Once underway, the project was delayed again after construction crews ran into an ancient villa, possibly that of Nero's mother Agrippina—who, like Saint Peter, was also ordered killed by the ruthless, quite possibly mad Nero.

The crypt of the Capuchins whose monks built elaborate decor out of human bones to drive home the transience of mortal life.

Given the concentration of priceless historic artifacts beneath Rome, it is understandable that constructing more modern urban services is difficult. The city has a two-line subway, lines A and B, constructed in an X-pattern across the city. But the system is relatively new and small. The underground portion is only about twenty miles long, and the system has merely two dozen stations, versus several hundred stations in the subways of other major cities (New York has almost 500). Rome's first subway line did not open until 1955. The first stage of the second line only became operational in 1980. Construction of a third line, Line C, has been repeatedly delayed as engineers encounter unanticipated archeological ruins in the tunnel's intended path, despite the fact that the line's planned depth is eighty-six feet beneath today's metropolis.

Romans have a love-hate relationship with their underground past. Befriend a resident of the city's center, and he may proudly show you some bits of mosaic tile or marble columns that intrude into his own basement. But many Romans keep these private finds quiet, out of fear that if authorities find out, archeologists will descend on their households and restrict what they may do. It's tantalizing to ponder how many basement artifacts are secretly guarded—but even more tantalizing to imagine the undiscovered worlds that still lie buried under modern Rome, unknown to anyone alive today but nonetheless part of this ancient Italian city's lost memory.

# London

T O A ROMAN CITIZEN, LONDINIUM, A city on the empire's northern edge, was a provincial backwater. To get there, a traveler had to traverse the Alps or circumvent them via Provence, trek across Gaul, navigate the stormy Channel to Britannia and then journey up a winding river to arrive at the small walled outpost. There, after hundreds of miles, the ship would dock at massive oaken quays, while other vessels delivered wine and took on passengers to carry back to Rome.

Although the course of the Thames River has shifted substantially in 2,000 years, London's ancient Roman origins can still be seen under the modern city. Excavations beneath Lower Thames Street, about 110 yards (100 meters) from the present waterline, have revealed the oak timbers of those Roman quays. Archeologists calculate that the quays must have originally been 600 yards long and 55 yards wide (550 by 50 meters).

Other traces of Londinium continue to be unearthed to this day: during big construction projects in London, fragments of colored Roman floor tiles are still surfacing and artifacts pertaining to daily life in the ancient settlement continue to emerge.

Even more significant is the way that English London still reflects Roman Londinium, as Paris reflects its Roman origins in the ancient city of Lutetia. The path of London Bridge, for example, is thought to follow the route of the principal Roman roads in and out of town. The famous Leadenhall Market, a delicate structure of iron and glass built in 1881 that still stands, rests on the site of a great hall the Romans built as part of their city's reconstruction after barbarians sacked Londinium about AD 60. Londinium recovered from that onslaught and continued to function for several centuries after that, but by the fifth century it had been largely abandoned, as the Roman Empire as a whole disintegrated. The town began to reemerge as a trading center only in the late seventh century.

As Londinium grew from an outpost on the edge of a Mediterranean empire to a city at the center of a global one, it

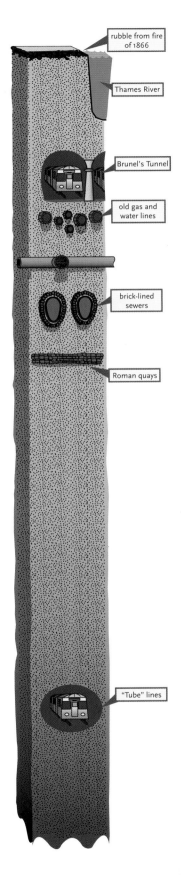

rubble from fire of 1866

Thames River

Brunel's Tunnel

old gas and water lines

brick-lined sewers

Roman quays

"Tube" lines

spread out, up—and down. From dungeons built by England's medieval kings to "priest holes" for hiding outlawed Catholic religious leaders to the bomb shelters designed by Winston Churchill, London has one of the most varied and fascinating of the world's underground urban domains.

Although it is not the prettiest or most well ordered, this city that is famously confusing aboveground, with its jumble of streets lacking any semblance of a pattern, also has perhaps the most chaotic and confusing underworld of any capital. Steen Eiler Rasmussen, in her 1934 book, *London: The Unique City,* calls it a "scattered city," and the term applies as much belowground as it does above. Between the medieval dungeons and the twentieth-century war bunkers came brick-lined sewers; nineteenth-century water tunnels built by private companies; a thirty-two-story inverted skyscraper to house the national archives; and of course the city's sprawling, amazingly comprehensive subway system, the London Underground, nicknamed "the Tube." Older sections of the Tube are undependable and in need of repair, but stunning new lines and stations show the progress that has been made.

The most recent addition to the world beneath London is an entire eight-story building, part of the newly relocated British Library, at St. Pancras station, that opened in 1998 after thirty years of fighting over its design. (France has put much of its new national library below street level, too.) Less conspicuous is a new water main, eight feet in diameter and fifty miles long with an average depth of forty-three yards or forty meters that encircles London. Competing for space are the remnants of roughly a dozen streams and rivers. Some of the city's most important thoroughfares, such as Fleet Street, are named after the rivers that used to be in their path. Parts of the Fleet tributary remained open into the nineteenth century; others, such as Walbrook, Tyburn, Westborne, and Counter's Creek, were covered in medieval times. Hydrology and archeology experts estimate that there were once more than 100 miles of waterways in what is now Greater London. Besides lost rivers, they have detected

50,000,000 BC

43 AD

Oceans cover what is now London, leaving deposits of seashells and other fossilized sea life that are still found today beneath the city.

The Romans found Londinium.

**Country:** United Kingdom

**Location:** Southeastern England, on the Thames River

**Population:** "City of London": 7,185; Greater London: 7,172,091

**Area:** "City of London": 1.1 square miles (2.9 square kilometers); Greater London: 659 square miles (1,705 square kilometers)

the remains of a receded sea. In the chalky clay soil beneath the metropolis, seashells and fossilized sea lilies, starfish, and sea urchins lie buried.

London's complex underworld reflects its hydrology: many of the old waterways have been incorporated into the sewer and storm-water system. But the seemingly random layout of the underground systems also mirrors the cultural and political history of England. Beginning with King John's forced signing of the Magna Carta in 1215, yielding some of his power to landed nobles, British political muscle became more and more decentralized over the centuries; dominance and responsibility gradually became divided among multiple jurisdictions, localities, corporations, and authorities. That is why the "City of London" technically consists of just

1216

1666

Henry III is crowned king of England at the age of nine. He goes onto install water pipes and a rudimentary sewer system for his own Palace of Westminster, but the city as a whole would have to wait more than 500 years.

London burns down. The city's complicated system of property rights, with both long-term leases and outright ownership, helps prevent implementation of Christopher Wren's plan to redesign the city, which included plans for water and sewer systems.

one square mile around St. Paul's Cathedral, with a population of just a little over 7,000 people.

Unlike Paris (a city that grew under the watchful eye of a centralized national government, especially after Napoleon), the national government of Great Britain could not as easily expand its capital's borders as the city grew physically, nor could it order the thirty-two separate boroughs of London to do its bidding. But with so many different entities responsible for a divided landscape, it was inevitable that the underground systems would be fragmented as well. Below London, roughly forty abandoned subway stations (almost certainly more than under any other city) remain unused, all of them parts of lines planned by competing companies. Similarly, there are far more extraneous water, sewer, gas, and electrical lines here than anywhere else. By comparison, in Paris, centuries of largely top-down centralized authority have left that city with neat, orderly, and efficient urban systems underground, as manifested in its gleaming Métro and its spacious, well-mapped sewers.

With virtually no comprehensive record of what has been built in the past under London, upgrades are difficult and expensive. "It's a very London problem, because the characteristics of London don't come from the vision of one planner or architect," said Roland Paoletti, architect of the city's new Jubilee Line extension, in a 1999 interview. "It's chaotic down there. You can't believe what's going on."

Despite the problem of subterranean construction, some architects and builders have pursued new projects fearlessly; the eight floors beneath the new British Library being one of the most noteworthy new underground spaces. Designed by Sir Colin St. John Wilson, the building is a blessed haven for scholars but provokes the ire of architecture critics because of its controversial design that features plain flat walls faced with unadorned red brick. Prince Charles famously said the new British Library resembled a training school for the secret police.

As with the new French National Library in Paris, whose design was also controversial but which the powerful French bureaucracy took only a few years to approve

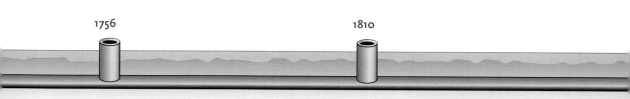

**1756**

The king of Corsica dies in London while on a mission to raise funds for new kingdom. His grave is still located at St. Anne's church in the Soho section of London.

**1810**

Some 200,000 cesspits serve a population of a million people, making London the biggest city in the Western world. But inadequate drainage from cesspits breeds disease and turns the Thames into a polluted mess.

Workers tear up Fleet Street in preparation for installing infrastructure, perhaps sewers.

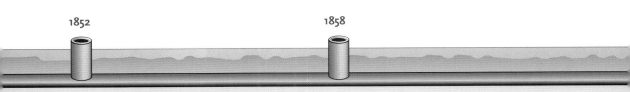

1852

1858

Parliament passes the Metropolitan Water Act, which requires the half-dozen private water companies to filter their water when drawing it from Thames and to move the intake valves upstream. The city's death rate by disease quickly drops.

"The Great Stink" from the Thames prompts the nearby House of Commons to pass and fund construction of a sewer system.

Depiction of sewers underneath Fleet Street.

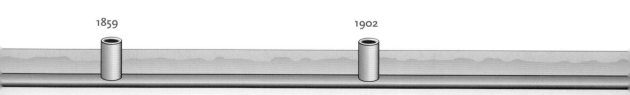

1859

1902

Joseph Bazalgette, chief engineer of the Metropolitan Board of Works, comes up with a plan to convert underground rivers into large main sewers called "interceptory sewers." Bazalgette builds almost 100 miles of sewers, all of which are in use today.

London nationalizes its water system, which until now has been run by private companies. The Metropolitan Water Board is created.

and build, most of the collection of the British Library is stored in vast, football-field-size floors underground. Construction of this type is amazingly expensive, and it's one reason the final price tag for the library was about $800 million dollars. But it makes sense to have gone ahead with the project, for both practical and political reasons: for books, as with wine, underground storage means temperature and humidity control is far easier than in tall buildings that must be protected from the glare of the sun and the variable temperatures of the changing seasons. Creating such a space underground also circumvented the fact that building "up" in London is a difficult proposition: the city is not one of towering giants but of low-rise townhouses and other modestly scaled buildings. Altering the city's skyline is sure to provoke a political fight.

The unwieldy nature of London both physically and politically is one reason some residents call it "the city that doesn't work." Ongoing attempts to improve the Underground are, for many, a textbook example of this nickname. The Tube was the world's first, but today, as subways all over the world have improved their service, London's subway system is struggling to return to a place of leadership. Westminster, Piccadilly, and many other well-known, heavily used stations have at times suffered from dirty platforms, broken escalators, and unpredictable service. Although the system is improving, relying on the Tube can sometimes be a gamble. Londoners tell of simple journeys taking hours instead of the expected minutes, as they are forced to reroute around stations or lines closed because of fires, crowding, or equipment failures. Londoners almost seem to revel in pointing out how bad their once-great subway system has become. A headline in the *Independent* newspaper summed it up in 2001: THE UNDERGROUND WAS ONCE A SOURCE OF PRIDE, BUT NOW IT SHAMES THE COUNTRY AS A WHOLE. Maxwell Hutchinson, writing in *Underground to Everywhere,* put it this way:

**May 31, 1915**

Germans planes drop bombs on the outskirts of London. Thousands take refuge in subway as the raids intensify. Both the bombing and the seeking of shelter in the Underground foreshadow the much larger events of World War II a generation later.

**1940**

Londoners escape the Blitz by going into the Underground. On September 27, 177,500 people were recorded as sleeping in the train stations.

It is sad indeed, at the beginning of the third millennium, that this awe-inspiring concoction of engineering achievements has become such a vile object of hatred. . . . [I]t is sad that a younger generation of Londoners will not see the tube as I saw it for the first time. For them, it is unreliable, expensive, over-crowded, dirty and, with the rise in street crime, potentially dangerous.

This is perhaps overstating it a bit. Overall, most of the system is clean and quiet and has effective amenities like electric signs that announce incoming trains. But it's also true that the Underground has accumulated an enormous and expensive to-do list of badly needed maintenance after decades of relative neglect. Much of the political infighting recently has been over who will perform these repairs and who will pay for them. Perhaps this is the burden that comes from being first.

The Tube was not always thus.

Opened in 1863—four decades before either New York or Paris had a subway—the Underground began as the Metropolitan Railway, a single line that ran between Farringdon Street, a stone's throw from St. Paul's cathedral in the old city, out to Paddington Street near Regent's Park.

Over the next generation, different private companies built relatively small competing lines and attempted to solve various technical problems. Chief among them was how to vent vapor from the steam engines used to haul the cars. It was not until 1890 that the Prince of Wales, the City, and South London Railway opened the world's first electric underground train line, from King William Street in the City of London under the River Thames to Stockwell.

Competing private companies continued to expand upon London's early lines. Most were built after 1906, during the same era when New York, Paris, Budapest, Boston, and other cities were building subways. These businesses laid out lines such as the Bakerloo, the Piccadilly, and the Hampstead in attempts to capture the most traffic, and without regard to creating an efficient, comprehensive network. The result

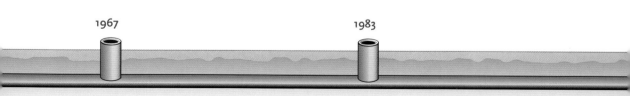

**1967**

The Greater London Council, a political body representing the metropolitan area, takes over responsibility for the management of the Underground.

**1983**

Prime Minister Margaret Thatcher does away with the Greater London Council, which is run by Ken Livingstone, a leader from the rival Labor Party. Thatcher hands the duties over to new body called London Regional Transport.

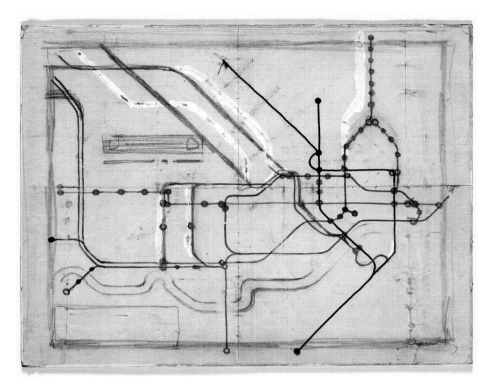

This map of London's underground by Henry C. Beck set a new standard for clean, rational design. A version of the map is still in use today.

is that London's network of subway lines is particularly disordered. After the London Underground was put under government control in the 1920s, duplicate or less necessary stations were abandoned. They include the old British Museum and Downing Street stations, both closed in 1932, and more recently the Aldwych station, closed in

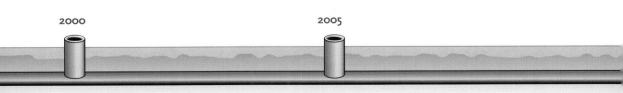

**2000**

**2005**

Transport for London, a new organization created by the national Labor government, takes over management of the London Underground.

Terrorist plant multiple bombs in several stations under central London, causing deaths, injuries, and massive traffic jams at street level when the Tube shuts down.

1994. Although proposals to adapt the unused stations for other purposes have surfaced, they generally lie vacant, occasionally used as locations for filming music videos.

In the 1920s and '30s, Frank Pick, chief planner for the British government's new Underground Group, an administrative agency created to run the newly nationalized subway system, led the system to its "golden age" after the competing lines were put under centralized government control. Pick supervised the construction of art deco stations such as Southgate and Clapham South, designed by Charles Holden. Pick also hired Henry C. Beck, a graphic designer, to create a comprehensive map that rationalized the crazy quilt of lines. A version of Beck's famous, easily readable map, updated over the years, is still used today. And under Pick's tenure, designer Edward Johnston came up with the distinctive red bar-and-circle Underground logo, which has evolved into a symbol of London itself.

After World War II, some new subway lines were built and ridership increased. But the national and regional governments, busy with new initiatives like national healthcare, began to slack off on maintenance. Similar trends toward negligence were underway in New York City. As the London Underground fell into disrepair, various political leaders tried to avoid responsibility for its upkeep or pushed it off onto someone else. In the postwar period, the bureaucracy governing the Underground was reorganized about a dozen times, but the system continued to decline.

In the 1980s, London's underground transportation issues were fought out at street level in Parliamentary skirmishes. Conservative Prime Minister Margaret Thatcher and Ken Livingstone, liberal Labor leader of the Greater London Council, warred over the Tube's management and fate. Thatcher initiated privatization of the national train lines, and she wanted to do the same to the Tube or at least to drastically reduce national government funding. In this time period, Livingstone began his "Fares Fair" campaign to lower Tube prices—a slap in the face of Thatcher, as this would have required more government funding, not less. In response, Thatcher slashed funding for the Tube and used her power to dissolve the London Council that Livingstone led. But the Labor leader returned to power in 2002 as the first elected mayor of a new regional London government. There he continued to advocate for better Underground service, and in 2003 he gained political credibility with his traffic management system for central London that received positive early reviews (a system charging a fee to incoming automobile commuters).

In 2003, Prime Minister Tony Blair gave Livingstone's regional government authority over the Tube, but only on the condition that it accepted a partial privatization of much of the service, something Livingstone had strongly opposed. As laid out in 2,800 pages of contractual language, private companies under the supervision of the government would run the trains and maintain the tracks. Although critics

The Southwark underground tube station is part of London's new Jubilee
Line, which stands in sharp contrast to the older, often poorly maintained parts of the system.

predicted disaster, proponents said the setup would save money and improve service.
Besides improving service, the major goal was to stop the increasingly common
accidents caused by poor maintenance. One of the worst disasters occurred in 1987,
when thirty-one people died in a fire at the King's Cross station after someone
dropped a lit match on an escalator.

"It's been so under-invested in the last decade that [the Tube] is in a fairly perilous
state," says William Parks of Transport for London, the new group under Livingstone
that manages the subway. Parks claims the Tube ". . . does need a huge investment to
bring it up to scratch."

Joseph Bazalgette, chief designer of London's first comprehensive sewer system, stands atop one of his trunk line brick sewers under construction.

Fortunately, London is resilient as well as wealthy, and the city is embarking on an effort to improve the Underground. The new Jubilee Line extension has been completed, the first line south of the Thames to run roughly parallel with the river. With a price tag of about five billion dollars, it includes eleven new stations (bringing the total to 275 city-wide), each planned by a different architect. The Canary Wharf station, designed by Sir Norman Foster, features a soaring glass canopy that carries light deep into the station. On the platform, passengers wait behind glass walls—shielding them from the tracks—that automatically open as the sleek, high-speed trains pull into the station.

But renovating the older lines in the system is more difficult. It means raising and spending huge sums to put in new tracks, renovate stations, upgrade signaling and replace trains. And Londoners, who may need to hold their nose in certain stations, aren't holding their breath.

Along with more conventional repairs and renovations, the lethal bombing attacks of July 7, 2005 in the Tube have raised the question of whether the tunnels and plat-forms, many a century or more old, can be better protected against such attacks. It's not a new question.

Londoners endured decades of tension from the 1970s to the turn of the century during struggles with the Irish Republican Army, which frequently exploded bombs in the city. The London Underground has long lacked public trash cans so that terrorists would not have an easy place to plant explosive devices. After the 2005 attacks, it was not immediately clear just how the system could be made more secure.

At least Londoners don't have to think much about their wastewater. Before its sewers were built, London relied on more than 200,000 unsanitary cesspits under buildings. As in Paris, this effluvium found its way to the River Thames, the principal source of the city's water. Consequently, for centuries, epidemics of cholera and typhoid periodically raged through London. The novelist Tobias Smollet wrote in the eighteenth century that "If I drink water I must quaff the mawkish contents of an open aqueduct exposed to all manner of defilement, or swallow what comes from the River Thames, impregnated by all the filth of London and Westminster."

In nineteenth-century London, a half dozen or more water companies, all drawing water from the Thames, competed for business. J. C. Wylie, in *The Wastes of Civilization,* notes that, "Despite high death rates, fortunes were made out of the supply of poisonous waters," and that "some streets had three separate pipe lines with three sets of laborers digging them." With the Metropolitan Water Act of 1852, Parliament ordered companies to filter water and to move their intake valves upriver. Death rates in the city quickly dropped.

In spite of growing health concerns, the city might never have developed its sewer system in the nineteenth century if not for "The Big Stink" of 1858. That year, the Thames turned putrid from all of the waste feeding into its current. Streets in central London, with old river tributaries beneath them, literally radiated heat because of the fermenting sewage below. Parliament, whose offices sat directly beside the Thames, could scarcely ignore the problem—especially after curtains soaked with lime were hung over the windows of the House of Commons to keep out the smell. Soon enough, members broke their long-standing opposition and voted on allocating money for a comprehensive sewage system.

The man who designed the city's graceful brick-lined sewers, which still serve much of London, was Joseph Bazalgette. His French-sounding surname is apt, given that he influenced Baron Haussmann in Paris, who at the same time was building that city's own comprehensive sewer system. For thirty-three years, Bazalgette was chief engineer to the Metropolitan Board of Works, London's first metropolitan government. Bazalgette designed his tunnels in an upside-down egg shape, which caused the water toward the bottom to run faster, thus scouring the tunnel clean of its collected waste. Between 1859 and 1865, he diverted underground rivers into six large interceptor sewers, many along the banks of the Thames, sewers that are still used today. He produced an estimated 100 miles of these interceptor sewers, 400 miles of main sewers, and 13,000 miles of smaller local sewers. Thanks to Bazalgette's efforts, London's sewage today flows not into the Thames but into the Beckon Works treatment plant facility, which opened in 1865.

## UNDER THE BLITZ

The air-raid sirens sound and, in what is becoming a practiced routine, you take your children and head into the Underground. On the platform by the tracks, you huddle with hundreds of other families in the cold and damp. You try to sleep but squeeze in only a few hours as you and your family lie next to people you don't know. Decades later, you remember small pleasures: a cup of tea and a game of cards with strangers who became new friends; a feeling of closeness and community with your family and neighbors that you would never experience so intensely again aboveground.

Such was life in London during World War II, as the Nazis pursued a strategy of aerial bombardment with planes and dronelike V2 rockets. The London Underground was the city's principal bomb shelter, and time spent there came to symbolize the country's indomitable spirit during the war.

Initially, authorities prohibited taking refuge in the subway, posting large signs reading UNDERGROUND STATIONS MUST NOT BE USED AS AIR RAID SHELTERS. Although there seemed to be some bureaucratic reflex in this prohibition, the official logic was that using subway stations as bomb shelters would disrupt the functioning of this essential service. But Londoners went down anyway. Because most of the Underground was tunneled several stories below city streets, the stations offered ideal protection. Soon the official policy was changed. Shortly after the aerial campaign began, while policy was still being sorted out, authorities counted 117,000 people taking refuge on subway platforms. Eventually seventy-nine deep Tube stations were designated as official shelters.

They soon developed their own culture and lifestyle. Several stations published newsletters, such as *The Swiss Cottager,* named after the Swiss Cottage station in South Hampstead. An intershelter darts league was organized, as were lending libraries for books.

Even so, life underground was decidedly unpleasant. Many stations had only buckets for bathrooms. Eventually, some stations were equipped with toilets that used compressed air to jettison waste up to the public sewer system, which ran above the level of the station tunnels. People slept end to end and side by side like sardines in a can. Henry Moore, the famous sculptor, was in London at the time, and made sketches of people sleeping on platforms and stairs. They look like lost souls in purgatory. One bulletin helpfully advised, "Vibrations due to heavy gunfire or other causes will be felt much less if you do not lie with your head against the wall."

German bombs still found their way into these lairs of safety, despite the subway's depth. One bomb broke through street pavement, entered into a church crypt, and bounced down a flight of escalator stairs before exploding in the midst of the Bank station, killing 117 people. In another incident, more than 600 people died when a German bombshell burst a water main, flooding a station.

During the war, Winston Churchill approved the construction of ten additional shelters, deep underground. Eight of these shelters, each of which consisted of two 1,200-foot-long tunnels, eventually were built—four for the public and four to be used as military headquarters. General Dwight D. Eisenhower, commander of the Allied forces in Europe, made his headquarters in one of these underground bunkers during the latter years of the war. The shelters were constructed beside or beneath existing subway stations, in the hope that after the war they would become stations for a new express line service, similar to the RER in Paris. The new line was never built, and today the World War II tunnels have been left to the vagaries of time.

Churchill himself spent much of the war in a special underground shelter known as the Cabinet War Rooms, located between the prime minister's official residence at 10 Downing Street and the Houses of Parliament. Its chambers included a map room, a conference room, and private quarters for Churchill's family. From here the pugnacious prime minister directed the bombing of German cities and the movement of troops, as well as broadcast his famous BBC radio speeches. Today the Cabinet War Rooms complex is a popular tourist attraction.

A musical concert during an air raid in 1942 makes time spent underground in the tube more bearable.

But it would take London far longer to establish a truly public water system and deliver clean water to all of its citizens. For that, Londoners had to wait until 1902, when the Metropolitan Board of Works took over the private water systems.

More recently, the city's water woes are the result of an overabundance of the resource. While many cities are seeing their water tables sink because of overuse by industry, London has the opposite problem. With the decline of heavy industry in and around London, the city's water table is actually rising. The London Underground is also threatened by the climbing water. According to city officials, in 1905 the water table at Trafalgar Square was 110 yards (100 meters) below the surface. In 1999, it had risen to just 44 yards (40 meters) belowground. To counter this, London is boring holes around the city to siphon off billions of gallons of water annually.

As with the water lines, private companies initially laid out most of London's other underground infrastructure. Beneath the city are remnants of the London Hydraulic Power Company, which supplied power by forcing pressurized water through underground pipes. It operated for more than a century, until the mid-1970s. This system was similar to the practice still used in New York City, where building are heated by centralized steam power. For many decades, the Gas Light and Coke Company was a powerful force within London. This company, after breaking or buying out its rivals, owned most of the city's gas lines, which lit street lamps, powered industry, and warmed homes. Complaints against the company's rates and service were legion, as were unsuccessful attempts by its workers to unionize. In the nineteenth century, Charles Pearson, the solicitor of the City of London and a reformer, tried to break its monopoly by founding a competing, semipublic company, but he was unsuccessful. (Pearson had better luck with the city's first subway line, which he promoted and helped to start.) The new Labor government after World War II nationalized the Gas Light and Coke Company in 1948, effectively eliminating unproductive competition among London's utility companies.

And so the history of London's underground realms rolls on, with each generation reinventing the map of services and functions to be carried out for the benefit of its citizens, just beneath the pavement. As part of one of the world's oldest cities, the London underground is also, understandably, one of the most complex. Perhaps nowhere else is the tangle of infrastructure—new and old—with history and geology more intriguing or problematic.

# TUNNELING UNDER THE THAMES

Although bridges have spanned the River Thames since the Roman era, it wasn't until the early nineteenth century that technology suggested the possibility of tunneling under the river. The impetus came from an odd sort of adventurer and inventor named Marc Isambard Brunel. A Frenchman by birth, Brunel arrived in London via the United States, to which he had fled during the French Revolution. He fancied himself an entrepreneur but spent time in debtor's prison after one of his ventures failed to pay off. In prison, he developed a technique on paper for efficiently boring through the earth. Similar in principle to more advanced techniques still in use today, it involved a screw drilling behind a shield designed to hold back earth, water, and debris.

Brunel began his carriage tunnel under the Thames in 1815, believing it would only take three years to build. Instead, Queen Victoria opened it twenty-eight years later, in 1843, after countless setbacks and cave-ins had claimed ten lives. At one point the tunnel collapsed on Brunel's son, who by luck was somehow sucked up to the surface of the river and survived, although others died in the same incident. As with John Roebling, the architect-engineer of the Brooklyn Bridge, a generation later, Brunel was thwarted by the little-understood phenomenon of changing air pressure underground, which made his men sick with "the bends." Eventually the British government stepped in to finish the project.

While more than 50,000 people strolled through the tunnel on the first day, after the novelty wore off it was not widely used. There was not enough money—after all that work—to build ramps that would allow carriages to enter and exit the tunnel, forcing Londoners to negotiate stairs at each end. Brunel had hoped to make money by charging a toll, but low demand made his plan unfeasible and Brunel's dark, dank tunnel came to be frequented by prostitutes and thieves. In 1869, the East London Railway took it over, and it is now part of the Underground subway system: at the Wapping Tube station on the East London line, visitors can have a look into London's tunneling past.

Brunel's tunnel under the Thames floods in 1828 while under construction.

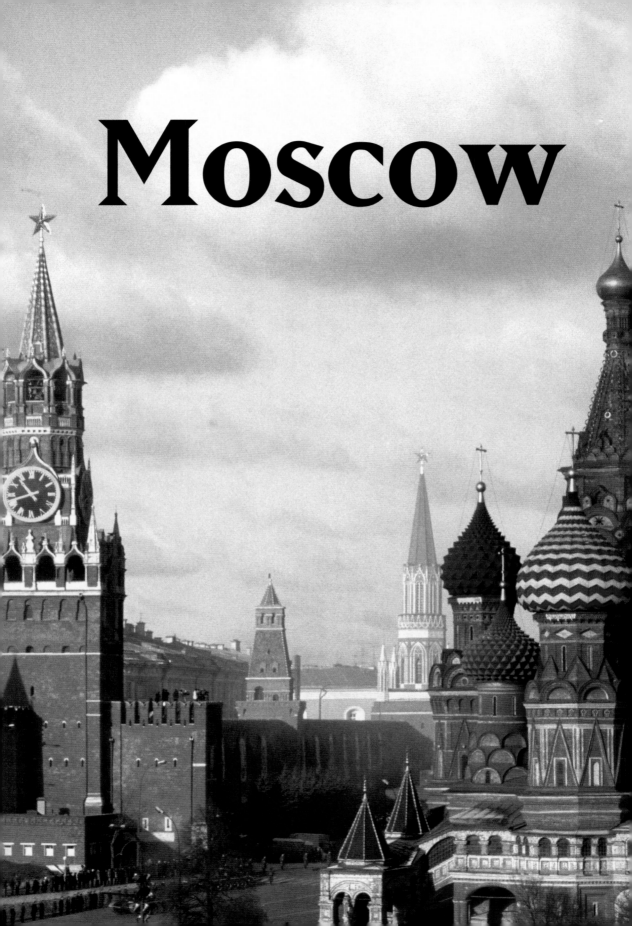

# Moscow

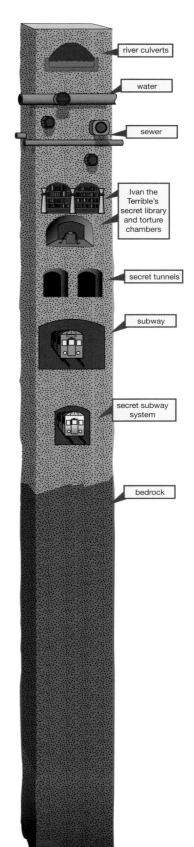

river culverts

water

sewer

Ivan the Terrible's secret library and torture chambers

secret tunnels

subway

secret subway system

bedrock

OOKING AT THE GLEAMING GOLDEN domes of the Cathedral of Christ the Savior standing on the bank of the Moskva River not far from the Kremlin, it would be easy to assume that this center of the Russian Orthodox Church has stood proudly for centuries. In fact, the monumental cathedral, visible from most of the city, was built in 1997. The original cathedral, a Moscow institution since 1326 whose leadership vied with the czars for authority, looked very much like the reconstruction. Soviet premier Joseph Stalin tore it down in 1933 as a sign of the primacy of the state over the Russian Orthodox Church. In its place he built a public swimming pool.

Some traces of the original cathedral remain—in the Kropotkinskaya subway station in central Moscow for instance, a series of marble columns support gothic arches recycled from the old church. Using materials from a church to build a subway for the common man had a symbolism that no doubt pleased the communist, secularist Stalin.

Winston Churchill famously said in 1939 that Russia was "a riddle, wrapped in a mystery, inside an enigma." Whether he knew it or not, his words certainly apply to what lies beneath Moscow, including a secret subway for communist leaders and myriad cold war command centers. Reputedly, there are even tunnels built by the American Central Intelligence Agency (CIA) and equipped with bugging devices—a leftover from the heyday of cold war espionage. But Moscow's underground mysteries date back much farther than the recent communist era. Deep below the city are secret passageways built by the czars as well as—possibly—the lost library of Prince Ivan III (also known as Ivan the Great), thought to contain thousands of books encrusted in gold and jewels.

More affordable baubles can be found beside the Okhotny Ryad subway station near the Kremlin, where the city's most elite shopping mall of the same name extends four floors beneath Manezhnaya Square. Completed in 1997, the Okhotny Ryad shopping mall has become a symbol of the new, glitzy, capitalist Moscow, and was the first of a series of underground shopping malls that the city of Moscow has helped finance with private developers. In 2005, the Moscow City Hall approved spending $200 million to build a 115,000 square foot shopping mall underneath Paveletskaya Ploshchad square in central Moscow. At Pushkin Square in one of Moscow's better residential neighborhoods, shoppers can browse the kiosks of vendors that line the *perekhods*, or underground passageways, beneath a busy intersection. Modern Russia's role in the free-market world still may be somewhat uncertain, but the fall of communism has added these new commercial layers to a city whose underground geography reflects centuries of tumult.

Moscow sits on a bend of the winding Moskva River, and beneath the city streets are as many as 150 underground tributaries, the remains of small creeks that once drained into the river but which have been converted into culverts lined with brick and stone. The valley that contains the course of the river is composed of deep bedrock, formed millions of years ago. Closer to the surface are giant boulders and rocks, left by the glaciers that swept across the area in the Pleistocene era. As a result, the landscape of Moscow is uneven, broken by low hills and depressions. A central ring road, the Garden Ring, forms a division between inner and outer Moscow. Outside of this artificial divide, blocks of severe, rectangular Stalinist-era apartment buildings stretch in every direction, inside the ring streets are lined with trees and lower-rise buildings, some five centuries old. It is this more attractive architecture that gives the city its European flavor.

Moscow has been the political center of Russia since the Middle Ages, when the city's ruling princes held off the Mongol hordes and then conquered or absorbed neighboring principalities. As Paris grew to become the capital of France, so did Moscow become the capital of Russia. After the fall of Constantinople in 1453, Muscovites began calling their city "the Third Rome," and in 1547, Ivan the Terrible became the first Russian ruler to call himself "czar," a word derived from "Caesar."

At the center of the city is the mighty Kremlin—a fortress of palaces, onion-domed Russian Orthodox churches and the vast expanse of Red Square—the nexus of Russian government since the fifteenth century. It was then that Ivan the Great built

**1147**                                                        **1453**

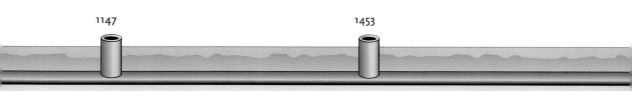

Prince Yuri Vladimirovich Dolgoruky founds Moscow on the banks of the Moskva River. In coming years, he builds wooden walls around the small town. The town is at the center of several trade routes and grows in size and power.

Constantinople, capital of the Byzantine Empire, falls. Sophia Palaeologa, the niece of the last emperor, smuggles from the city a precious collection of medieval and ancient handwritten manuscripts.

**Country:** Russia

**Location:** Located about 600 miles from the Polish border

**Population:** City proper: 9.3 million

**Area:** 386 square miles (1,000 square kilometers)

the core of the Kremlin complex  as well as the rumored underground library that is still considered a holy grail of urban archeology.

The story of the prince's lost library has fascinated scholars and explorers for centuries. Just before the fall of Constantinople (the last center of the dying Roman Empire) in 1453, a precious library of early books handwritten in Hebrew, Egyptian, Greek, and Latin was removed from the city. The library passed through various hands and finally made its way to Moscow with Sophia Palaeologa, niece of the last Byzantine emperor and wife of Ivan the Great. The story is that she had an Italian architect, Aristotle Fioravanti, build for her a safe home for the precious library—a home *underneath* the Kremlin.

**1472**

**1533**

Sophia Palaeologa marries Ivan the Great, who has a home built for his wife's precious library under the Kremlin by Italian architect Aristotle Fioravanti. Ivan the Great starts to refer to himself as *czar*, after Caesar, and calls Moscow and the lands it rules "the Third Rome."

Ivan Grozny, who eventually earns the nickname Ivan the Terrible, becomes czar. He expands the library and has copies made of many of the volumes, while restricting access to it. The library becomes known as "Ivan the Terrible's library."

Ivan the Great's grandson, Ivan the Terrible, took possession of the library when he ascended the throne in 1533. Despite his moniker, Ivan the Terrible was a learned man who restructured the Russian government in his fifty-one-year reign and created many of the lasting foundations of the Russian state. He treasured the ancient library. But Moscow at that time was repeatedly threatened by Mongols and was in fact burned down more than once. To guard the library, Ivan kept its location secret and had its books translated into Russian. He reportedly let no translator see the entire room of books. The collection, which expanded under the care of the czar, eventually numbered many thousands of volumes. But at its core were at least 800 priceless handwritten manuscripts.

Toward the end of Ivan the Terrible's reign, the aging czar went on a murderous rampage in an effort to control the country's feudal nobles, called *boyars*, whom he blamed for Russia's loss in a previous war he had started. Historians speculate that Ivan may have gone insane in his last years. It was during this period that he built extensive tunnels beneath the Kremlin, which he used as torture chambers, prisons, and secret passageways. In one of these rooms, the library is still believed to exist. While it may be true, subsequent leaders of Russia, from Peter the Great to Nikita Khrushchev, have searched without success for the legendary library.

In the 1990s, Moscow mayor Yuri Luzhkov sanctioned several campaigns to find the library, and contributed public money for metal detectors and other equipment. The campaign fit with Luzhkov's idea of making the underground rooms a tourist attraction. The leader of the exploration, the businessman and amateur historian Gherman Styerligov, did make one discovery: a tunnel filled with the skeletons of Russian nobles murdered by the Oprichniki, Ivan the Terrible's secret police. But the library has yet to be found. One historian, Apalos Ivanov, at age eighty-seven, said in 1997 that he believed he had located the treasured collection on a map, but he died not long afterward before getting a chance to test his theory.

One problem in locating the library has been the reluctance of the Russian military

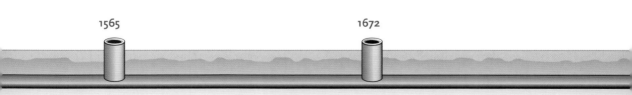

**1565**

Ivan the Terrible, growing ill, violent, and possibly insane, builds a labyrinth of tunnels underneath the Kremlin, which he uses in part to store the bodies of the thousands of political enemies he has killed. Subway construction in the twentieth century will uncover some of Ivan's tunnels and their bodies.

**1672**

Peter the Great becomes czar and moves the capital of Russia to a city he names St. Petersburg. Moscow remains the home of the Russian Orthodox Church and the site where Russian czars are crowned.

Muscovites in the archetypical Russian winter hats exit from the Kropotkinskaya metro station that opened in 1935. Its interior features columns scavenged from the Cathedral of Christ, razed during Stalin's reign.

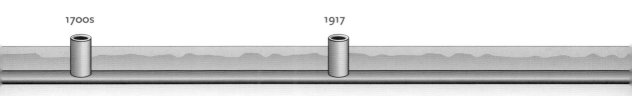

**1700S**

**1917**

Workers mine limestone around the city, to construct imperial buildings. As with the catacombs of Paris, this mining leaves dozens of abandoned quarries underneath the surface of the city.

Czar Nicholas II abdicates after leading the country to disastrous losses in World War I. A few months later, Nikolai Lenin seizes power in the Bolshevik revolution and eventually orders the czar and his family killed. The era of the Soviet Union as the world's leading communist state begins.

Underneath the famous minarets of Red Square and the Kremlin are mythic treasures and horrors, ranging from medieval libraries to forgotten torture chambers.

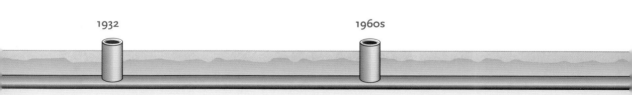

**1932**

**1960s**

Soviet president Joseph Stalin authorizes construction of the Moscow subway. His appointee, Lazar Kaganovich, designs and constructs lavish station interiors as "people's palaces" to serve as a counterpoint to the private mansions barred from ownership under communism. It will become the busiest subway in the world.

Soviet president Nikita Khrushchev appoints a special task force to hunt for Ivan the Terrible's secret library beneath the Kremlin. When he is removed suddenly from power in 1964, Khrushchev's task force is disbanded.

to open up restricted sections of the Kremlin's underground network. A resolve that has only strengthened with the global war on terror that includes Russia's fight against Chechnyan terrorists seeking independence in the twenty-first century. Walk into Moscow's central Arbatskaya subway station, past the streams of commuters and the vendors hawking their wares, to a dark alley in an out-of-the-way corner. There you will find a very solid metal door, and probably a police officer guarding it, who will encourage you to sightsee elsewhere.

The door is one of the few visible entrances to Moscow's secret subway system, which in turn is part of a larger network of tunnels, chambers, and even an entire underground city. The tunnels were built using parts of Ivan the Terrible's old network and these passageways are for use only by top government officials in emergencies; in fact, many were built during the cold war as part of the country's preparations for a nuclear confrontation. It's no coincidence that the Arbatskaya station lies just below the Ministry of Defense.

Although with the collapse of communism parts of the secret subway have been integrated into the public subway, the full extent of the government's exclusive system is not commonly known and this isn't likely to change. Russian newspapers, not always accurate, have reported that the Federal Security Service controls the hidden subway and that the system consists of more than 320 kilometers of track and employs 8,500 people. Since the dissolution of the Soviet Union into the Russian Federation, the secret subway exists in an odd kind of limbo. Authorities no longer deny its existence, but they will also not publicly say how extensive it is or whether the trains keep any kind of regular schedule. Much as with restricted information in other countries, information about Moscow's secret subway comes out in bits and pieces from ex-officials and others who no longer respect the old vows of secrecy. One fact is certain though: a branch of the hidden subway connects to the city's Vnukovo airport, seventeen miles from downtown, and to a secret underground city in Ramenki, a suburb six miles southwest of the Moscow center.

1970s          1991

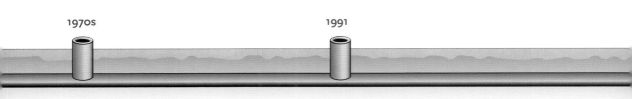

Soviet president Leonid Brezhnev completes construction of a secret underground city outside Moscow in the suburb of Ramenki, designed to protect leaders and ensure continuity of government during a nuclear war. The city is 900 feet deep, close to a square mile in size and has streets for automobile traffic.

Russian president Boris Yeltsin, the former mayor of Moscow, climbs on a tank in Red Square and confronts coup plotters that seek to end the reforms of Soviet leader Mikhail Gorbachev. The coup fails. Gorbachev resigns, and the Soviet Union is disbanded.

This underground city in Ramenki is yet another relic of the cold war. As the arms race escalated after World War II, both the Soviet Union and the United States built underground bomb shelters to house essential government employees in the event of nuclear attack. The Americans constructed a massive complex beneath the mountains of West Virginia, a short drive from Washington, DC. In Russia, the secret police of the Soviet Union—the KGB—and other directorates built the underground city in Ramenki, accessible quickly and safely from the Kremlin via the underground train line.

The underground city in Ramenki, say various observers, is as large as 500 acres and includes a swimming pool, a movie theater, and streets wide enough for two lanes of automobile traffic. Warehouses are reportedly stocked with enough food for 30,000 thousand people to live in relative comfort for years. What's more, this subterranean city is 900 feet deep, making it able to withstand a direct nuclear blast overhead. The bulk of Ramenki was built in the 1960s, but wasn't fully completed until the 1970s under Soviet president Leonid Brezhnev.

It would be interesting to see whether the secret subway is as handsome as some of the city's public subway stations. Since the end of the Soviet Union, much of the city's public infrastructure, from medical care to sewage treatment, has fallen into disorganization or disrepair, but not the subway. It's true the trains themselves need upgrading, but they remain spotlessly clean—as do the stations, which feature intricate mosaic tile work, high ceilings with cupolas, chandeliers, and art displayed along the platforms. There is an odd contradiction between the refined civility of these aspects of Moscow's public subway system and the paranoid, even frightening history of the tunnels built by the czars and the leaders under communism.

About 3.2 billion trips are taken on the Moscow subway system annually, making it the busiest in the world by far, more than twice as much yearly traffic as New York's. Considering the intensity with which it is used, Moscow's system is surprisingly small. It includes roughly 170 stations—more are being added every few years—and

1998

Moscow Mayor Yuri Luzhkov envisions turning the city's extensive underground domains into a tourist attraction. He renews efforts to find Ivan the Terrible's secret library.

about 5,000 cars. New York, by comparison, has close to 490 stations and 6,210 cars. Moscow's transit network is extensive nonetheless, it crisscrosses just about every section of the city, and includes a complete Circle Line, opened in the 1950s, that follows the path of the ring road. The high frequency of subway use in Moscow may reflect the fact that until recently very few people could afford to own automobiles.

Besides being clean and attractive, Moscow's subway system is notable for its extreme depth; most stations lie ten to thirty stories underground (roughly 100 to 300 feet down). Riding the escalators at stations like Mayakovskaya is like looking backward into a telescope—or "like taking a trip to hell on an escalator," said Douglas Birch, Moscow correspondent for the *Baltimore Sun*.

The construction of a subway in Moscow had been discussed for decades in the late nineteenth and early twentieth centuries, even before the 1917 communist revolution. But it would take the iron hand of Stalin to make it a reality. In the 1920s and '30s, during the forced industrialization of the Russian national economy under Stalin, central Moscow doubled in population to four million people. To cope with his rapidly expanding metropolis, Stalin ordered the creation of a subway system. With its lavish design, it was built to be a monument to the communist ideal of the

Red Square and the State History Museum in Moscow.

The opulent Komsomolskaya metro station features chandeliers and beaux-art plaster that could grace the finest French chateau.

New Man and the worker's paradise. Relying in part on forced labor, Stalin's chief architect and engineer Lazar Kaganovich completed the first line in 1935 after just one year of construction.

The stations, including both entrances and platforms, are each ornate and luxurious, but they vary in style. The effect is like walking from the rooms of one beautiful mansion to another, as if you had many wealthy friends with strikingly different tastes in architecture and decor. Some stations, like Smolenskaya that opened in 1953, have a classical feel, with Greek columns and marble benches. Others, like the Komsomolskaya station, unveiled in 1935, feel almost decadent in their lushness, with gold-plated chandeliers hanging from a vaulted ceiling decorated with Beaux Arts–style plaster bas-relief that wouldn't be out of place at Versailles. A mosaic on the ceiling here shows a armored knight on horseback prancing across a Russian landscape. Still others, like Novoslobodskaya station that first received passengers in 1952, seem almost medieval with stained glass windows depicting flowers and garden scenes. The Mayakovskaya station has floors of black and white marble set in patterns of squares and lines. The rich decor of each station almost defies belief, so different are they from the utilitarian feel of even the most well-kept subway in any other Western city.

The Mayakovskaya station, designed with a cool pattern of black and white tile, lies deep underground like most of Moscow's metro system.

## THE MOLES OF MOSCOW?

Vadim Mikhailov, founder of the clandestine "Moscow Diggers" and the city's most famous underground explorer, says he is not sure what led him to spend much of his life sneaking through tunnels under his country's capital. As the son of a subway train driver, perhaps it was in his blood from birth. But for whatever reason, Mikhailov, now almost forty, has been popping through manhole covers and wading through half-flooded tunnels since he was twelve years old. He told the *Chicago Sun-Times* in 1997, "The change of light and darkness, and the tunnels branching off sideways fascinated me. I knew these concrete caves of civilization were another world—a fairyland."

Even though his activities are illegal, Mikhailov and his fellow diggers are tolerated by authorities because they know more about the city's underground than anyone else. After the attempted coup against President Boris Yeltzin in 1991, Mikhailov helped the army find rebel forces taking refuge in Moscow's tunnels. His most famous moment came in 2002, when Mikhailov ushered police to a secret entrance providing access to a downtown Moscow theater where Chechen rebels had held eight hundred people hostage for three days. In another incident, Mikhailov led television crews to a dangerous quantity of radioactive waste that had been dumped underneath Moscow State University.

Mikhailov has shown reporters fleets of dusty military vehicles sitting idle on

underground highways, complexes of seemingly forgotten underground apartments with kitchen appliances and furnished living rooms, stacks of skeletons dating back to Ivan the Terrible's murderous reign, and a sarcoph-

Vadim Mikhailov leads the "Moscow Diggers;" and is reputed to know more about the city's underground than anyone alive.

agus from the Byzantine era. He firmly believes that the forgotten library and other treasures remain to be found beneath the Kremlin.

Mikhailov says that with the collapse of the Soviet Union, many of the public service components of the city's underground, like its drainage tunnels, are neglected and becoming polluted. Perhaps more seriously, he says the city is vulnerable to underground terrorist strikes. "The Diggers believe that, regardless of barriers, one can pass unnoticed under the ground," Mikhailov told the *Ottawa Citizen* in 1997. "There should be a monitoring system established that could, to my mind, control such places as the Metro's ventilation shafts."

Ironically, the very same underground systems that were designed to make Moscow safe from a nuclear war could now be used to cripple the city from below.

"It fit the Socialist ideal of the communal space being more important than the private space," said Birch. "While people might be sharing an apartment with fifteen or twenty people, they can commute to work while looking at art as though in a museum. It's precisely the opposite of the way cities in the West usually work." This approach to building an underground urban transportation system reflects a decidedly different notion about the meaning of "beneath the metropolis." While many cities treat the underground as merely utilitarian or as a place not worthy of cultural enrichments, the Russians, in their premier city, Moscow, envisioned a subterranean realm where civility, beauty, and safety all coalesced into an achievement of which they could be justly proud. They then chose to repress the memories of forced labor and torture chambers, suggesting that the cultural meaning of an underground space is not just a matter of architecture or engineering, but also involves controlling the narrative of urban history itself. Although at first glance the subway station ornamentation in Moscow can appear more Louis XIV than Joseph Stalin, the wall paintings or bas-relief statues often depict Soviet heroes and scenes. Many mosaics feature a hammer-and-sickle emblem, the symbol of the former Soviet Union, once emblazoned on its national flag.

Moscow's subway is still not finished. It is a sign of hope for the citizens that even in today's chaotic political and economic climate, new stations and lines continue to come be added. In May 2003, the Park Pobedy metro station opened, which at fully thirty stories below ground may be the deepest in the world. It was built so far down because the tunnels had to run under large pockets of water in the earth closer to the surface. Its heavily decorated interior was designed to show that modern, free-market Moscow can build public-works projects as grand as those from the communist era. Although the use of marble is nowhere near as extensive as in many of the older stations, the new station does have black and gray granite floors and walls of red and white marble. Park Pobedy is a fitting successor to Moscow's grand subway stations of the past—even if there isn't a hammer or sickle anywhere in sight.

The painted tiles of the Komsomolskaya metro station show the classic socialist-realism style depicting the worker's struggle.

## PACKING THEM IN

**Annual Subway Ridership, 2002**

Major Cities of the World

| | | |
|---|---|---|
| 1. | Moscow | 3.3 billion |
| 2. | Tokyo | 2.6 billion |
| 3. | Seoul | 2.2 billion |
| 4. | Mexico City | 1.4 billion |
| 5. | New York City | 1.4 billion |
| 6. | Paris | 1.2 billion |
| 7. | London | 970 million |
| 8. | Osaka | 960 million |
| 9. | St. Petersburg | 821 million |
| 10. | Hong Kong | 786 million |

Source: Metropolitan Transportation Authority, New York

# Cairo

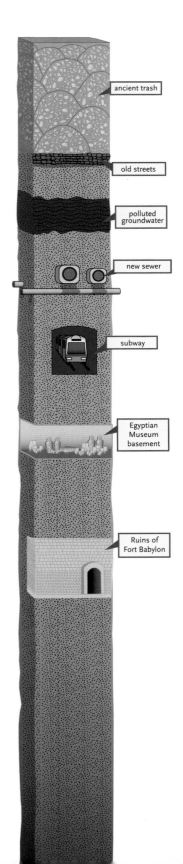

ancient trash

old streets

polluted groundwater

new sewer

subway

Egyptian Museum basement

Ruins of Fort Babylon

D EEP WITHIN MEDIEVAL WALLS THAT once protected Cairo from invaders but are now surrounded by the sprawling modern city, lambs gather around water troughs on an ancient street scarcely wider than a man's outstretched arms. People who are out shopping or on some other business—for this is a regular city street, as well as a stockyard—squeeze by the animals without irritation. In a few days, the herders of these animals will take knives to the lambs' throats, in preparation for the annual Islamic festival Eid al-Adha, the Feast of Sacrifice, that takes place in early February. By tradition, families buy a freshly slaughtered lamb and then give much of the meat away to the poor. The act is meant to show a family's generosity as well as its wealth.

The blood from the animals' throats, once cut by their keepers, will run down the gutters, past streets, homes, and mosques dating back as much as a thousand years. The entrances to these homes usually sit several feet *below* the street—evidence of the layers of history at this Mediterranean crossroads originally called al-Qahira. Some of the spilled blood will find its way into the city's inadequate sewer and storm water system. But much will simply soak into already waterlogged soil, mingling with the vast quantity of polluted groundwater that lies just under the surface in Cairo. While life flows on uninterrupted aboveground, this contaminated groundwater leaches into the ancient buildings, rotting them from below.

A few miles away from this simultaneously ancient and modern pastoral scene is busy Tahrir Square in Cairo's downtown business center, built comparatively recently in the mid-nineteenth century. Although there are no lambs in the square, crowds of commuters descend like sheep into Sadat Station (named after former president Anwar Sadat), part of the city's new subway system. Two major subway lines opened in the late 1980s and '90s, and a third is under construction. A recent addition to the subterranean landscape, already close to 2 million people a day use this relatively small system. Some women on the platform have their faces shrouded by the black *niqab*, a scarf worn over the face with only a tiny slit for the eyes. Others wear the less severe *hijab*, a scarf that covers the head but leaves the face exposed. Both articles of clothing enable them to follow an Islamic rule that requires a woman to hide her face, limbs, and other potentially sexually appealing features from the prying eyes of strange men. But in more cosmopolitan Cairo, unlike in Riyadh, Saudi Arabia or other more orthodox Islamic cities , only a minority wears this traditional dress, although the percentage is growing. The majority of women you see on the streets of Cairo—Egyptians and others—wear more conventional Western dress.

These women riders on Africa's only subway, dressed as they are in such contrasting styles, provide a reminder that in Cairo, the old and the new, and West and East, exist in uneasy proximity. Some of that tension between past and present is echoed beneath the crowded streets.

If Paris, London, and Moscow are cities that grew into nations and empires, Cairo is a city that emerged from the nations and empires of others. The occupation began in 520 BC, when Persia conquered the city then known as Heliopolis, and it did not end until 2,500 years later in 1952, when an army officer and future Egyptian president, Gamel Nasser, declared the country's independence and kicked out the British, the country's last colonial masters. In between, Cairo was ruled by Greeks, Romans, Fatimids, Mamluks, Ottomans, French—everyone, it seems, but the local population, who are descended from the Pharaonic Egyptians, even though after millennia of being ruled by outsiders, there has been extensive intermingling.

Inevitably, Cairo's underground reflects this history of multiple occupations and constant change. As a measure of their significance, successive empires and conquerors often built a new Cairo rather than occupy the old. As each new city went up beside the previous one, the metropolis came to encompass several different "old" and "new" Cairos, each with centuries of history beneath it.

A surprise to many visitors who associate Cairo with the pyramids is that very little of that history dates to the Pharaonic period. Although the 4,500-year-old

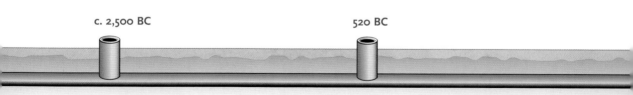

c. 2,500 BC

520 BC

The pyramid at Giza is constructed. Today, Cairo's Line Two subway ends here.

Persians seize Egypt, beginning millennia of occupation and control by foreigners including Greeks, Romans, Fatimids, Mamluks, Ottomans, French, and British.

**Country:** Egypt

**Location:** On the Nile River, at the head of the delta, near the Mediterranean Sea

**Population:** 20 million (metropolitan area) Cairo is the largest city in Africa and the Middle East. Some 18–20 million people live in greater Cairo, and the population is growing by about 1 million every year. It is the only African city with a subway.

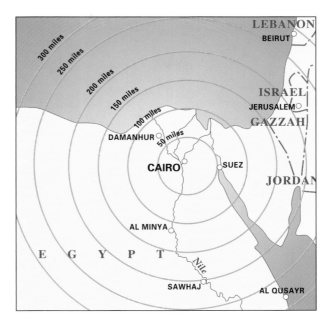

pyramid at Giza—where Cairo's Line Two subway terminates—is visible from all over the city, Cairo-proper has few ancient Egyptian relics beneath it, with the exception of the basement of the magnificent Egyptian Museum, built by the British in 1902. This museum houses the world's greatest collection of mummies, golden beds, and other antiquities from ancient Egypt, and its basement is reportedly stuffed with more than 200,000 objects that the museum does not have space to display.

When the Pharaohs were building the pyramids at Giza, the land under what has become modern Cairo was used to grow food for the workers who built them. There were small towns or cities nearby, principally Heliopolis and Memphis, the capital of

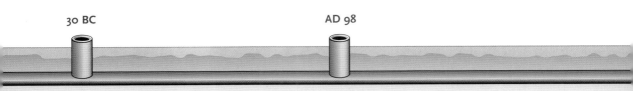

**30 BC**

**AD 98**

Roman emperor Augustus, pushing out the Macedonian Greeks, takes control of Egypt.

Roman emperor Trajan establishes the fort of Babylon by the Nile River on land that will become modern Cairo. Egyptian slaves there establish secret Christian sect that will become the Coptic Church.

## A PARK GROWS FROM A HISTORIC PILE OF GARBAGE

For a thousand years, high stone walls surrounded al-Qahira, the very heart of Cairo until the nineteenth century. Nowadays al-Qahira is known as medieval or Islamic Cairo. These walls were built around AD 1000 to hold back the Crusaders from Europe, who were expected to lay siege to the city but never quite made it this far south. Inside the walls, people built houses, mosques, and businesses. Outside the walls, they buried their relatives in the City of the Dead—and discarded their trash.

Lots of trash. A thousand years of trash. The pile of garbage outside the city's northeastern wall grew and grew. In 1652, French traveler Jean de Thévenot noted that piling debris had nearly covered the walls. By the early twentieth century, the walls on the northern edge had been completely buried under trash and dirt.

Today, this giant mound of refuse is being transformed into a thirty-seven-acre public park. In a city with very few green spaces, al-Azhar Park (named after the thousand-year-old mosque just inside the walls) is a much anticipated amenity. "We have almost no open space in Cairo," says Maher Stino, one of the park designers, leading a visitor around the park site. Nearby, workers chiseled away at slabs of limestone for the park's restaurant, the Lakeside Cafe. Underneath the new park are three enormous water reservoirs, each 262 feet/80 meters in diameter installed in the late 1990s. The cylindrical concrete tanks are part of a plan to improve the water supply of the city and distribute purified water more widely, evenly, and consistently. Cairo draws its water from the Nile and from underground aquifers, both of which are heavily polluted. The water goes to sixteen treatment plants scattered around the city.

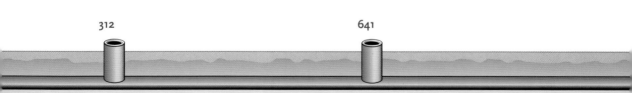

312

641

The Catholic Church, made the official state religion of the Roman Empire, begins centuries of efforts to suppress the Coptic Church in Egypt, seeing it as a competitor. Nevertheless, the Coptics establish the Hanging Church of Babylon inside Roman fort.

Islamic Arabs, followers of Muhammad the Prophet, take control of Babylon from the Romans, and establish new settlement outside the fort called "al-Fustat."

Since opening in 2004, al-Azhar Park's tree-lined central promenade, orchards, and pond have seen many visitors. Part of the construction included an excavation of the old city walls. Stino hopes the park will educate Cairenes, in more ways than one. "We want to help the public understand what a park is, and how to appreciate plants and nature," he says. "We also want something unique to Cairo."

That much is certain. Park visitors are able to walk under the walls of the old city and into the historic city itself. This new park, which is using an ancient dump to simultaneously help the city solve its water problems and give the city badly needed open space, is a hopeful sign for Cairo's future.

Cairo's new Al Azhar park, constructed on an ancient pile of garbage outside the old city walls, gives the city a major new park and a place for underground water storage tanks beneath the park.

969

1171

The Fatamids, a Shiite tribe of Muslims, conquer Egypt and establish the walled city of al-Qahira, meaning "the Victorious," a few kilometers away from the Sunni population of Fustat. Italian merchants call the new city "Cairo."

Salah ad-Din, aka Saladin, a Sunni Muslim and a Kurd, conquers the city and becomes one of its most famous sultans. He builds the Citadel, a mammoth walled palace on a hill, to defend against Christian attacks during the Crusades.

Centuries ago the home on the right in this photo was at street level. Now its doorway lies several feet below the street because the city has gradually risen around it.

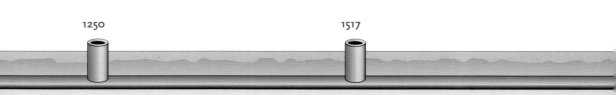

**1250**

The Mamluks, a caste of slaves trained as soldiers to protect the Sultan, seize power in a coup d'état. They and their descendants establish an empire that rules much of the Middle East for centuries, with Cairo as its capital.

**1517**

The Ottoman Turks, based in Istanbul, conquer Cairo. The Ottomans and the Mamluks vie for control of the city and country over the following centuries, sometimes sharing power.

Egypt during the Old Kingdom (c. 2575–c. 2130 BC). But the area that would grow into what we know as Cairo was not settled until the Roman emperor Augustus took control of Egypt from the Macedonian Greeks in 30 BC. The location, where the Nile begins to fragment into a wide delta before draining into the Mediterranean, was a convenient juncture for maritime traders.

The Roman emperor Trajan established the fort of Babylon, now in the southwestern section of Cairo, in AD 98, an area that is still a center of Coptic worship—the branch of the Christianity dating back to the time of Trajan and predating the establishment of the Roman Catholic Church. The Coptic Hanging Church was so named because when it was originally built in the third century AD, it overlooked the outer wall of the Roman fort. The United States, through its Agency for International Development (USAID), is funding archeological excavations that have uncovered the walls of the Roman fort. Once over sixty feet high, the walls have been completely buried underneath the growing city.

Fort Babylon was the center of Cairo until AD 641, when Islamic Arabs, the first followers of the Prophet Muhammad, wrested control from the Romans. They set up a city outside Babylon called Fustat. The Fatimids, who conquered the area next in AD 969, built al-Qahira a few miles north of Fustat. That settlement is what eventually became known as Cairo. In 1171, the Ayyubic leader Salah al-Din, or Saladin, built the Citadel, an immense walled palace and garrison overlooking al-Qahira. The Citadel and al-Qahira were the city centers for the next 700 years until the 1860s, when Khedive Isma'il, then ruler of Egypt under the Ottoman Empire, laid out a European-style city of broad avenues and roundabouts on marshy land near the river.

Cairo's new Metro ties much of this sprawling grid together. Line One, which opened in 1987 and cost $585 million, is twenty-seven miles long and has thirty-four stations, five of which are underground. The line incorporated existing aboveground commuter train lines and stations. Line Two, completed in 1999

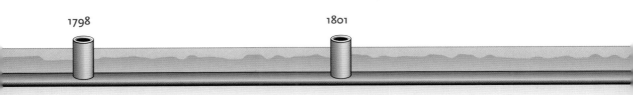

1798

1801

Napoleon Bonaparte invades Egypt, slaughtering 10,000 Mamluk horsemen who are attempting to defend Cairo with medieval cavalry tactics.

Ottomans regain control of Cairo from the French.

at a cost of $3 billion, is even more ambitious. The route includes a tunnel under the Nile to the pyramids plus eighteen stations, most of them underground. An east-west Line Three, still in the planning stages, will bisect the center of the city and connect to the airport.

The new subway is a big step for Egypt. It is a point of pride that Cairo now has the only metro system in Africa. Through projects like this, Cairo, a sprawling third-world city, is transforming itself into a more physically integrated first-world city, with a greater reliance on such public systems as water, sewer, and transportation.

At the Opera station on Line Two, the walls are adorned with large, colorfully decorated mosaics. They show modern interpretations of ancient images of women in Pharaonic dress, with stereotypically clipped hair and long skirts. One women plays a lute. To a Cairene (as the people of Cairo are called), as to an American, these are images of an Egypt from many thousands of years ago, with little or nothing to do with the daily life of a contemporary Islamic Arab. A few stations down the line however, the walls are adorned with an abstract geometric pattern of lines and circles. Every subway station is visually distinct. The designs are entertaining, but they also identify stations graphically for Cairo's many illiterate citizens. In addition, northbound lines (toward the Nile) are colored blue, while southbound lines (toward the pyramids) are yellow; in the center city, where all lines meet, the color changes to green.

"This helps people figure out where they are," said Ezz Eldin Fahmy, a principal and architect with EHAF Consulting Engineers, a firm that helped design Line Two. "When they see the triangles look like boats, they know they are in Rod El Farago station. We had the theme of boats because this used to be the only port on the River Nile."

1868

1910–15

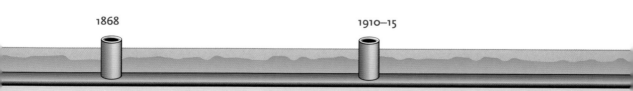

The Sultan Isma'il, inspired by the example of Paris that is being transformed under Napoleon III and Baron Haussmann, designs a new European-style city of avenues and traffic circles next to medieval Cairo.

The British build first modern sewage system for Cairo, which then has less than a million people.

Excavations around the ancient Coptic Hanging Church have uncovered the even older remains of Fort Babylon, the Roman military encampment that began Cairo in 100 AD.

**1952**

**1956**

Future Egyptian president Gamel Nasser declares Egypt's independence, evicting the last occupying colonial power, the British.

Britain, France, and Israel invade Egypt to take back control of Suez Canal after Nasser nationalizes it. The invasion fails after President Eisenhower denies American support.

Cairo's Metro is comfortable and clean. The platforms and corridors are wider than in New York or Paris, a welcome feature in most subways but particularly necessary here, in an already heavily used system. Unlike on the city streets, there is virtually no trash to be found. Yet this is not a contradiction. "To an Egyptian, the underground is a sacred space," says Abdel Halim, an architect with Community Design Collaborative in Cairo. "It's where you go to get a glimpse of God, of the Afterlife. It makes sense to them that the Metro is clean and orderly, and they want to keep it that way." This imagery, of course, reverses what the European

Workers construct a tunnel under the Nile River to link the two sides of Cairo in its subway system.

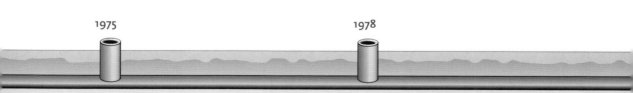

1975

Grossly overloaded, Cairo's sewer system fails regularly and floods neighborhoods with raw sewage. Cholera is common.

1978

Work begins on the Cairo Wastewater Project, a planning effort that results in the construction of an entirely new sewage system. The United States finances most of the cost, which runs to billions of dollars.

Christians see in their cosmology: the sky above is the sacred space of Heaven while the dark underground below is the portal to Hell.

That characteristically Egyptian view may change, Halim says, as Cairenes become accustomed to life belowground and begin behaving there as they do on the streets. "But now, you can see it," he says. "People keep things clean. It's not part of the messy world aboveground."

Nonetheless, Cairenes have still not mastered the art of getting on and off the subway in an orderly fashion. Crowds push in, even as throngs force their way out. The drivers close the doors before people have finished entering. And this at 1:00 PM on a weekday. Despite these lapses in subway etiquette, Cairenes have embraced their new subway as an easy way to travel around at least a small part of their congested city.

The Metro is, by Egyptian standards, a pricey world. The subway costs a few score piastres, less than one Egyptian pound, or ten to fifteen cents in American dollars, but substantially more than a bus, and a high price in a country where the annual per capita income is $1,500 US dollars. But the choking congestion of battered taxis, buses, and private cars on the streets above makes the Metro a popular choice. Almost too popular.

Line number one carries 1.2 million travelers a day during the week. Line number two carries 600,000 daily, for a total of 1.8 million, an enormous number on a fairly new system. By comparison, the Washington, DC Metro system, which includes five lines covering much of the surrounding region, took twenty-five years of operation before reaching the current number of 625,000 riders daily. Clearly, Cairenes needed a subway.

The subway is a big step forward toward modernization for Cairo, but its other underground systems are still very much rooted in the developing world. An estimated one-fourth of all households in the city still lack running water and sewer connections; many others are poorly served by an outdated sewer system that leaches human and industrial waste into the subsoil.

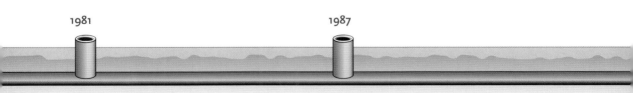

**1981**

President Anwar Sadat is assassinated. Construction begins on the city's first Metro line, with the French supplying money and engineering.

**1987**

Cairo opens its Metro to link far-flung parts of a now sprawling city.

Although Cairo lies in a desert, the ground underneath the city is in fact quite wet. When the ground gets saturated with polluted water, the ancient, porous limestone buildings (made of the same material as the pyramids) wick up the excess moisture, to as much as six feet aboveground. There, the hot sun evaporates the water but leaves the crystallized salts and living microbes that are carried in the polluted mix. These salts and microbes eventually crack the buildings' foundations. A similar process is rotting the foundations of Venice, Italy, which suffers from frequent flooding and whose waters are also polluted. In Cairo, to make matters worse, the air is also heavily polluted, which also damages the buildings.

"It's a case of environmental pollution attacking the stone from the two primary sources of life, air and water," says Anthony Tung, author of *Preserving the World's Great Cities*. "It's causing the buildings to decay very rapidly."

To combat the problem, Cairo has embarked on the construction of what may be the largest new sewer system in the world.

Until the 1990s, the sewers backed up more than 100 days a year, flooding the streets with dangerous and unsightly raw waste. The city's only modern system was one built by the British just before World War I, for a city of about one million people. As the population grew, this sewer soon became grossly inadequate. And so, out of necessity, Cairo over the last two decades has begun to construct an entirely new system, including an enormous sewage treatment plant north of the city—a task nearly equal to the problem in magnitude.

Because the old sewer system was so overburdened, it could not simply expand. "They had to rethink the whole network," says Mona Serageldin, professor of urban planning at Harvard Design School and a Cairo native who teaches a course on the city. "It was a major challenge in design."

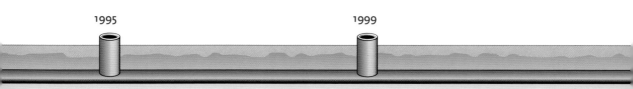

1995

Despite extensive work, an estimated one out of every four Cairenes live in homes that still lack water or sewage.

1999

Metro Line Two is completed. Planning is underway for Line Three.

In a sewer system, you have thousands of small pipes that descend from the toilets, sinks, and showers of individual homes and businesses. These connect to larger branch-line pipes, that eventually connect to just a few or even a single *trunk line*—large pipes, tunnels really, that carry all the collected wastewater to a river, the sea, or, ideally, to a treatment plant. A trunk line is always the largest part of any system and the most expensive.

In Cairo, because the old British system was so inadequate, the old trunk line had to be abandoned and a completely new central trunk line designed and installed in the ground. This new trunk line is 16.4 feet in diameter and extends in a sloping,

Raw sewage backs up into the streets of Cairo in 1992. This frequent occurrence is a major reason for the construction of the city's new sewer system, a multi-billion dollar project.

## THE TBM: A REVOLUTIONARY MECHANICAL MOLE

Visit the construction site of a big tunnel these days, whether it's for a train, a highway, a water line, or something else, and you will often find a TBM—a tunnel boring machine—at work. These enormous, expensive contraptions have revolutionized the construction of every sort of tunnel. In Cairo, a TBM bored the tunnel for the newest subway, Line Two.

Costing in the tens of millions of dollars (prices vary dramatically depending on the job and conditions), a TBM is like a gigantic, motorized serpent, intent on eating earth and rock and spitting it out the other end. This serpent is enormous, a football field or more in length. For example, the TBM the United States government used to bore out a long-term storage site for radioactive waste in the Yucca Mountains, eighty miles east of Las Vegas, weighed 860 tons and was 460 feet in length.

Using a ferocious-looking spinning wheel lined with giant teeth, a TBM methodically grinds away at stone and sediment. Meanwhile, a stream of water in the body of this serpent converts the debris into a "slurry" and carries it away. At the same time, another part of the machine slides prefabricated supports into the freshly bored tunnel, in preparation for lining with concrete or other materials. Depending on geologic conditions, a TBM can bore a thirty-foot-wide tunnel at a rate as fast as 20 feet an hour.

Although casually referred to as a TBM, there are actually many types of TBMs, because they are always extensively modified to fit a specific project. A hard material, like stone, is usually cheaper and faster to cut through than mud or sand. Europeans, particularly the French, and the Japanese have taken the lead in developing and improving the modern TBM because the countries in these regions have had a far greater number of "megaprojects," from train lines, to subways to underground highways. Specially designed TBMs were used in building the thirty-one-mile "Chunnel" under the English Channel, completed in 1994, and in the fifteen-mile Laerdal highway tunnel in Norway, which opened in 2000. Deep below the avenues and alleyways, A TBM is constructing New York City's third water tunnel which will give the metropolis the capacity to repair and maintain its first two distribution tunnels.

As the technology of TBMs improve, the cost of major tunnel construction keeps dropping. This has led to some rather spectacular predictions by the technologically entranced. Fred Hapgood, in the April 2003 issue of *Wired,* the magazine, declared that it would soon be feasible and cost effective to construct projects like "the ultimate TBM mega project: a supersonic world subway." Hapgood sees a future of magnetically levitated trains traveling through TBM-bored tunnels under the oceans between continents.

While this is difficult to accept as anything but fantasy, it's undeniably true that TBMs operating under the world's great cities have made possible projects that would have once been unthinkable. And Cairo enjoys the results of one of the best of them in its subway, Line Two.

A huge tunnel boring machine is assembled in Lesotho in Africa in preparation for a water project there.

gravity-fed descent from south to north through the city until it ends by the new treatment plant, at a depth of 82 feet. Still unfinished but with the bulk of the trunk line complete, the project has already cost several billion dollars.

Interestingly, the United States is paying for most of the cost of Cairo's new sewers. From 1978 to 2002, Egypt received more than twenty-five billion from USAID. Great Britain also participates. This substantial foreign aid began to flow after Egypt made peace with Israel in 1978, when President Anwar Sadat of Egypt, Prime Minister Menachem Begin of Israel, and President Jimmy Carter of the United States met in Washington, DC, to hammer out a peace treaty. The underground development of a city can be directly shaped by the intricacies of international politics.

Money aside, it may be a long time before the blood of lambs slaughtered during Eid al-Adha drains into a proper wastewater treatment system. Experts believe it will take decades before all of Cairo is connected to the new underground system—if ever.

With sewage as with drinking water, transportation, and other services, Cairo, like many third-world cities, is in a race against its own ceaselessly growing population. Immigration from the rest of country and a high national birth rate present those officials who attempt to manage Cairo with an unending challenge.

"It is a megacity," says Serageldin. "You have to look at the speed at which it is growing. A megacity grows from its own internal dynamic. It's not easy to contain."

In the shadows of the pyramids, workers labor on Cairo's new sewer system, much of which will be paid for by the United States.

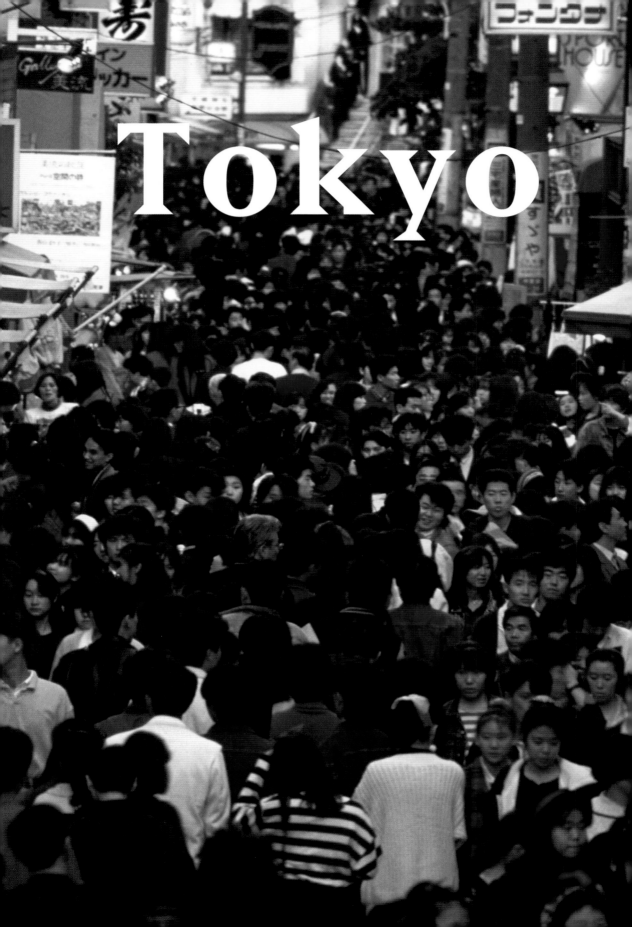

Tokyo

EVERYWHERE IN TOKYO, ONE IS REMINDED just how valuable space is. Dizzyingly tall buildings rise from narrow lots, apartment blocks squeeze beneath elevated railway lines, with trains rumbling overhead at regularly scheduled intervals. Dozens of tiny businesses cram themselves together within a few yards of available real estate, so that finding a particular vendor can be difficult even when standing right in front of it. Adding to the abundant confusion is the odd fact that Tokyo has no formal system of numbered addresses.

Until the economic crash of 1989, Tokyo had the highest property values on the planet. Most apartments in the city are minuscule by Western standards, and renting a bed for the night can mean just that—a bed in a pullout drawer more akin to a filing cabinet than a hotel room. And there are not many parks or other green spaces to offer some relief from the congestion. Tokyo has just 54 square feet of park space per person, compared to 311 square feet in New York, a city many Americans consider "crowded."

Nowhere is Tokyo more tightly packed than in the downtown Shinjuku district, a jarring riot of skyscrapers, bright lights, sex shops, and elite boutiques west of the Imperial Gardens. There is even the Times Square Shopping Center, named after its inspiration in New York that iconic symbol of modernity that Shinjuku resembles in its unlikely mix of activity. All of this is laid out on a jumbled quilt of streets that seem to lack any order or coherence.

At the center of the hubbub is Shinjuku Station. More than a dozen subway and commuter train lines meet underground here, and the station itself forms a boundary between high and low—separating the corporate office towers from the red-light district, the designer boutiques from the noodle shops. It may be the busiest subway station in the world (more than two million people a day pass through its corridors), but it is also a subterranean city in itself, with bars, restaurants, stores, and more than fifty entrances.

Pity the foreigner who wanders into Shinjuku Station without a guide. Christopher Sanford, a travel writer from Seattle,

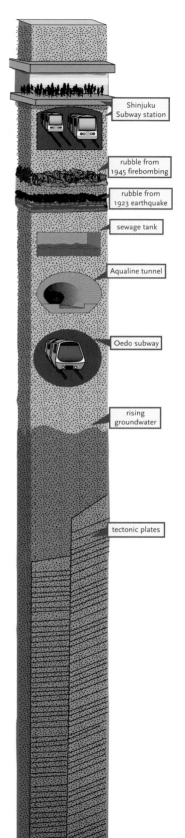

Shinjuku Subway station

rubble from 1945 firebombing

rubble from 1923 earthquake

sewage tank

Aqualine tunnel

Oedo subway

rising groundwater

tectonic plates

Washington, made the mistake of straying beyond the boundaries of his carefully memorized route. "I recognized nothing," Sanford wrote in an essay in the *Seattle Times*. "Commuters swarmed as though they'd received conflicting information on escaping some cataclysm. Clothing stores and restaurants filled every vista. I trudged up and down flights of stairs; I struggled to maneuver my luggage through a ticket chute designed for one thin, luggage-less person. . . . Whenever I paused—to attempt to decipher a sign in Japanese, to try to determine which of multiple tunnels might lead to my train platform—people massed behind me, then flowed past on either side like water past a sandbar." Hours later, Sanford emerged from the station, chastened but wiser.

Shinjuku Station illustrates Tokyo's two defining qualities, both good and ill, which are intensity and density. Above- and belowground alike, Tokyo has more people and services packed into smaller spaces than just about anywhere else on the planet. There is no room to spare. Japan, boasting the world's second-largest economy, is a country geographically about the size of California but with 125 million people (or nearly 3.7 times more populous than America's most heavily populated state). On top of that, approximately 25 percent of them, or 30 million, live in Greater Tokyo.

And yet, if Tokyo were a wheel, it would be a spinning whirl of energy around a peaceful hub—the Imperial Palace, set in a large garden in this space-conscious city. The palace occupies the center of the city, near the harbor. Around this placid core are constellations of furious activity, business and shopping districts like Marunouchi and Ginza on either side of the high-speed train tracks, Roppongi and Shibuya to the southwest, Harajuku and Shinjuku. Beneath all of them are equally lively underground activities.

The underground world of Tokyo has most of the same components of a Western industrialized city, but they are laid out differently and in dissimilar quantities. Tokyo has more of some things—subways, freeways, shopping centers—and less of others—

**1400**

The town of Edo—later to be called "Tokyo"—is founded on the site of a fishing village. The town thrives due to the patronage of the shoguns.

**1657**

An earthquake and subsequent fire destroys most of the city and kills about 100,000 people. In coming centuries, earthquakes will repeatedly smash the city.

**Country:** Japan

**Location:** The south-east coast of Honshu, on Tokyo Bay

**Population:** 11.8 million in city proper in an area of 836 square miles. There are an estimated 27 million in the  greater metropolitan area.

**Area:** 844 square miles

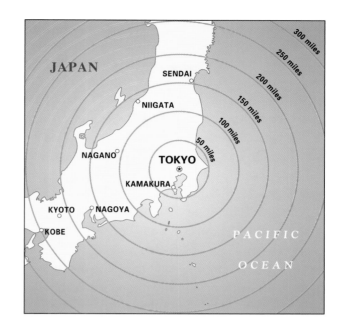

like sewers and storm water systems, old or new. These differences, impacted by geography and historical developments, reflect social and political values.

The stores around Shinjuku Station comprise just one of many underground shopping districts in Tokyo. By one estimate, there are thirteen major complexes, with a total of 2.2 million square feet, the equivalent of two aboveground malls in the United States. The Yaesu Underground Mall by the Japan Railways (JR) Tokyo station, for example, has more than 300,000 square feet and boasts 189 stores and restaurants—a dizzying array of choice and redundancy for any shopper.

No less strange to Westerners are Tokyo's subways themselves. White-gloved attendants courteously answer questions about directions—then forcefully wedge passengers

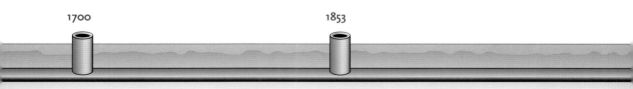

**1700**

The population of Edo reaches a million people—twice as many as London, the largest Western city at the time. Although there are also large Chinese cities, Edo is probably the largest city in the world.

**1853**

U.S. Commodore Matthew Perry drops anchor in Tokyo bay and demands that Japan opens its markets to Western goods.

into overstuffed trains. The subway system carries 7.2 million riders every weekday. That's more than twice New York's daily ridership, on a system that has half as many cars. In recent years, lines have operated at an average 180 percent capacity. (100 percent capacity is when every passenger is either seated or can hold a ceiling-mounted strap.) That's down from the average 230 percent capacity in 1975, but some lines remain seriously over-utilized; the JR Keihin Tohoku Line currently operates at 240 percent of capacity. By comparison, New York's most congested line (the Lexington Avenue IRT, or 4/5/6) functions at 130 to 140 percent capacity, evoking chronic complaints from an unhappy public.

"I know overcrowding is very serious in New York, but it's not as bad as it is here in Tokyo," said Carol Riddle in *The Daily Yomiuri,* an English language newspaper in Tokyo. Riddle is an American who teaches English at a private Japanese high school. She spends three hours a day traveling between Suginami Ward and her home in the Machida district to the south. "The trains are so packed," Riddle observes, "it looks like there is no room for water to run between passengers."

Nonetheless, the Tokyo subway stations have clean restrooms and other comforts, such as a lending library. Subway riders in New York enjoy none of these amenities. Yet on the Tokyo trains, much of the reading material is clearly not from any library— instead falling into the category of lurid pornographic comic books, which men read without compunction or embarrassment. Worse, women passengers often contend with the wandering hands of *chikans*—gropers. Subway officials have begun a campaign to stop groping, but the practice is deeply ingrained in a culture where women were long considered servile. One Tokyo sex club even features a mock subway car full of (real) women, who can be touched for a fee. In 2005, Tokyo introduced several "women only" cars on a few of the most crowded subway lines to combat this issue.

Surprisingly, groping is the only widespread crime on Tokyo subways, but a major new fear is terrorism—especially after the March 1995 subway attack by members of

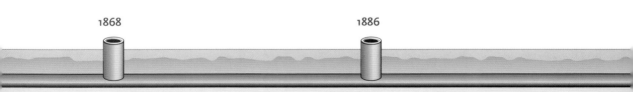

**1868**

Emperor Meiji moves his residence and the country's capital from Kyoto to Edo and renames the city Tokyo, meaning "the Eastern Capital."

**1886**

Sensai Nagayo, director of the city's first public health bureau, is inspired by Baron Haussmann's efforts in Paris and designs the city's first comprehensive sewer system.

People make their way to Shinjuku Station, whose size and complexity can overwhelm visitors who lose themselves in its corridors lined with businesses and dozens of entrances.

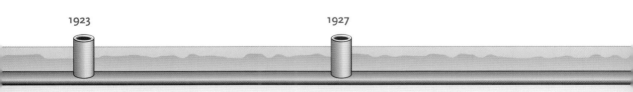

**1923**

**1927**

A massive earthquake destroys much of the city's low-rise wooden buildings and kills an estimated 140,000 people.

Tokyo's first subway line, the Ginza, opens as a small private railway in what is then the city's downtown but is now considered "old Tokyo." A decade later it is extended to include eighteen stations along nine miles of track.

A subway official, wearing white gloves, suggesting gracious behavior, nonetheless stuffs rush hour commuters into an overpacked train.

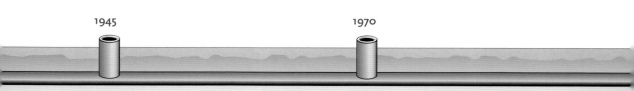

**1945**

**1970**

U.S. Air Force General Curtis LeMay oversees the firebombing of Tokyo. American bombers destroy half of the city and kill an estimated 80,000 people. In coming decades, underground bunkers used during the war will come to light during the construction of subways and other projects.

Japan Railroad's central Tokyo Station, built 87 feet below the street, opens.

the religious cult Aum Shinrikyo. The terrorists punctured bags of the colorless, odorless liquid chemical weapon sarin and tossed them on subway cars, killing a dozen people, injuring thousands more, and terrifying the entire city. In response, subway authorities took a number of new security measures, ranging from sealing off coin-operated lockers to reassigning transit police in new, undercover operations.

However crowded the ride in a Tokyo subway car may be, the train almost always arrives precisely at the scheduled minute—unless it has been delayed because someone jumped in front of it. Hundreds of people in Tokyo commit suicide in this grim fashion every year, a serious problem. (The Chuo line, near the city's center, seems to be the favored route for jumpers.) In an attempt to control the number of suicides, authorities have brightened platform colors, installed mirrors, and stationed more guards, but to little avail. The high rate of suicide in urban Japan reflects the pressures people feel to compete and succeed in their overheated economy. Yet Tokyo's subway remains so efficient that its trains arrive on schedule in each station nearly 100 percent of the time. If a train is late, subway staff will issue a note to take to your employer or school, if the boss or principal needs more than a verbal excuse.

Meanwhile, the subway's congestion is what keeps the semiprivate train network profitable. Unlike most countries, which heavily subsidize their subways and inter-city trains, Japan finances urban public transport differently: The Tokyo trains are largely dependent on revenue from the fare box. Thus, there is little incentive for the private companies to ease crowding. Nonetheless, officials are now discussing a system of state subsidies that would begin to relieve congestion without endangering the system's financial health. The $8.7 billion Number twelve O-Edo subway line, which the government did subsidize between 1991-2002, runs ninety-five feet underground for twenty-five miles and is the most spacious and comfortable.

The Japanese government has been considerably more beneficent when it comes to auto tunnels. Recently opened projects include a 53-mile Tokyo ring road called the Gaikando, with tunnels 52 feet in diameter and 131 feet underground; and the

**1995**

Shoko Asahara, leader of the cult Aum Shinrikyo, orders his followers to toss bags of the liquid chemical weapon Sarin into subway cars. A dozen people die and thousands are injured.

**1997**

Tokyo Gas constructs a new gas main 230 feet beneath the streets. At that depth, shaking is minimized during an earthquake.

Tokyo Bay Aqualine, an eleven-billion-dollar freeway across Tokyo Bay that includes two artificial islands and a 5.8-mile stretch of tunnel. The highway eliminates 50 miles from the journey between Kawasaki and Kisarazu.

Japan has been unusually active in improving and expanding its infrastructure over the past fifteen years as it attempts to spur the nation out of a long economic slump with the classical Keynesian economic remedy: massive public works projects to create employment and new businesses. Lacking space on the surface, much of the new infrastructure is underground, despite the nation's notorious proclivity for earthquakes.

Given the city's waterfront location, there are plenty of opportunities for expensive infrastructure investment. Like many great cities, Tokyo's bay and protected harbor are what made it an ideal settlement when traveling by water, which once was paramount. This one-time advantage can prove expensive when a city tries to build roads, train and water lines. The city was established in the 1400s as a fishing village, then called "Edo" (a name borrowed by the aforementioned subway). Thanks to trade and the patronage of shoguns and emperors, Edo grew rapidly. By 1700, a million people lived in the city—far more than in any European center of the time. In 1868, after the overthrow of the shogun, Emperor Meiji moved the capital of the country from Kyoto between Lake Biwa and Osaka Bay to Edo, and the city was renamed Tokyo, meaning "the Eastern Capital."

But by then, earthquakes had already taken their toll on Tokyo, situated at the point where the edge of the Pacific Continental Shelf slides under the Japanese archipelago. A major trembler (and subsequent fire) destroyed the city in 1657, killing perhaps 100,000 people. Another massive quake hit the city in 1855. Still others came later, in 1894 and 1923—the last killing an estimated 140,000 people.

All of these disasters produced rubble, and in Tokyo there is nowhere to put it. The city rebuilds on top of itself. Consequently, Tokyo has become a leader in deep tunneling, drilling roads, subways, sewer pipes, and other underground infrastructure

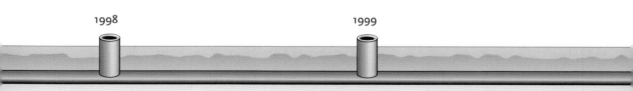

**1998**

The Tokyo Bay Aqualine expressway, which includes one of the world's longest underwater automobile tunnels, opens across Tokyo Bay. The tunnel portion is 5.8 miles long and is constructed between two artificial islands.

**1999**

A record 212 people jump to their death in front of the trains of the commuter railroad JR East in Tokyo. The company responds by installing sensors to warn people away from platform edges, and brighter lights so guards can more easily spot potential suicides.

Stricken passengers await medical attention after followers of the cult Aum Shinrikyo tossed bags of nerve gas into the subway cars.

**2001**

Tokyo opens its twelfth subway line, the Oedo, which forms an 18-mile loop under the central city. Ultra advanced tunnel boring machinery gouges out deep tunnels for trains that run on cushions of air using electromagnetic technology.

165 to 330 feet down, deep enough to avoid the rubble, abandoned war shelters, and other debris closer to the surface. Most of this deep tunneling is done with gigantic automated boring machines (see sidebar "A Revolutionary Mechanical Mole"). This push to locate so many services underground also prompts Japanese authorities to attempt to limit individual property rights below a certain depth, perhaps 130 feet. If successful in their efforts, authorities could build a new subway or gas tunnel without getting permission or buying rights from individual property owners above this depth. Just as "air rights" are an issue in aboveground urban development, the cost of subterranean property rights is a major factor in financing a city's infrastructure.

Despite Tokyo's high-tech tunneling, the city lags far behind Western capitals in other underground services, due largely to Japan's different historical context. Most Western cities have at least some semblance of a coherent street system. Romans, who used orderly grids, founded many European towns and cities. Later the French laid out streets in geometric patterns of circles and radiating spokes. But the Romans and French had little influence on Japan. The Japanese have a lesser notion of "public space" than Western cultures do, except perhaps in their temples and gardens. The absence of a concept of organized public space influences how they develop public services, resulting in the haphazardly planned streets of Tokyo. The same goes for what lies beneath the pavement.

Although its subway and commuter train system is extremely advanced, the majority of Tokyo's electrical and telecommunications cables are still carried on poles aboveground, adding to the chaotic jumble along the streets. "Tokyo's infrastructure is not as modern as that of other advanced countries in the world," writes Toshio Ojima in *Japanese Urban Environment*. "Its transportation system along with its urban supply and dispersal facilities such as electricity, gas, water supply, sewage disposal, telecommunication, garbage collection, district heating and cooling, etc. are estimated to lag thirty years or more behind the development of the infrastructure of various cities in Europe and the USA."

(Top of opposite page)
The new Aqualine Freeway across Tokyo Bay includes two artificial islands and a 5.8 mile tunnel. It is part of a massive public works program meant to spur the Japanese economy.

(Bottom of opposite page)
The image of a station official reflects in a large mirror in Tokyo's Ogikubo station, a mirror meant to discourage potential suicide jumpers by startling them with their own images.

## No Sewer? No problem!

The million residents of eighteenth-century Edo (now Tokyo) managed to live in close proximity and in good health without a sewer system. Their secret, practiced in many Asian cities, was collecting human waste and selling it as fertilizer. "Night soil," as it was called, was so valuable that it had its own elaborate distribution system. Ships arrived in Edo's port bearing vegetables from the countryside, and returned loaded with human waste to spread on the fields.

Complex laws and customs governed the sale of sewage. Landlords usually had the right to sell their tenants' night soil, although the renters retained rights to their urine (which had value for its phosphorous. Tenants would often dump chamber pots full of urine into larger barrels on street corners, where the distributor paid them a small sum.

"The most important difference between waste disposal in Japan and in the West was that human excreta were not regarded as something that one paid to have removed, but rather as a product with a positive economic value," writes Susan Hanley, a professor of Japanese history at the University of Washington in Seattle, in "Urban Sanitation in Pre-War Japan," in the *Journal of Interdisciplinary History*.

This system of waste collection kept Edo surprisingly clean. In Europe during that same period, authorities developed rudimentary sewer systems and pushed private building owners to install cesspools and indoor toilets. But these initial attempts at public sanitation actually increased disease, scholars say, because the waste still eventually flowed into major rivers and into the groundwater, from which the city usually drew its drinking water. The results, in terms of disease, were often calamitous.

Sewer systems were built in Tokyo during the nineteenth century, after merchants from the United States and Europe forcibly opened the country to international markets and Western influences in general. Tokyo's first sewers were modeled after those Baron Haussmann designed for Paris. In the Chiyoda Ward at the center of Tokyo, the egg-shaped Kanda Gesui sewer system, built in 1886, is still in use today.

For example, Tokyo has no citywide storm water drainage system. But it has recently started a program to encourage the construction of privately owned underground tanks that will collect rainwater to be reused. The first built was a 35,000-cubic-foot tank underneath the Kokugikan National Sports Stadium. The collected water is recycled to flush toilets and irrigate plants. Smaller collection tanks are currently under construction, beneath homes and businesses.

Compounding Tokyo's drainage problem is, like London, the city's rising groundwater as it transitions from a manufacturing to a service economy. During Japan's economic boom in the 1960s, hundreds of factories drew down Tokyo's water table, and the city imposed restrictions on water use. Now, with factories moving out of the crowded city to the suburbs, rising water under the city threatens subway tracks and stations. Japan Railroad's Tokyo Station was built at eighty-seven feet below street level in 1970. By the year 2000, the water level had risen to sixty-five feet. Engineers have had to anchor the track with steel blocks to prevent it from floating away on the rising tide of water. Similar work has been done on other stations, and the government spends several hundred million dollars annually to pump out an estimated eighty-four million cubic feet of water that leaks into the system each year.

The rising groundwater under Tokyo raises concerns that, when the next big earthquake hits, the city's saturated soil will *liquefy* and swallow collapsing buildings. As a first line of defense, the city does have an extensive earthquake monitoring system, although some experts question its value. Hundreds of underground monitors are buried as deep as 600 feet. When the meters show seismic movement, technicians alert officials at the Japan Meteorological Agency and a special committee of scientists quickly evaluates the data for signs of imminent danger. But foresight in seismology is difficult. A similar set of monitors failed to predict the massive Kobe earthquake near Osaka in 1995, which killed 6,000 people.

The earthquake and subsequent fire in Tokyo in 1923 destroyed the city and killed an estimated 140,000 people.

Tokyo: a city of the future or the past?  As with all great cities, it's both. Ultrafast, remarkably clean subways—some riding quietly on cushions of air—and glittering underground shopping malls: these characteristics might make a visitor think that Tokyo is a world leader in exploiting its underground territory. But the confusing tangle and high cost of other utilities below street level, not to mention the ominous threats of rising water and the likelihood of earthquakes, make underground Tokyo a hotbed of challenges for the future.

Despite the city's technological prowess, Tokyo's telephone and other telecommunication lines are still carried in a confusing jumble on poles on the street.

## Real Estate in the Cellar

Both Tokyo and Calcutta are crowded cities, but only Tokyo has freeways and shopping malls underground. Why is this? India and Japan each have a great many people per square mile, so it's not merely an issue of space. To understand the reason why, try looking at something that varies tremendously between Calcutta and Tokyo: real estate values. It's very expensive to put subways, parking, shops, and other services underground. Building downwards only makes fiscal sense when eliminating the need to buy additional land aboveground compensates for the higher cost.

A condominium in Tokyo in 1990 cost about $2,000 per square foot. After the stock market crash of 1990–91, an economic depression set in. The same condo in recent years would have sold for about $500 per square foot. This is a big drop, but still comparable to New York, San Francisco, London, and other cities known for their expensive real estate. These high prices are why building downward or upward can make sense, rather than spreading out horizontally.

To take a mundane example, consider the decision of whether to build an underground parking lot. Each parking space on the ground level of a parking lot costs about $1,000 to construct. In a parking garage aboveground, it's about $10,000 per space. Underground, the cost rises dramatically to about $50,000 per space. The only reason to proceed with the latter scenario is if it is cheaper than buying additional land aboveground. To do so is seldom a wise choice in the suburbs, where land is cheaper, but can make very good sense in a densely packed city with high land prices, like Tokyo or New York.

A similar set of calculations goes into decisions to build a subway, which can cost a billion dollars per mile versus lesser sums for a highway or streetcar line. Only when a city needs the enhanced people-moving capacity of a subway does it make sense to spend the additional sums on building underground rather than developing new roads or highways on the surface. As seen in New York, Paris, or Tokyo, the phenomenon tends to build on itself. As subways and train lines create a dense city, things get crowded, which generates public pressure to build even more subway lines. Once completed, these transportation solutions create an even denser, more crowded metropolis as people are drawn to the entertainment and job opportunities. There is no stopping the cycle.

O N A NARROW STREET IN A CORNER OF Beijing hangs an unremarkable sign reading *Underground City*. A small doorway leads down into the earth, opening onto miles of below-ground tunnels and rooms. These spaces, some of which are enormous, are remnants of the recent past in years but very distant in terms of the cultural and political changes that have taken place in China since this netherworld was constructed.

Produced at the direction of aging supreme ruler Mao Tse-tung in the 1960s and '70s, Beijing's "Underground City" is part of a subterranean network hundreds of miles in length. It is also a remnant of cold war paranoia and of a time when one man had the power to command millions to dig an elaborate civil defense system using only hand tools. Now skyscrapers and shopping malls rise above this labyrinth of tunnels and, in some cases, the shopping malls now sit right inside it.

Its vast, underground civil defense network is just one of many vestiges of the past that contrast with the city Beijing is fast becoming. A walk anywhere around the city gives a lesson in how quickly things are changing. Cranes at work on new office towers dominate the skyline in all directions, and scaffolding appears to be a new architectural style in itself.

Yet some parts of this sprawling, feverishly modernizing city are still mazelike warrens of *hudons*—small alleys lined with simple communal houses built around a courtyard, often lacking plumbing or other basic public services. The hudons are getting harder to find these days, a fact that seems to bother Western visitors in search of "old Beijing" more than it does the Chinese themselves. Everywhere in Beijing, billboards proclaim the glory of the future, which includes hosting the Twenty-ninth Summer Olympiad in 2008, the first Chinese city to host the games. Condominiums rise skyward. Suburban tract housing developments (with Western names like "Vancouver Forest" or "Santa Fe Ranches") stretch toward the horizon like a bamboo forest.

Like other cities, Beijing is using Olympic fever to justify major urban renewal. Chinese citizens who have left Beijing

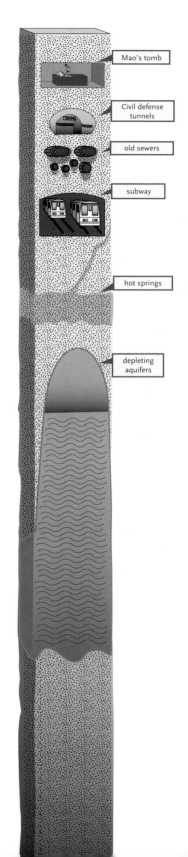

Mao's tomb

Civil defense tunnels

old sewers

subway

hot springs

depleting aquifers

for a few years return to find old neighborhoods virtually erased, replaced by new highways and ring roads, towering office buildings, and sprawling parking lots. The metropolis morphs, seemingly overnight, from an eerily calm capital—where residents in red and blue tunics pedaled bicycles on quiet streets past one-story structures—into a megacity of skyscrapers proclaiming their international corporate allegiances, Kentucky Fried Chicken franchises wedged beneath their imposing shape. Cars, once a rarity, now compete for more space with bicycles and rickshaws on the high-traffic roads, and contribute to appalling and dangerous levels of air pollution. Still, Beijing rushes onward towards its capitalist/communist future.

Until the twentieth century, change came slowly to Beijing, one of the few major world cities not built around a waterway. Situated about 100 miles from the Yellow Sea's Gulf of Chihli, commonly known as "Bo Hai." Beijing developed as an overland trading center for caravans making their way across the country. With mountains opening like a V to the west, travelers naturally funneled into the area that became the city of Beijing.

Although it had existed as a trading center for several thousand years, Beijing as a proper city was founded in 1267 when the Mongols, who governed this region of China at times, built their capital, Tatu, here. "Beijing," as the native Chinese named it, became the political center of China during the fifteenth century. (In the West, the city was also known as Peking, a spelling based on an alternate system of translating Chinese characters.) Despite the rise and fall of many dynasties, Beijing's urban street pattern changed little over the centuries, with a broad grid of straight avenues emanating from the Forbidden City, the home and court of the emperor.

The Chinese monarchy ended in 1924 with the Nationalist Revolution, led by Chiang Kai-shek, but the 600-year-old Forbidden City remains the ceremonial and spiritual heart of Beijing, and a place of considerable mystery and intrigue. At the primary entrance to the Forbidden City is Tiananmen Square, an enormous plaza comparable to Red Square in Moscow or the Zócalo in Mexico City. During the centuries of

**3000 BC**

Earliest settlements near contemporary Beijing, a place recognized from the outset as a crossroads connecting Han Chinese farmers from the south and west to the nomadic tribes from other surrounding areas.

**1027–256 BC**

First political capital city built on site of present-day Beijing, by Zhou (Chou) dynasty. Over the coming millennium, different rulers would give the city a succession of names.

**Country:** China

**Location:** Northeast region, between the Yellow Sea and the Hsingan Shan mountains

**Population:** 14,000,000

**Area:** 6,484 square miles

monarchical rule, access to this imposing "forbidden" walled complex of 172 acres was highly restricted—a situation guaranteed to breed speculation about what went on inside. Only the emperor himself could use a central arched bridge into the compound.

With the triumph of the Communists, led by Mao Tse-tung, over the Nationalists in 1949, Beijing entered an era of rapid growth as the country began the still continuing process of converting from a peasant society into an industrialized nation. Mao ruled the country through top-down directives that consolidated his power, including the vicious Cultural Revolution in the 1960s and '70s, an internally sponsored revolution meant to purge China of non-Communist thinking. During the Cultural Revolution, students were encouraged to denounce and bring down figures of authority, including political, artistic, academic, and industrial leaders.

AD 1215

Mongol king Genghis Khan burns the city to the ground. Kublai Khan, grandson of Genghis Khan, founds the Yuan dynasty and renames the city Dadu, meaning "Great Capital."

1368

Mongols are expelled and Ming dynasty established. The city is renamed Beiping, meaning "Northern Peace." The capital moves to Nanjing in the south.

It was during the Cultural Revolution that Mao embarked on one of the most unusual underground projects in the world: an incalculably vast network of civil defense tunnels and shelters under Beijing and other Chinese cities. The tunnels make their appearance in the oddest places. In many small shops in Beijing, a floor can be rolled up or pushed aside, and stairs will lead down to the maze. Tunneling began in 1969 after the Soviet Union seized the disputed Zhenbao Island on the Amur or Heilong River, which runs along its border with China. Relations between the two Communist giants had deteriorated badly since Mao had taken power in 1949 with the Soviet Union as an ostensible ally, and both sides feared a nuclear clash was imminent. "Dig deep, and store grain everywhere!" Mao told the people in an oft-repeated motto. And dig they did. For ten years they excavated, mostly with hand tools and bamboo baskets to carry out the dirt. They often dug at night, after working full days at regular jobs. Many died when poorly built tunnels collapsed, but the tunneling went on, in an estimated seventy-five cities throughout China. (Meanwhile, the Soviets were busy building tunnels in their own country.)

"In those days we didn't mind working after dinner every night," Wang Jun Liang told the *Chicago Tribune* in a 1991 interview. "We were happy to make people safe. We brought our own food and our own tools. We sang, we cursed the Soviets and shouted a lot of slogans."

Work on the underground system faded out in the late 1970s, as Mao grew old and lost power, and China turned to a more capitalist-style economy under Deng Xiaoping, a leader ousted during the Cultural Revolution but who regained authority in 1978, two years after Mao's death. Today the slogan is "New Beijing, Great Olympics," and the old concrete-lined tunnels are very much a part of the city's vibrant makeover. In Xicheng to the west of central Beijing, old air-raid shelters have been converted into a vast wholesale food market, with more than 1,000 stalls, managed by the Xicheng District Air-Raid Shelter Office. Under Wangfujing Street just

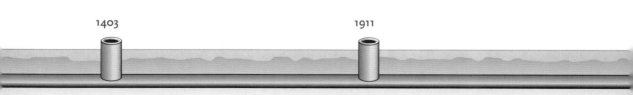

**1403**

The capital moves back to Beiping, renamed Beijing, meaning "Northern Capital."

**1911**

Nationalist Party overthrows Qing dynasty and ends roughly three thousand years of rule in China by its emperors. The monarchy is dead.

Beijing's underground city was built mostly by hand between 1969 and 1979 as a defense against a potential Soviet attack. Its extensive tunnels lie under much of the city.

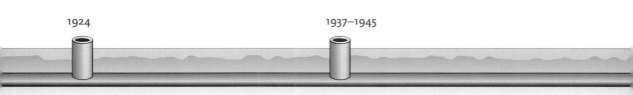

**1924**

**1937–1945**

Nationalist leader Chiang Kai-shek moves country's capital again to Nanjing, and gives Beijing back its older name, Beiping.

Japanese occupy Beijing during World War II, but the city escapes major destruction.

This underground shopping mall at Wang Fujing in central Beijing demonstrates one of the many uses the Chinese have found for once-passive underground spaces beneath the city.

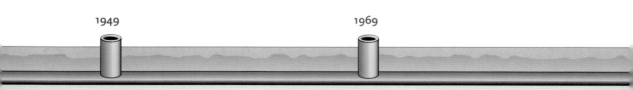

1949

1969

After the Communist Revolution, the city takes back the name Beijing and becomes capital of the People's Republic of China, under the leadership of Mao Tse-tung.

Construction of first subway begins.

east of the Forbidden City, there is a shopping center, a restaurant, and a youth hostel. This immense complex has been expanded in recent years from its civil-defense origins, and now includes three million square feet of retail and office space spread over three underground floors.

Many of Beijing's belowground areas have been turned into hotels, creating 10,000 to 40,000 subterranean beds. In hyper-busy Beijing, these hotel rooms have a bonus that to many visitors makes up for the absence of direct sunlight: quiet. Beijing is a notoriously noisy city. But the noise can't be escaped entirely by retreating underground. Various restaurants cater to diners under Xidan Street in the Xidan district. And below Da Sha La Street near Tiananmen Square are a theater, sports hall, and a roller-skating rink.

Although Yan Huang, deputy director of the Beijing Municipal Planning Commission, calls the cold war "long ago history," the army and related defense departments still own the subterranean network, which includes underground schools and hospitals. The West City District Civil Air Defense Enterprise Management Company, for example, owns the Chang'an Hotel and Dongtian Restaurant, which is located six stories beneath Xidan Street. Below ground, then, as above, contemporary China is nothing if not adaptable.

No one knows the full extent of the underground network beneath Beijing, but some claim it is capable of housing anywhere from 300,000 to 5 million people. Some say the tunnels here in Beijing connect to others around the country, and that the entire national network is thousands of miles in length. The existence of at least one very broad tunnel, an underground highway wide enough for trucks, running between the Great Hall of the People at Tiananmen Square and the Communist Party leadership compound outside the city is certainly a reasonable hypothesis. After army troops suddenly materialized in Tiananmen Square in 1989 to put down student protesters, many observers speculated they must have arrived from tunnels under the square itself—tunnels generally unknown to the public.

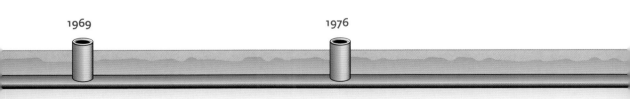

**1969**

The Soviet Union invades Zhenbao island, disputed territory on the Chinese-Soviet border. Fearing nuclear attack, Mao initiates a huge network of civil defense tunnels and shelters under Beijing and other cities.

**1976**

Mao dies.

The future Olympic village under construction for Beijing's 2008 games.

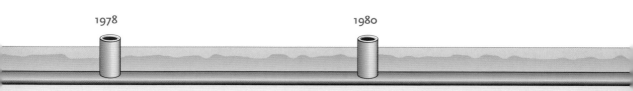

**1978**

**1980**

Deng Xiaoping, purged during the Cultural Revolution, becomes president and stops work on the underground civil defense network, turning the country's focus to developing a capitalist-style economy.

Beijing's second subway line opens—a loop around city, following the path of the old city walls.

In 2002, the Beijing Municipal Office for Safety Control in Underground Spaces began a survey with the intention of producing a three-dimensional map. In a related effort to organize and better use these underground spaces, Yan Huang's office recently embarked on a two-year "Underground Space Planning" project, a grand-scale mapping project that has precedents in Chinese and Southeast Asian history. In the 1930s, the Mao-led Communists had also built a network of tunnels to penetrate the territory in Northern China occupied at that time by the Japanese. Tunnels were also used prior to 1949 at various locations in China during the civil war against the Nationalists. Throughout the 1950s and '60s, Vietnamese Communist leaders, then allies of the Chinese, toured these primitive tunnel networks, then returned to Vietnam and built tunnels of their own to use against the French and then the American armed forces. Military hardware, soldiers and food moved not only through the jungle but beneath it, thwarting the more technologically advanced but less inventive French and American armies.

Only a small portion of Beijing's underground network has been left in a state similar to how it was when the country was preparing for nuclear war against the Soviets. This is the so-called Underground City, which, as of 2005, authorities had opened exclusively to foreign tourists. The small entrance on Damochang Road near the Quianmen district, is easy to miss, with a sign overhead that reads (in Chinese and in English), UNDER GROUND CITY. After paying a small fee, an attendant leads visitors down a staircase to the "city": mostly bare concrete tunnels, no more than four feet wide, that seem to continue on forever. A flashlight beam pointed down side tunnels reveals only more inky blackness. But eventually the tunnels open into vast rooms: a cinema, a school, and a hospital. Clearly these enormous shelters were designed to be inhabited for long periods of time.

Although crudely carved through rock and soil, the shelters were equipped with ventilation shafts and massive steel doors in sections that could be closed to keep out gases and radiation. In the few tunnels lit by bare lightbulbs hanging from the

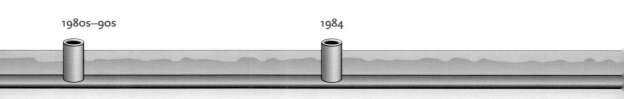

1980s–90s

1984

Beijing converts concrete-lined tunnels and air raid shelters into food markets, shopping centers, restaurants, youth hostels, hotels, and business offices; some reach three stories underground.

City completes drilling of forty deep-water wells to tap underground hot springs in southeastern Beijing to heat homes, businesses, and mineral baths.

ceiling, portraits of Communist heroes such as Karl Marx still hang, and walls are painted with cold war slogans such as DEFEAT THE AMERICAN EMPIRE! and PREPARE FOR WAR! At the end of the section open to tourists, women work in one of the rooms, making silk scarves.

And yet, other than the civil defense network, Beijing hides relatively little beneath its surface, particularly compared to other great metropolises. The city is still struggling to improve basic underground services like water and sewer lines,  storm water management systems, as well as electrical and telecommunications lines. It is not hard to imagine how much better off Beijing's citizens would be today if Mao had led an effort to complete these urban services networks, rather than tunnels for use in a nuclear war. Now the city is doing its best to catch up. Nevertheless, to some observers it appears that China, at least in its major cities, will accomplish in one generation what it took Western cities nearly a century to do. The aptly named "Olympic Action Plan" calls for major upgrades in water delivery and aquifer protection, as well as broad-based sewage treatment, all on short order by 2008.

One bright spot is Beijing's small but rapidly expanding subway system. In fact, it may grow to become one of the largest in the world by the time of the 2008 Games. Until just a few years ago, Beijing had only two subway lines—Line One (construction began in 1969), traveling east-west across the city, directly beneath Tiananmen Square; and Line Two (opened in 1980), tracing the footprint of the ancient city walls to form a loop around the old city. Having since extended the reach of its service, Beijing's subway stations and trains are clean and utilitarian in appearance. Yan Huang

(Opposite Page)
Tourists in Beijing's sprawling Tiananmen Square may have no idea about the enormous network of underground spaces beneath the pavement.

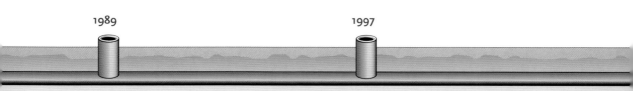

**1989**

Chinese Army puts down student protests in Tiananmen Square. Observers surmise the soldiers arrived by tunnels under the square.

**1997**

Some Beijing neighborhoods sink as the city depletes its groundwater (for industrial development and domestic use).

Beijing's Municipal Office for Safety Control in Underground Spaces begins survey for a three-dimensional map of the city's vast underground realms.

of the Beijing Planning Commission says that today's relatively modest system of 35 miles of track will be extended to more than 150 miles by 2008—a growth of almost 330 percent! No other city or economy in the world is this explosive.

Work is under way that will expand the number of subway lines from two to five. The twenty-four-mile-long Line Three, called the "Olympic Subway Line," cuts through the city's downtown and some of its busiest intersections linking several Olympic game sites. Lines Four and Five are also under construction, as well as a fast-rail connection to the airport. By 2008, the estimated capacity of the entire system will be 1.74 billion riders annually, putting it in the big leagues of city subways. In time for the Olympics, says Yan Huang, probably understating the accomplishment, "the subway system will be a significant contribution to the transportation of this city."

In its fevered pace of subway construction, Beijing (along with other rapidly developing Chinese cities, such as Shanghai) resemble Paris, New York, and London of old, all of which built enormous subway systems consisting of multiple lines and hundreds of stations in just a few decades at the turn of the century. New York's first subway line, running almost the entire length of the island of Manhattan (about thirteen miles), took less than four years from start to finish. Such a pace of construction is unimaginable in today's modern cities, even though tunneling technology is far more advanced than it was a century ago. There seems to be something about a developing city (its civic pride and political energy perhaps) that allows it to harness the resources and finances to get big infrastructure jobs done quickly.

Although subway construction is expensive, it is the only type of transportation that makes sense for a large, rapidly industrializing city whose population is still relatively poor. In this sense, Beijing can be expected to follow in the footsteps of Mexico City, which had no subway lines before 1969 but whose subway ridership now ranks in the top five worldwide.

Beijing's rapid modernization has brought other infrastructural problems besides simply developing new transportation systems. As a growing population and industrial base consume ever more water in northern China, the region's underground aquifers have dropped alarmingly—diminishing by an average of five feet per year. Greater Beijing uses about 220 million tons of water per year from surrounding aquifers—the principal local source of fresh water, like Mexico City. And, as in the Mexican capital, this increased usage is causing Beijing to sink. A 1997 study showed that some neighborhoods in the city have dropped more than a foot since the mid-1980s, when China's industrialization began to take off. This slow, continual shift downward wreaks havoc on building foundations and walls.

To help reduce water consumption and the sinking of the city, authorities are considering raising the price of water to discourage consumption. Longer-term plans include ending the city's exclusive reliance on groundwater by bringing in water from

The hungry teeth of a tunnel boring machine digs a tunnel for a new subway under Beijing. Shanghai, Beijing, and other Chinese cities are leading the world in subway construction.

the Yangtze River to the south, a difficult project because the water would have to be pumped uphill—again a drawing a parallel to Mexico City's water dilemma.

Sewage is another problem facing Beijing. The city has the remains of a fifteenth-century sewer system underneath it, but this network gradually failed to work in the centuries that followed due to lack of maintenance. In the 1950s, Beijing finally built its first modern sewer system. These new sewer lines, as well as water mains, usually ran to the blocks of apartment buildings that were under construction on what was then the periphery of the city. At the time it was considered too expensive to dig a sewer system underneath the older parts of Beijing and authorities have begun to sign contracts with international companies to put in new sewer lines throughout the entire city. New buildings such as conspicuous Western-style hotels or sports stadiums are easy to plan for and finance, but connecting sewers to the thousands of smaller, older buildings throughout the city takes more time and political will. Presently, only an estimated 40 percent of Beijing is equipped to the public sewers. Per person, that means almost 8.5 million residents do not have proper sewage disposal. The public health implications are staggering. As Beijing industrializes and increases its population density, it becomes more important to add modern infrastructure that can handle water and sewage. When the city was essentially a gigantic village, it could survive with wells and septic systems, even if there were some health problems. This is no longer true. In its Olympic Action Plan, the city proudly proclaims a goal of having 90 percent of Beijing's sewage treated by 2008.

For all its growing pains, Beijing does have one unusual resource beneath it: hot water. The city is situated over a series of deep geologic faults, which place groundwater under pressure and convert some of it into steam. Scientists estimate there may be as many as thirty-nine square miles of hot springs beneath Beijing, most of them more than a half-mile below street level. Entrepreneurs have drilled dozens of wells to tap these hot springs which are used to heat buildings and to power certain industries. But like everything else in Beijing, the hot springs have found new life under capitalist modernization: one such spring feeds a luxurious spa in the Xinqiao Hotel, a short distance from Tiananmen Square.

(Opposite Page)
Deep faults under Beijing produce numerous hot springs in the city. Bathers at Xiatangshan enjoy a warm, comforting soak.

## SUBWAY WISHES AND PIPE DREAMS

With several new subway lines under construction, Beijing's public transportation network will soon rival those of many Western capitals causing other developing cities around the world to look at Beijing with envy. Major population centers in Latin America, Africa, and Asia desperately need subways to accommodate swelling legions of citizens, few of whom own cars. Case in point: by 2010 Tokyo, Bombay, Lagos, São Paulo, and Mexico City, are expected to be the largest cities in the world. Without public transportation, job growth in such cities will remain stagnant, even as millions more poor people flood into them from economically depressed or politically unstable rural areas.

Many Asian cities, such as China's Shanghai or Seoul, South Korea, are completing new subway systems at a rate that matches or exceeds the construction of the great subway systems of Paris, New York, and London a century ago. But cities in Africa and Latin America, lacking the explosive economic growth that many Asian cities now enjoy, have not been able to achieve such a pace. One bright spot for these hopefuls is automated tunnel boring technology, which brings down the cost of subway construction (see sidebar in "Cairo"). Here are a few highlights in the worldwide subway race:

Seoul, South Korea, whose subway system was begun in only 1971, now has an eight-line network that is one of the busiest in the world. Its rapid expansion came in the 1990s, with the addition of more than 100 miles of new track.

Algiers, Algeria, has been constructing a small subway system for more than a decade, but the project is beset by numerous delays and cost overruns—all occurring against a backdrop of persistent political instability.

Santiago, Chile, has about twenty-two miles of underground lines in three lines —a small start in a national capital that lacks a strong industrial base. A fourth line is expected to be completed late in 2005.

Buenos Aires, Argentina has the oldest subway system in Latin America, dating back to 1913. But it remains relatively small, only about 26 miles altogether. Keeping pace with population expansion however, the extension of several lines is already underway.

São Paulo, the industrial center of Brazil, has a moderately large system with eight lines covering much of the city and more under construction. Brasilia, the nation's capital, has a much smaller network with only two subway lines. Not surprisingly, Brazil has South America's strongest industrialized economy.

Kolkata (Calcutta), India, has a small subway system, a single ten-mile line, and Delhi opened its first of three subway lines in December 2002. India pursues high-tech industrial development aggressively and has become a net exporter of certain foodstuffs, but the nation as a whole is still relatively poor. The country is attempting to change this with intensive investment in infrastructure in specific areas.

Shanghai, China currently has four lines in its subway system, and like Beijing, Shanghai's subway network is growing at a rapid pace. The system, which first opened for service in 1995, may soon take its place as one of the world's busiest.

The new subway in Shanghai—here, busy with commuters—is expanding rapidly.

# Sydney

**L**IKE MOST CITIES BRACING TO HOST ONE million daily visitors for the Olympics, Sydney prepared for the summer 2000 games by sprucing up its parks, streets, and monuments. Unlike most cities, it also started digging—just about everywhere. Sydney, perched on verdant peninsulas that meet the ocean in a series of coves, inlets, and brilliant white beaches, built the Southern Railway Tunnel to connect the airport to the Olympic Park at Homebush Bay, west of downtown. It built a new Olympic Park Railway Station, with a sprawling canopy housing an underground train line to the city center. It built the Eastern Distributor highway, much of which is underground, and created pedestrian paths and parking garages below street level. Sydney even built an enormous new storm water system—the $300 million, fourteen-mile Northside Storage Tunnel—to channel dirty water away from the city's showpiece harbor. Many of these underground projects had been discussed for decades, but the Olympics provided the impetus to make them happen.

So when the games came to town, athletes and spectators easily shuttled between the main stadium at Homebush Bay, volleyball at Bondi Beach, triathlon at the Sydney Opera House, and boxing at Darling Harbour.

But Sydney's tunneling did not stop with the Olympics. After the games in October of 2000, Sydney started building the (US) $480 million Cross City Tunnel that connects the center city from east to west, followed by the $580 million Lane Cove Tunnel—both for car traffic. The Sydney City Council, perhaps anticipating further development, has even allocated funds to create a three-dimensional map of the city's subterranean spaces. Railways, too, are beginning to reserve rights of way underground. The city is now trying to determine who owns such spaces, and at what depth. As in Tokyo, authorities in Sydney are trying to find a legal way to limit property rights beyond a certain depth to facilitate government-driven construction, while landowners are claiming property rights down to the center of the earth.

Tunneling is nothing new to Sydney. We think of it as a

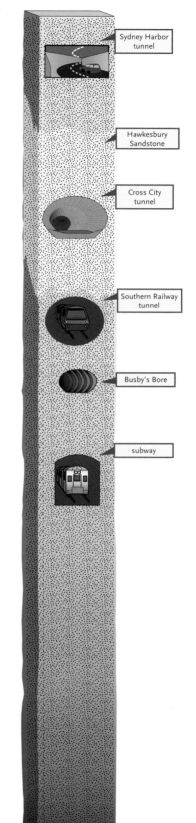

Sydney Harbor tunnel

Hawkesbury Sandstone

Cross City tunnel

Southern Railway tunnel

Busby's Bore

subway

modern city, much younger than, say, Rome or Beijing, but it has a full subway system, built in the early twentieth century, which continues to be extended today; and water tunnels that were put in place in the nineteenth century. The city's underground amenities even include four elegant public restrooms in central Sydney, ornamented with decorative ironwork. These facilities—all for men, since in those times women were not expected to use a toilet outside the home—were installed around 1900 in a prissy Victorian-era effort to keep public toilets out of sight. Sadly, most of these historic restrooms are now abandoned and closed.

But in every other way, establishing and occupying underground spaces has become a rallying cry in Sydney, perhaps the most underground-obsessed urban place in the world. While other cities decide to build great projects below street level on a case-by-case basis, Sydney has made "go-underground" a strategic approach to improving the urban area as a whole. "We are realizing it's a sensible place to put things," says Robert Mitchell, head of the Warren Centre for Advanced Engineering at the University of Sydney. "You want the people to live above ground."

In 1995, Mitchell's Warren Centre initiated its Underground Space Project. Their 314-page report became a blueprint for this kind of development. Essentially, the Warren Centre advocates putting not only major components of infrastructure such as cars and trains below ground, but also light industry, shopping malls, warehouses, and practically anything else that fits.

In many ways Sydney is ideal for underground expansion. Geographically, the city spreads out on a series of points and peninsulas that are best linked by tunnels. And its citizens have an unusually high interest in city planning, observers say, which makes it easier to gather public support for something as politically and technically challenging as tunneling. "It's a city which is very self-conscious of its future," says Martin Wachs, a transportation consultant from the University of California–Berkeley who has worked in Sydney. "The plans for city development seem to be much more widely discussed and better circulated there than in American cities."

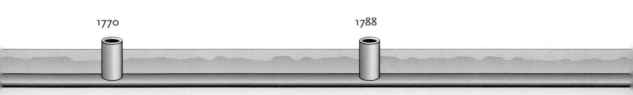

**1770**

Captain James Cook discovers Australia and claims it in the name of the British King George III.

**1788**

Admiral Arthur Phillip sails into the harbor of what will become Sydney with a shipload of convicts and their jailers. Over the next half century, Great Britain sends thousands of convicts to Australia.

**Country:** Australia

**Location:** Southeastern coast, on the South Pacific Ocean

**Population:** 24,000 for the small central city; in the metropolitan area, 4.1 million

**Area:** 4,790 square miles (metropolitan area)

National and urban pride may be at work here, too, or it could be the same plucky, competitive streak that makes Aussie sailors, tennis stars, and rugby players famous worldwide. Finally, Sydney is well suited for tunneling because much of the ground is Hawkesbury sandstone, a relatively soft sedimentary rock that is easy to bore through but strong enough to withstand crumbling when trains, autos, and trucks run through it or pass just overhead.

Even so, the range of underground activity is unusual for a city as sprawling, suburban, and relatively young as Sydney. When English ships deposited Sydney's first "settlers"—convicts banished to Australia—in the late 1780s, most of today's big

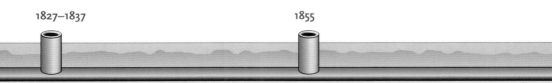

**1827–1837**

Using convict labor, English surveyor John Busby constructs Busby's Bore, a meandering tunnel through solid rock, giving Sydney a reliable water supply.

**1855**

The government-owned railway company builds one of the earliest train tunnels in the world, about a mile long. The tunnel is still in use today.

cities were already major urban centers. It was an inauspicious start for Sydney but one the Australians eventually overcame.

Until 1776, England had used its North American colonies as a dumping ground for criminals, paupers, and religious dissenters. But with the American Revolutionary War and the states' independence came the need for a new British penal colony. The first load of prisoners arrived in Australia 1788 on a ship under the command of Admiral Arthur Phillip. They disembarked in an area that would later become Sydney. There, in a secluded cove next to a freshwater stream in what is now Port Jackson, Phillip founded a colony of about a thousand prisoners and their jailers. Over the next five decades, England sent thousands more prisoners to this new land, "down under" and on the other side of the world. The convicts—thieves, political prisoners, and prisoners of war—working alongside free settlers, gradually built a new country and a thriving city.

By the 1850s, based largely on the success of sheep farming, Sydney had grown into a major port and commercial center, and Australia had evolved into a prosperous young nation. Many former convicts and their free descendants had become prominent citizens, and contemporary Australians pride themselves on tracing their ancestry back to criminals, taking pleasure in a national story based on an ironic reversal of fortune.

Sydney's colorful past has even inspired some underground mythology. Many Aussies claim that secret tunnels still exist under Sydney that allowed convicts to travel from their cells to the shoreline. Another story maintains that a tunnel ran from the city's Government House to the coast, so the colony's governor could escape in case of a prisoner uprising. Such tunnels have never been found but prisoner labor did figure in the construction of the city's first large tunnel, a water main known as Busby's Bore.

John Busby, an engineer and mineral surveyor from England, supervised the construction of the tunnel, which meanders 1.8 miles through solid rock from

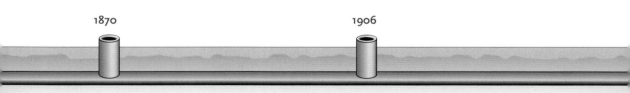

**1870**

**1906**

Fearing invasion by Russia after the Crimean War, the Australian army places large guns in a series of tunnels dug into cliffs overlooking Sydney's key harbors. The tunnels are later used to store ammunition during World War II, and for training during the Korean and Vietnam wars.

Sydney Central railway station opens, which includes more than two dozen platforms and tracks underground, as well as work areas and offices.

The canopy of the Olympic Park Railway Station, one of the many underground projects completed for the 2000 Olympics in Sydney.

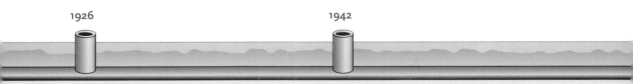

**1926**

**1942**

First Sydney subway line opens. The system grows into the present day CityRail system, which brings thousands of commuters into Sydney daily.

The Australian military builds the three-story Air Defense Control Centre underneath the ground in the suburb of Bankstown, south of Sydney.

Thousands of Sydney denizens walk through the New Cross City Tunnel after its official opening in January 2005.

the Lachlan swamps, now the site of Centennial Park, to Oxford Street at the corner of Hyde Park in the heart of the city. Convicts using pickaxes and shovels dug the tunnel from 1827 to 1837 and when it was done it carried almost a half million gallons of water to the thirsty population each day. It was the city's principal conduit of fresh water for the next half century.

**1992**                                    **1995**

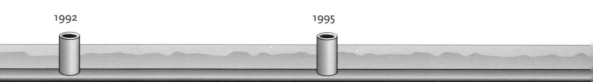

After a century of debate, Sydney Harbour Tunnel is completed at a cost of $532 million.

The Warren Centre for Advanced Engineering at the University of Sydney releases its Underground Space Project, a comprehensive report and strategy intended to utilize Sydney's underground in a comprehensive and systematic way.

During a drought in 1872, city workers entered Busby's Bore to measure and clean it. They found that the dank passage varied substantially in size, from as narrow as three feet, to almost 9 feet in height. They also found numerous false starts and dead-end side paths. Without accurate documentation, historians can only guess at the reasons for these occurrences. It's possible that Busby and his foremen were reluctant to enter the tunnels and supervise the work of the convicts. Or, maybe, the convicts were trying to dig their way to freedom.

In the late nineteenth century, Sydney built additional water tunnels, and by the 1930s Busby's Bore had been largely shut down, with parts of it filled in to prevent the streets and buildings above from collapsing. But most of the "bore" is still intact, and it has become a popular gathering spot for the city's clandestine underground explorers known as "Drainers." Many Drainers are members of a club called the "Sydney Cave Clan," which is dedicated to exploring, often illegally, the myriad underground spaces beneath Sydney. Members have coined their own vocabulary, which includes the salutation "Good draining!" Each year, at the Clannie Awards, the group presents its Golden Torch to an explorer who has shown the most initiative in underground exploration.

Another popular haunt of the Drainers is the original stream that Admiral Phillip discovered when he chose the site of Sydney for his penal colony. To ensure plentiful drinking water, Phillip settled at the mouth of this stream in Sydney Cove, now in the shadow of the Sydney Opera House. But as the penal colony grew, the stream silted up from development along its banks. Fearing the consequences, and in an early effort at watershed management, Phillip banned timber cutting and animal grazing along the banks. He also ordered the construction of three tanks to hold the water of the diminishing stream, which came to be known as the Tank Stream.

But the Tank Stream quickly became polluted anyway. Despite its inadequacies, the stream was the settlement's principal source of water for four decades, until the construction of Busby's Bore. Drainers gather at the site of the Tank Stream once a year, when the Sydney Water Board opens up the culvert for inspection, to catch a glimpse

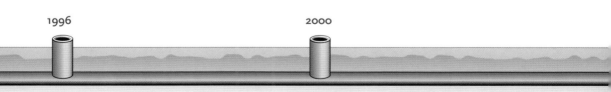

**1996**

**2000**

A community group called "Sydney Cables Downunder" campaigns to put more of the city's power lines underground.

Sydney's third subway, the Airport Line, opens in time for the Summer Olympics.

of this historic waterway. After the ceremony, some make their way down ladders to explore the old tunnel.

While scavenging for water in the 1800s, Sydney was also constructing some of the earliest train tunnels in the world. In 1855, a tunnel still in use today was excavated from the Sydney railyard to Darling Harbour, a distance of less than a mile. Between 1926 and 2000, the City Circle, Eastern Suburbs Railway, and the Airport Line were opened to service the Central Business District. As a result, Sydney currently has an efficient three-line subway network and is at work on a fourth line—the $1.1 billion Chatswood to Epping link in the northern suburbs, scheduled for completion in 2008, with 8 miles of tunnels and a series of spacious new stations.

The new subway will have to compete with Sydney's new underground highways however. The 1.3-mile Cross City Tunnel, begun in January 2003 and opened to traffic in July 2005, runs from Darling Harbour (one of the city's main docks for goods and people), underneath Hyde Park, the oval-shaped landscaped park in the city center that was originally a horse-racing track, and continues to Kings Cross. The Cross City Tunnel also connects with another major tunnel, the Eastern Distributor, completed in 1999. Expected to carry 90,000 vehicles a day, Cross City Tunnel is part of the city's strategy to route heavy traffic underground and reserve surface streets for cyclists, pedestrians, and lighter automobile traffic. This is a plan similar to Boston's efforts to relocate underground formerly elevated major highways that once sliced through its historic downtown. The new look at street level includes well groomed parks and plenty of pricey real estate development—while traffic flows silently underneath it all, out of sight.

But surely, Sydney's most famous automobile tunnel is the Sydney Harbour Tunnel, completed in 1992 at a cost of $532 million. The tunnel runs under the water between the opera house and the Sydney Harbour Bridge, which was completed in 1932 and remains one of the longest steel-arch bridges in the world. The tunnel's construction came after a century of debate and planning. In the 1890s, a train tunnel

**2003**

Work begins on the 1.3-mile Cross City Tunnel. Scheduled for completion in 2005, it runs directly underneath the central city and is expected to carry ninety thousand vehicles a day, leaving surface streets available for more walking and bicycling.

was proposed for the city's North Shore, but the idea was dropped because of the projected cost. In the 1920s, a tunnel was again proposed, but the bridge was built instead. Tunnels are usually preferred to bridges under important bodies of water because tunnels do not obstruct shipping, but they are almost always considerably more expensive to construct.

Increasing traffic put the Sydney Harbour Tunnel back on the public agenda in the decades following World War II. A private international consortium built the four-lane, 1.4-mile tunnel, with the right to operate it for thirty years, until 2022. At that point the tunnel is to be transferred to the city, debt-free. This novel financing method was the end result of almost four decades of bickering among supporters and opponents of the tunnel about how to pay for it. The construction under the harbor involved sinking eight 23,000-ton tunnel sections made of reinforced concrete. These sections lie in a trench, covered with boulders, to protect the tunnel from dragging anchors, sinking ships, and other maritime hazards in the harbor waters overhead. Variations on this technique are a common way of building tunnels underneath

Sydney's new Cross City Tunnel that travels between Rushcutter's Bay and Darling Harbour.

A painting depicts The Botany Bay Penal Colony, around 1788, marking the beginnings of a settlement that was to become the city of Sydney.

bodies of water. In some cases, when building in deep or dark waters, tunnel engineers use GPS (Global Positioning System) locators to help position tunnel sections exactly in alignment with one another underwater. Projects as short as the tunnel under Boston's harbor or as long as the mammoth Malmo/Copenhagen tunnel between Sweden and Denmark (2.2 miles ) have used this "underground" (underwater) construction method. It was more difficult in Sydney because before being placed into position, the tunnel sections had to be transported over open seas. But the construction proceeded without major mishaps. Now, more than 75,000 drivers each day pay about two dollars to use the tunnel.

As Sydney has learned, while tunnels solve some problems, they also create problems of their own. Vehicles in those tunnels generate clouds of exhaust, which are ventilated through powerful blowers out of stacks located above the ground. Some residents of neighborhoods near these stacks now complain that the emissions are a health hazard. Consequently, many in Sydney have banded together to form Groups Against Stack Pollution (GASP), to fight automobile tunnel expansion. Not surprisingly, easy solutions have yet to be found. Perhaps the advent of hybrid cars with reduced emissions will bring an answer to this vexing situation.

Despite these obstacles, Sydney seems intent on exploiting its underground realms to a degree unprecedented in comparison to other major cities. The gleaming auto, train, and pedestrian tunnels are a long way from Busby's Bore, hacked out of the earth in a ragged fashion in the 1800s by a band of convicts, working inch by inch with picks and shovels. Even members of GASP are likely to concede that Sydney has come a long way since these humble beginnings.

# DEFENDERS: TAKE YOUR POSITIONS . . . UNDERGROUND

Alone—with New Zealand—at the bottom of the world, Australia has never experienced any major foreign invasion, although an unannounced American naval scientific expedition did assert their presence, in the dark of night, without permission in the Sydney harbor in 1839.

This incident along with later geopolitical fears prompted the country to build tunnels and bunkers over the next two centuries, despite the continent's isolated location. For instance, the Australians had a long-standing suspicion about Russia who was often at odds with the mother country (England) and sometimes sent ships into Australian harbors while en route between "European" Russia and Russian colonies on the Asian Rim or in North America. In 1870, after the Crimean War, fearing invasion, the Australian army built a series of tunnels for gun installations in the cliffs overlooking Sydney's key harbors. They were later used to store ammunition during World War II and for training during the Korean and Vietnam wars, both of which drew the Western powers into nasty underground guerrilla war combat in Asia.

A much more extensive series of underground bunkers and tunnels was built around Sydney after the Japanese attack on Pearl Harbor in 1941, when federal and local authorities went on a frenzy of bunker building to guard against a dreaded Japanese invasion. After the war, authorities closed the bunkers, many of which were classified as secret, and forgot about them. In the subsequent decades, casual explorers often accidentally uncovered them, or comments slipped out in reminiscences from former soldiers and government officials. One of larger underground defense complexes came to light in 1971 after a military journal made reference to its existence. This was the three-story secret Air Defence Control Centre at Bankstown, a suburb to the south of Sydney. Built in 1942, this command center intended for use during a bombardment of Sydney was equipped with kitchens, dining rooms, and bathrooms. Vandals set fire to and destroyed the bunker in 1973, but the remains still lie underneath the township's central park.

Australian authorities also pressed subway tunnels into service during WW II, just as the British did in London. The St. James subway station was originally constructed with four tunnels underneath it, in anticipation of additional subway lines to come in the future; two of those unused tunnels were put to use as bomb shelters during the war. American General Douglas MacArthur, who knew Japan's imperialist war plans better than anyone, established his headquarters in a special bunker built just past one of those subway tunnels. The Australian Cabinet also took refuge here. Recent attempts by intrepid Cave Clan members to find these underground headquarters from which Australia safely oversaw its substantial contribution to the war effort have been thwarted by flooding in the passageways.

Sydney's Cave Clanners or "Drainers" stand inside one of the city's sewers.

# CONCLUSION

IF YOU COULD FLIP A MODERN CITY UPSIDE DOWN AND LOOK AT WHAT'S underneath, as if it were a houseplant removed temporarily from its pot for inspection, you would see not a mass of roots but an amazing assortment of wires, tubes, and structural supports, interspersed with dirt, stone, and assorted debris from ages past.

The particulars of this urban underside would vary from city to city—because each city is different above ground—but there would also be patterns of development beneath each city that could be sorted into common categories and trends. As we look back on the twelve cities described in this book, and to the future of these and other cities, what can we say about each environment that could help us predict what its underground realm might look like a decade, or a even a century from now?

For one thing, a city's underground assumes different roles, depending on its stage of historical development. In cities that have not yet industrialized—think of London in 1600, Moscow in 1900, or Beijing in 1975—those spaces may be *rich in potential* but their functions are usually more *passive* in nature; in other words, serving as places to store or hide things or persons, such as books in a library, manacles in a torture chamber, or people in a fallout shelter.

It isn't until cities industrialize and develop intense commercial economies prizing speed and efficiency that they add the more active systems below street level to move water, sewage, electricity, gas, people, and, now, bits and bytes of information to and from their inhabitants and businesses. Rapidly industrializing cities, like New York in 1900 or now Beijing a century later, find their undergrounds indispensable in helping them compete economically, and they find the resources to add these critical infrastructural components, and to add them quickly, despite the great expense usually involved.

Beijing is particularly illustrative of this point. Until the mid 1970s, the capital of China was akin to a large village. There were few water or sewer lines beneath it, and no subway lines. A home or business—almost all of them state-owned in China under Communism—was likely to rely on wells and cesspits for water delivery and removal and the occupants depended on walking or bicycles for transportation. Except for the bicycles, this is similar to how Paris or New York functioned in 1800, before industrialization and modernization changed them irrevocably.

Now, early in the twenty-first century, Beijing will soon have five subway lines complete that are expected to carry close to two billion passengers annually. In about a generation, a mere blink in time for a city with such a long history, China's capital will have built what is often a city's most expensive component, a subterranean delivery system for its people. Other quickly developing urban centers, such as Shanghai and Mumbai (Bombay), are making similar journeys toward full industrialization and, thus, toward a thoroughly new adaptation of their underground spaces. The development experiences of these cities compare with New York, London, and Paris, all of which completed the bulk of their extensive subway construction in about a generation.

Nowadays, however, these advanced industrialized cities add new infrastructural systems more slowly. London and Paris have each opened only a single new major subway line in the last half-century, and these came at great expense and political effort. New York has been planning a new line along Manhattan's east side, the Second Avenue Subway, since the 1950s, but still has not managed to assemble the funds and political willpower to construct it. This great American city is also working on a third water tunnel, but after thirty-five years of construction, it remains incomplete.  These delays are not just the result of interruptions for wars or economic recessions, nor do they always indicate a lack of funding. It is often absence of political will that stalls further underground development.

It would seem that cities go through distinct historical epochs as far as their respective underground infrastructure is concerned. When the moment is right, cities add water, sewer, power, and transportation at a furious rate, becoming "mature," and then do so less rapidly for another, longer period of time. But what else can we say about such infrastructures that might help us to predict how they will develop in the future?

The substrata of cities are among the most important and durable of all the pages on which history records the past. Each epoch a city experiences deposits a layer of physical evidence that archeologists and historians can later try to interpret, although often this task is highly difficult. In a city like Rome, historians spend their entire careers assembling and analyzing its colossal underground record. Often, this book of subterranean history tells stories that cities would prefer to forget. New Yorkers, for instance, discovered in the late twentieth century that their cosmopolitan metropolis had been a slave-trading city for much of the seventeenth and eighteenth centuries, a truth all but forgotten in popular memory until workers digging the foundations of a new office building unearthed an African Burial Ground.  The realms beneath most cities will continue to play this role of psychic mirror, forcing their citizens to confront unpleasant truths about themselves or their ancestors, much as the unconscious mind can do the same for an individual.

Still another pattern likely to remain important in our study of urban undergrounds is that what exists below street level will usually reflect a city's enduring political culture. New York and London have highly complex, multifaceted, fragmented political economies, and what lies beneath them is similarly complex. Paris, on the other hand, has a more hierarchical, state-led political economy that values beauty and advanced engineering, and the Parisian underground infrastructure reflects this more orderly way of planning and building infrastructure. It seems likely, too, that the emerging megacities of India, China, Korea, and other Asian nations will produce belowground environments that reflect their own political cultures, distinct in various ways from those of the Western world.

Regardless of their exact forms, what is built by man beneath the world's great urban places will retain their primary importance in our understanding of how cities grow, perform, and sometimes decline. Much like the organs of the human body, today's urban underground supplies water and heat, carries electrical currents and information, and disposes of waste. And like a human's internal organs, the systems beneath a city, of course, are usually out of sight and out of mind, that is, until they break down. As cities add new telecommunications systems or other technologies not yet imagined, it seems likely they will locate them underground because, despite the expense, it is more efficient in the long run. In Paris, new fiber optic communication lines are strung along the old roofs of the arching brick ceilings of Haussmann's cavernous sewers, built in the 1850s. Other cities have to dig new passages for the same kinds of communications systems, and at great cost and effort, but places for them *are* being found beneath the streets.

Although we can make general predictions about the future of urban development, knowing exactly what is happening and can happen beneath each city will remain the domain of the civil engineer, the archeologist, and the geologist. In all probability, no truly complete record of any great city's underground can ever be assembled. Except for such metropolises as San Francisco and Tokyo, which over time face the threat of severe earthquakes, it's unlikely that a great city will ever be literally turned upside down like the houseplant on the potting shed bench. We can never see all of a city's underground systems and foundations. Some chapters of a city's story will always remain buried, misunderstood or wholly undiscovered, contributing to the continuing allure of exploring beneath the busy streets and avenues. But whether the whole story comes to light or not, we know that what lies below helps to sustain the visible structures above ground—the evidence of our own collective activity—and in many subtle ways uniquely reflects the power, productivity, and beauty of the changing human habitat.

# SOURCE NOTES

## NEW YORK

### INTERVIEWS

Christopher Choa (architect, New York City).

Greg Dreicer (museum curator and expert on infrastructure systems, New York City).

Larry Furlong (President, Electric Railroaders Association. New York City).

Andrew Hoffman (Vice President, JPMorgan Chase Bank), interview with the author, May 2003.

Ken Kruckemeyer (professor of civil and environmental engineering, Massachusetts Institute of Technology).

Charles J. Maikish (executive vice president in charge of facilities, JP Morgan Chase).

Natalie Milner (public relations, Department of Environmental Protection [water department], New York City).

Robert Olmsted (former planning director, Metropolitan Transit Authority), interview with the author, June 12, 2003. This long interview with Olmsted was very helpful in understanding the city's transit system more comprehensively.

Ed O'Shea (global facilities manager, JPMorgan Chase Bank, New York City).

Bruce Rosen (planner, New York City Planning Department).

Junnko Tozaki (assistant director, New York City Transit Museum), interview with the author, June 6, 2002.

Robert Yaro (president, Regional Plan Association), interview with author, May 8, 2002.

Jeff Zupan (senior fellow for transportation, Regional Plan Association), interview with the author, June 11, 2003.

### BOOKS

Michael W. Brooks, *Subway City: Riding the Trains, Reading New York* Rutgers University Press, 1997).

Edwin G. Burrows and Mike Wallace, Gotham: A History of New York City to 1898. Oxford and New York: Oxford University Press, 2000). This wonderful book provided an extremely useful overview of the city's development, particularly with regard to the city's water system and its early history with slavery. Brian Cudahy, *Under the Sidewalks of New York: The Story of the Greatest Subway System in the World* (New York: Fordham University, 1995).

Joseph Cunningham, *A History of the New York City Subway System* Cunningham, 1993).

Robert Daley, *The World Beneath the City* (Philadelphia: J. B. Lippencott Company, 1959).

Peter Derrick, *Tunneling to the Future: The Story of the Great Subway Expansion that Saved New York* (New York: New York University Press, 2001).

Stan Fischler, *The Subway: A Trip through Time on New York's Rapid Transit* (Flushing, New York: H7M Productions Inc., 1997).

Dave Frattini, *The Underground Guide to New York City Subways* (2000).

Stanley Greenberg, photographer, Thomas H. Garver, introduction, *Invisible New York: The Hidden Infrastructure of the City* (John Hopkins University Press, 1995).

Clifton Hood, *722 Miles: The Building of the Subways and How They Transformed New York.* (Johns Hopkins University Press, Centennial edition, 2004).

Kenneth Jackson, *Encyclopedia of New York* (Yale University Press, 1995). Especially useful for information about tunnels.

Pamela Jones, *Under the City Streets: A History of Subterranean New York.* (Holt, Rinehart, and Winston, 1978).

Margaret Morton, *The Tunnel: The Underground Homeless of New York City* (Yale University Press, 1995.

*The New York Subway: Interborough Rapid Transit 1904* (New York: Fordham University Press. 1904, reprinted 1991).

John Stilgoe, *Metropolitan Corridor: Railroads and the American Scene* (Yale University Press, 1985). Especially strong on the development of Grand Central Station.

Jennifer Toth, *The Mole People: Life in the Tunnels beneath New York City* (Chicago: Chicago Review Press, 1995).

## Magazines and Newspapers

Henry L. Acossitt, "The World's Biggest Thirst," *Saturday Evening Post,* September 10, 1955.

"Amazing Maze Beneath the City" *The New York Times Magazine,* January 12, 1958.

"An Illustrated Evening Newspaper," *The Daily Graphic,* June 24, 1878. Cartoons showing the unpleasant effects of the elevated rail lines.

Mark Berkey-Gerard, "Keeping the City Running," *Gotham Gazette,* October 6, 2003.

Victor H. Bernstein. "Art in the Subways of New York," *New York Times Magazine,* April 11, 1937. Carl Bevelhymer, "Steam,"*Gotham Gazette,* November 10, 2003.

David Bianculli, "'Mega Tech' Gets under Apple's Skin," *Daily News,* November 6, 1998.

Col. Sydney H. Bingham, "New Ideas for Efficent Passenger Transportation,"

David Bird, "Holland Tunnel on Eve of 50th Birthday," *New York Times,* November 11, 1977.

Glenn Collins, "On View for Public Coveting," *New York Times,* January 10, 2005.

Jason Feldman, "Under the Streets of New York," *New York Construction News,* May 13, 2001.

Laura Forlano, "The Office of the Future Today," *Gotham Gazette,* November 10, 2003.

"From Croton to Town," Source not available, July 6, 1872. Viewed in archives at Museum of the City of New York. Article is about how the people of that era had entirely forgotten where their water came from.

Goodyear Tire and Rubber Co. and Stephen-Adamson Manufacturing Co., "Transportation for the Modern City,"

"Destinies of a Great Bank Depend upon Aaron Burr's Old Tank." Source unknown; newspaper article marked 2-10-1895. Viewed in archives of Museum of the City of New York. Article recounts how a rusty old water tank at Reade and Center streets is the foundation of the bank of Manhattan Company, because its charter depends on it being a water company.

Martin Gottlieb. "City Accepts Bid on Part of 3rd Water Tunnel," *New York Times,* February 25, 1983. Gene Guffini, "New York Underground," *New York Alive,* January/February 1985.

Gale Harris, Jean Howson, and Betsy Bradley; Marjorie Pearson, ed., Laurie Beckelman, supervisor, "African Burial Ground: The Commons Historic District Designation Report," February 1993. Provides essential information on the city's African Burial Ground.

Christina Hemphill, "Electricity," *Gotham Gazette,* December 8, 2003.

"Manhattan Streams Still Flow as Plague to Engineers," *New York Herald Tribune,* August 12, 1928. Describes how creeks and small rivers still course underneath the city.

Michael Markowitz, "The Sewer System," *Gotham Gazette,* October 10, 2003.

Akiko Matsuda, "Garbage," *Gotham Gazette,* December 8, 2003.

"Millions on the Move," special section on transit system, *New York Times,* July 11, 1971.

New York Metropolitan Transportation Council, "2000 Hub Bound Travel Report," May 2003.

W. Barclay Parsons, "Rapid Transit in New York," *Scribner's Magazine,* May 1900.

Robin Pogrebin, "Underground Mail Road," *The New York Times,* May 7, 2001.

222 Beneath the Metropolis

Anna Quindlen. "New York Abolishes Free Water and Cry Is Heard Round World," *The New York Times,* January 21, 1980.

Greg Sargent, "Why an Aqueduct?" *The New York Observer,* March 5, 2003.

Sidney Schaer, "Mail System down the Tube," *Newsday.* Provided information on the city's old pneumatic tube system.

"The Steel Threads that Built New York," *Transit Magazine,* November 1954.

Kate Stohr, "Water," *Gotham Gazette,* December 12, 2003.

Joel Swerdlow, *National Geographic,* February 1997.

"Terra Cotta Work in the Subway," special supplement on the subway in *The World,* October 2, 1904.

"Water Main Break on East Side Stops Subway for Hours," *New York Times,* August 25, 1983.

"Water Works Engineering—The Journal of the Water Works Profession Since 1877," Oct. 21, 1942.

Sam Williams, "Natural Gas," *Gotham Gazette,* October 13, 2003.

## WEB SITES

"Commemorating the African Burial Ground in New York City: Spirituality of Space in Contemporary Art Works," *Art eJournal of the African World,* http://www.ijele.com/ijele/vol1.1/frohne.html.

The Manhattan Office Market, http://www.reinet.or.jp/study/eng/5-manhattan/5-0112_e.htm.

"Midtown Manhattan Is the World's Most Expensive Shopping Location," Buildings.com, November 7, 2002.

New York Geology, American Museum of Natural History, http://research.amnh.org/earthplan/nyc_geol.html.

http://www.newyorkunderground.org/. This site, set up by Julia Solis, has fabulous pictures of the tunnels underneath New York City.

http://www.nycsubway.org.

http://www.rapidtransit.com.

Water Tunnel No. 3 in New York City, The International Tunneling Association, http://www.ita-aites.org/tribune8/fou4.html.

What Makes the Big Apple Grow, New York City Government, http://nyc.gov/html/dep/html/awareness.html. This site has great historic photos of the development of the water tunnels.

## Visits to Physical sites in New York City

Atlantic Street Tunnel, tour led by Julia Solis, Ars Subterranea: The Society for Creative Preservation. This fascinating old tunnel was built in 1844 and then closed in 1861 and forgotten until rediscovered in 1981. Visit htto://www.creativepreservation.org for more information.

New York Federal Reserve Bank, tour of gold held in vaults, August 2005.

Subway and commuter rail system, extensive visits to tunnels and stations.

# *Chicago*

## Interviews

Howard Decker (chief curator, National Building Museum). Decker provided great perspective on Chicago's location and its strategic importance.

Fred Deters (coordinating planner, Chicago Department of Planning and Development). A historian of the city, Deters offered an overview of the development of the city over its first two centuries and how that coincided with the city's physical development.

Bill Martin (urban planner, Chicago).

Ted Wolff (architect, Wolff Clements and Associates, Chicago).

Patricia Gallagher (executive director, National Capital Planning Commission, Washington, DC, and former parks department official in Chicago).

## Books

Bion Arnold, *Recommendations and General Plan for a Comprehensive Passenger Subway System for the City of Chicago* (Chicago: City of Chicago, Department of Public Works, 1911).

Harold M. Mayer and Richard C. Wade, *Chicago: Growth of a Metropolis—An Illustrated History* (Chicago: University of Chicago Press, 1969).

Frank Randall, ed., *History of the Development of Building Construction in Chicago* (1974). Good for information on the development of the raft foundations for the first skyscrapers in Chicago.

Alice Sinkevitch, ed., *AIA Guide to Chicago* (New York: Harcourt Brace & Company, 1993).

David Young, *Chicago Transit.* (*Northern Illinois University Press,* 1998.)

*This Fabulous Century, 1870–1900.* (Time-Life Books).

Daniel Burnham and Edward Bennett, *Plan of Chicago, 1909* (Chicago: Commercial Club of Chicago).

## MAGAZINES AND NEWSPAPERS

Don Babwin, *Account of 1992 Tunnel Flood,* Associated Press, April 12, 2002. Freight tunnel information.

P. J. Bednarski, "Loop Tunnels Stretch for 50 Miles," *Chicago Sun-Times,* April 13, 1992. Good information on the city's system of freight tunnels.

"Diversion Project to Rechannel 3.1 Billion Gallons of Water," *Midwest Construction,* August 2002.

## WEB SITES

Daniel Hudson Burnham, ArchiTech, http://www.architech.com.

Chicago Timeline, Chicago Public Library, http://www.chpublib.org.

Chicago Tunnel Company Railroad,
    http://www.Ameritech.net/users/chicagotunnell/tunnel1.html.

"Down the Drain: The Historic Development of an Urban Infrastructure," http://www.chpublib.org Good overview of the city's development, including the sewer system.

The History of Chicago, http://www.thehistoryof.co.uk/Cooking/Food/Onion.html.

Sears Tower, Great Buildings,
    http://www.greatbuildings.com/buildings/Sears_Towers.html.

Sears Tower, http://www.thesearstower.com/buildinginfo/SearsTowerInfo.pdf.

Sears Tower, Skyscraper Page, http://skyscraperpage.com/cities/?buildingID=5.

Sears Tower, http://web.bryant.edu/~ehu/h364proj/fall_98/gean/sears.htm.

# SAN FRANCISCO

## INTERVIEWS

Chris Arnold (architect working on earthquake preparation, Palo Alto, California)

Lucien Canton (director, Office of Emergency Services, City of San Francisco)

Mary Comerio (professor of architecture, University of California–Berkeley, and author of *Disaster Hits Home*)

Eric Elsesser (founding principal, Forell/Elsesser Engineers Inc.) Elsesser led the seismic protection renovation of the San Francisco City Hall.

Anthony Irons (Operations Department, San Francisco Unified School District) Irons supervised the seismic protection overhaul of San Francisco City Hall.

Jeanne Perkins (earthquake program manager, Association of Bay Area Governments)

Marcia Rosen (executive director, San Francisco Redevelopment Agency)

Jay Wilson (natural hazards videographer, Portland Oregon)

## BOOKS

Gray Brechin, *Imperial San Francisco* (University of California Press, 1999).

Encyclopedia Britannica, Macropedia. Articles on Earthquakes and San Francisco.

John Bernard McGloin, *San Francisco: The Story of a City* (Presidio Press, 1978). Provides information about the five principal tunnels in the city.

Amelia Ransome, *The Fantastic City: Memoirs of the Social and Romantic Life of Old San Francisco* (1932).

Gordon Thomas and Max Morgan Witts, *The San Francisco Earthquake* (Stein and Day, 1971). Discussion of what an earthquake would do to San Francisco and how likely it would be in the future.

## MAGAZINES AND NEWSPAPERS

Gerald Adams, "Underground Workers Find Gold Rush Ship," *Times-Picayune,* December 8, 1994.

William Allen, "Build on Sand: Soil Type One of Three Major Factors in Amount of Damage Done to Buildings in Earthquake," *St. Louis Post-Dispatch*, October 28, 1990.

Association of Bar Area Governments, "On Shakey Ground," April 1995.

_____. "Preventing the Nightmare: Designing a Model Program to Encourage Owners of Homes and Apartments to do Earthquake Retrofits," October 1999.

_____. "The Real Dirt on Liquification: A Guide to the Liquefaction Hazard in Future Earthquakes Affecting the San Francisco Bay Area," February 2001.

Michael Cabanatuan, "BART Searches for Answers after Retrofit Defeat," *San Francisco Chronicle,* November 7, 2002.

_____. "BART Needs $1.1 Billion Seismic Job," *San Francisco Chronicle*, June 4, 2002.

Robert Campbell, "Bay Watch: Boston Planners Can Learn a Lot from the Good, Bad, and Ugly of San Francisco Public Spaces," *Boston Globe*, May 14, 2002.

Lyn Duff, "City Harbors a Community of Sewer Rats," *San Francisco Examiner,* December 30, 1997.

Kevin Fagan, "Masons Restore Life to Once-Buried Bridge," *San Francisco Chronicle,* May 7, 2002.

Carl Hall, "Geologists Trace Fault Zone under S.F.," *San Francisco Chronicle,* December 15, 2001.

Joseph Hall, "San Francisco Nicknamed the 'Beirut of Transit,'" *Toronto Star,* November 5, 1998.

Phillip Matier and Andrew Ross, "Alarm Bell for Hetch Hetchy: Tiny Pin Nearly Brings System to Its Knees," *San Francisco Chronicle,* November 14, 2002.

Carl Nolte, "The Death of the Imperial City," *San Francisco Chronicle,* April 18, 1999.

_____. "Muni Builds Underground Train Yard to Fix Design Goof," *San Francisco Chronicle,* March 13, 1996.

Charles Petit, "Research Team Finds Quake Clues Deep in Mission District Soils," *San Francisco Chronicle,* October 17, 1991.

Ken Ringle, "1906 Legendary Disaster," *Washington Post,* October 19, 1989.

Walter Roessing, "San Francisco Cable Cars: An Engineering Feat Turned Landmark," *St. Petersburg Times,* May 15, 1988.

David Rosenbaum, "Surprise Bones of Contention," *Engineering News-Record,* June 6, 1994.

Ronald Rosenberg, "Tough Building Code Saved Many Newer Structures," *Boston Globe,* October 19, 1989.

San Francisco Public Utilities Commission, "San Francisco's Water System."

"UT Professor Studies San Francisco Earthquake," *Daily Beacon,* August 29, 1995.

## WEB SITES

All About Earthquakes, ReadinessInfo, http://www.readinessinfo.com.

The Biggest Earthquakes in North America, http://books.turnstonepub.com/storyinthe stone/sharedact/worksheets/landQuakes_wks.html.

History of Earthquakes, The Worst-Case Scenario Survival Handbook, https://www.worstcasescenarios.com.

San Francisco Earthquake History, Museum of the City of San Francisco, htpp://www.sfmuseum.org/alm/quake3.html#1989.

# MEXICO CITY

## INTERVIEWS

Jose Castillo (architect, Harvard University), interview with the author.

Leyland Cott (professor, Harvard University), interview with the author, June 9, 2003.

Robert Luchetti, (architect with Robert Luchetti Associates, Inc., Mexico City), interview with the author.

## MAGAZINES AND NEWSPAPERS

Naomi Adelson, "Water Woes: Private Investment Plugs Leaks in Water Sector," *Business Mexico,* March 1, 2000.

"All Systems Go for Mexico City Metro; Crash Program Pushes 70 km of New Lines," *Engineering News-Record,* October 22, 1981.

Katherine Barnhart, "Subway Construction Uncovers Archaeological Treasures: Digging Up Mexico's Past," *Business Mexico,* November 1993.

Christopher Claims, "How Water Leaks Can Sink a Huge City," *The Scotsman,* June 5, 1996.

Marla Dickerson, "It's a Dirty Job, But Somebody's Gotta Do It," *Los Angeles Times,* 2003.

Linda Diebel, "Teeming City Dies of Thirst," *Toronto Star,* May 9, 1999.

Sam Dillon, "Capital's Downfall Caused by Drinking ... of Water," *New York Times,* January 29, 1998.

Damian Fraser, "Stemming the Flow of Costs-Mexico City's New Water System Will Be One of the World's Most Modern," *Financial Times,* April 20, 1993.

Jan McGirk, "Mexico's Metro Keeps Women Safe from Roving Hands," *The Independent,* July 22, 2000.

Richard Meislin, "Tips for the Sophisticated Traveler: Notes from the Underground; Complete with Aztec Pyramid," *New York Times,* October 6, 1985.

"Mexico City Subway Job Runs Afoul of Antiquities," *Engineering News-Record,* January 12, 1984.

Molly Moore, "Refurbishing Spiritual Heart; Sinking Cathedral, Plaza Being Shored Up, Restored," *Washington Post,* August 27, 1998.

_____. "'Virgin of the Metro' Draws Faithful Underground; Crowds Flock to See Apparition in Mexico City Subway Station Despite Church Disclaimer," *Washington Post,* June 9, 1997.

Hugh O'Shaughnessy, "Designed by the French, Ridden by Mexicans; Mexico City's

Underground Is a Mix of Paris Design, High-Tech and the Country's Past and Present," *The Independent,* June 27, 1998.

Tod Robberson, "No Bounce in Mexican Rebound; Hard Times Fill Sewer Pipes with Children," *Washington Post,* May 22, 1995.

Danny Schechter, "Resurrecting the Cathedral; An Ambitious Project is Finally Reversing the Age-Old Problem of Uneven Sinking," *Business Mexico,* May 1997.

Danny Schiller, "Mexico City Subway Has Stops on Information Superhighway: Internet Cafés Booming There," *San Antonio Express-News,* October 19, 2002.

William Stockton, "A Subway Jolt for the Mexicans: The Three-Cent Fare," *New York Times,* August 1, 1986.

"Thin Walls Protect Subway Tunnels," *Engineering News-Record,* September 4, 1986.

Joe Tuckman, "How Do They Do It? Tube Systems That Work: Mexico City," *The Guardian,* August 22, 2001.

Tim Weiner, "It's a First-Class Gridlock, but No Easier to Unlock," *New York Times,* May 20, 2002.

_____. "Watchful Eyes on a Violent Giant," *New York Times,* January 2, 2001.

Michael Zamba, "Mexico's 'El Metro' More than a Subway," *Toronto Star,* January 16, 1988.

## WEB SITES

Ecologica-Agua, http://www.planeta.com/ecotravel/mexico/ecologia/97/0897agua.html.

Mexico City, Encyclopaedia Britannica, http://www.britannica.com/eb/article?eu=115539.

Mexico City's Water Supply, Improving the Outlook for Sustainability, http://lanic.utexas.edu/la/Mexico/water/ch3.html.

BTM, Sourcenotes, Mexico City, DE 9/22/05

# PARIS

## INTERVIEWS

Dominique Blanchecote (former official, RTPA [Régie Autonome des Transports Parisiens, which runs the Paris Metro or subway]).

Alan Cayre (supervisor of Météor line of Paris Métro), interview with the author, December 2002,.

Terrence Curry Loeb fellow, Harvard Design School, New York).

Greg Dreicer (Loeb fellow, Harvard Design School).

Tom Fox (Loeb fellow, Harvard Design School).

Glenn Garrison (Loeb fellow, Harvard Design School).

Peggy King (Loeb fellow, Harvard Design School).

Carol Lamberg (Loeb fellow, Harvard Design School, New York).

Clive Lamming (author of "Métro Isolite").

Bert McClure (director of Masters Program Planning and Urban Development of L'École Nationale des Ponts and Chausées, Paris).

Dr. Robert Paaswell (director of the University Transportation Research Center, and director of the CUNY Institute of Urban Systems).

Fei Tsen (Loeb fellow, Harvard Design School).

Tom Wright (executive director, Regional Plan Association).

Sally Young (coordinator, Loeb fellowship, Harvard Design School).

## BOOKS

Armand Bindi and Daniel Lefeuvre, *Paris: Histoire d'Hier à Demain* (Paris: Editions Ouest-France, 1990).

*Catacombs: General Guide,* English language edition. (Paris: Musées de la Ville de Paris).

Alain Clement, *Atlas du Paris Souterrain,* (Éditeur, 2001). This enormous volume is an encyclopedia, or "atlas," of everything underneath Paris, with marvelous photos and text.

Patrice Higgonnet; Arthur Goldhammer, trans.. *Paris: Capital of the World.* (Cambridge: Belknap Press, 2002).

Victor Hugo, *Les Misérables* (Signet reissue March 1987).

David P. Jordan, *Transforming Paris: The Life and Labors of Baron Haussmann.* (The Free Press, 1995).

Donald Reid, *Paris Sewers and Sewermen,* (Cambridge: Harvard University Press, reprint March 1993).

## NEWSPAPERS AND MAGAZINES

Paul Betts, "Metro Masterminds Export Drive," *Financial Times,* July 2, 1985.

*The Boston Globe,* January 12, 2001

Charles Bremner, "Paris is Sinking," *The Times* (London), January 6, 2001.

Ted Gup, *Smithsonian Magazine,* April 1, 2000.

Joanne Jacobs, *San Diego Union*-Tribune, May 26, 2002.

Stuart Jeffries, "London versus Paris," *The Guardian,* March 8, 2001.

Christopher Ketcham, "Spelunking the Empire of Death," *Salon,* June 19, 2002.

Lyn Kidder, Travel Section, *Toronto Star,* November 30, 2002.

Andrew Martin, *The Evening Standard,* April 9, 2001.

Mary E. Medland, "Sewers," *Pittsburgh Post-Gazette,* February 4, 2001.

"The Météor and the Métro," *Building Design Magazine,* September 3, 1999.

Paul Michaud, "International Construction," October 2001.

Claire Rosemberg, "Design of Métro," Agence France Presse, December 3, 2002.

Helen Rumbelow, *The Times* (London), April 20, 2001.


## WEB SITES

French National Library, http://www.bnf.fr/.

"Hector Guimard," Great Buildings Online,
    http://www.greatbuildings.com/architects/Hector_Guimard.html

Infiltration, http://www.infiltration.org/resources-france.html.

Paris, Encyclopædia Britannica, http://www.britannica.com/eb/article?tocId=9108530.

"Paris: Urban Sanitation before the 20th Century," Frederique Krupa's Design History
    and Criticism Papers, http://www.translucency.com/frede/parisproject/.

David Pirmann, "A Railfan's Guide to Paris," http://world.nycsubway.org/eu/fr/paris/.

## VISITS TO PHYSICAL SITES IN PARIS, IN DECEMBER 2002

Catacombs

La Défense business district

Les Égouts (sewer tour)

French National Library (subterranean portions)

Le Métro

Musée Carnavalet

Museum of the History of Paris

# ROME

## INTERVIEWS

Paul Bennett (travel agent, Context Rome).

## BOOKS

Ivana Della Portella; photography by Mark E. Smith, *Subterranean Rome*. (Konemann, 2000).

## MAGAZINES AND NEWSPAPERS

The Associated Press, "New Subway Line Opens in Rome," December 8, 1990.

Richard Boudreaux, "Pilgrims Coming to Rome, Ready or Not; Italy: The City is Dazzling and Chaotic as it Readies for the Start of the Holy Year," *Los Angeles Times*, December 22, 1999.

Roger Boyes, "Roman Rodent Holds the City to Eternal Ransom," *The Times*, July 4, 1987.

David Briginshaw, "Rome is Ready to Carry Millennium Pilgrims," *International Railway Journal*, December 1, 1999.

Elvira Cordileone, "The Roman Way," *Toronto Star*, July 21, 2001.

John Hooper, "Inside Il Duce's War Hideaway," *The Guardian*, January 3, 1998.

Louis Inturrisi, "An Eternal Search in Rome," *New York Times*, June 7, 1987.

Bruce Johnstone, "Escape Tunnel Found Beneath Mussolini's Palace," *Daily Telegraph*, May 31, 2002.

Peter Jones, "The Candour that Was Rome," *The Australian*, December 19, 2001.

Pietro Lunardi and Alessandro Focaracci, "Design and Construction of a Station on the Rome Metro," *Tunnels & Tunneling International*, March 1998.

Charles B. McClendon. The History of the Site of St. Peter's Basilica, Rome, *Perspecta* 25, 1989.

Paul Montgomery, "Italian Catacomb Reveals Ancient Jewish Site," *New York Times*, July 26, 1981.

Tom Mueller, "Underground Rome," *Atlantic Monthly*, April 1997.

Natalie Pompilio, "Tales from the Crypt: For New Orleanians Who Love Their Cemeteries,

Italy Is a Haven of Ghostly Catacombs, Caves and Cemeteries with Cool, Creepy, Fascinating Stories to Tell," *Times-Picayune,* June 4, 2000.

Peter Reina, "Italians Try Home-Grown Tunneling Method for Rail Line," *Engineering News-Record,* November 22, 1999.

Alessandra Stanley, "'God's Parking Low' Is in Conflict with Rome's Ancient Past," *New York Times,* December 3, 1999.

William Weaver, "The City Beneath Rome," *New York Times*, October 6, 1985.

Sofka Zinovieff, "Dolce Morte: It's What Romans Die For," *Financial Times*, August 5, 2000.

## WEB SITES

Cloaca Maxima, http://www.ku.edu/history/index/europe/ancient_rome/E/Gazetteer/
Places/Europe/Italy/Lazio/
Roma/Rome/Texts/PLATOP*/Cloaca_Maxima.html

Hidden History of Rome, The Discovery Channel,
http://www.discoverychannel.co.uk/hiddenhistoryofrome/feature2.shtml

Roman Subway, http://www.metropla.net/eu/rom/roma.htm

# LONDON

## INTERVIEWS

Robert Paaswell (director, City University of New York Institute for Urban Studies).

William Parkes (Transport for London), interview with the author,

Lucy Pringle (curator, Museum of London), interview with the author.

Hugh Robertson (curator, London's Transport Museum), interview with the author.

Jeffrey Zupan (Senior Fellow for Transportation, Regional Plan Association, New York City), interview with the author.

## BOOKS

Peter Ackroyd, *London, The Biography* (New York: Doubleday, 2001).

Felix Barker and Peter Jackson, *London: 2000 Years of a City and Its People* (New York: Macmillan Publishing, 1974).

Malcolm Billings, *London: A Companion to Its History and Archaeology* (London: Kyle Cathie Limited, 1994). A good section on the old Roman quays.

John Day, *The Story of London's Underground* (Middlesex: Capitol Transport, 1963).

Ken Garland, *Mr. Beck's Underground Map* (Capital Transport, 1994). All about the development of Henry Beck's famous map of the London Underground.

Stephen Halliday, *Underground to Everywhere: London's Underground Railway in the Life of the Capital* (London: Sutton Publishing, 2001). A critical look at what the author considers the severe decline of the London Underground in the late twentieth century, as well as discussion of the system's beginnings and history.

Charles Harper, *Queer Things about London* (London: Cecil Palmer, 1923).

_____. *More Queer Things about London* (Philadelphia: J.B. Lippencott, 1924).

Maxwell Hutchinson, Underground to Everywhere (2001).

Robert Kahn, ed., *City Secrets: London* (New York: The Little Bookroom, 2001).

*The New York Subway: Interborough Rapid Transit 1904* (New York: Fordham University Press, 1991).

Graham Norton, *London before the Blitz: 1906-1940* (London: Macdonald & Co., 1970).

Steen Eiler Rasmussen, *London: The Unique City* (Boston: MIT Press, 1934). A scholarly analysis of London as a "scattered" city.

Sheila Taylor, ed., *The Moving Metropolis: A History of London's Transport Since 1880* (London: Laurence King, 2001).

Richard Trench, *London under London: A Subterranean Guide* (1993). An entertaining guide to what is underneath London and the major events there over history.

J. C. Wylie, *The Wastes of Civilization.*

## Magazines and Newspapers

Chris Arnot, "Bunker Mentality: Nuclear Shelters are Rarely Comfortable and Never Pleasing to the Eye. So Why Are These Relics of the Cold War Enjoying a Peace-Time Boom?," *Daily Telegraph,* March 17, 2001.

Ruth Bloomfield, "Mayor or Nightmare?" *Time Out,* January 2, 2002.

Andrew John Davies, "Down to a Sunless Sea: Beneath Your Feet Lies Another London: A Strange Mix of Ancient Bones, Forgotten Passages, and Busy Modern Services," *The Independent,* September 26, 1994.

Stephen Glaister, "Rocky Road to a Smoother Journey; Londoners Want Better Quality and Cheaper Public Transport. With Limited Cash and Powers, Will the Mayor Be Able to Deliver?," *New Statesman,* April 10, 2000.

Philip Howard, "London Is Awash with Underground Romance Yet We Blindly Pass It By," *The Times,* February 21, 2003.

Mark Irving, "Open Space: The Real London Underground," *The Guardian,* October 23, 1998.

Angela Jameson, "Painful Progress of Public Private Partnerships," *The Times*, May 2, 2002.

Jill Lawless, "Going Under," *Courier Mail*, August 26, 2000.

"London Subway Work to Begin," *Engineering News-Record*, May 14, 2001.

Donald Macintyre, "The Voters Expect Their Trains to Run on Time," *The Independent*, December 11, 2001.

Nick Nuttall, "Boring Plan to Stop London Flooding," *The Times*, March 11, 1999.

"Observer Life Pages," *The Observer*, November 7, 1999.

Morag Reavley, "The Echoes Beneath Our Feet: From Ghost Tube Stations to Wartime Bunkers, Subterranean Britain Is a Warren of Man-Made Tunnels," *Sunday Telegraph*, January 19, 2003.

Byron Rogers, "Real Lives: The Burrowers," *The Guardian*, September 25, 1993.

Andrew Smith, "Tubeway Armies," The Observer, November 7, 1999.

Dougal Stenson, "Lives on the Line; Down the Tube: The Battle for London's Underground," *New Statesman*, March 3, 2003.

Deyan Sudjic, "Sold Down the River," *The Observer*, May 18, 2003.

Paul Waugh, "Money Down the Tube? London's Big Journey into the Unknown," *The Independent*, February 5, 2003.

Ben Willmott, "All Change for Staff with Tube PPP Deal," *Personnel Today*, January 14, 2003.

## WEB SITES

British Library, Encyclopaedia Britannica,

Cabinet War Rooms, http://www.iwm.org.uk/cabinet.htm.

The Great Stink, The Crossness Pumping Station, http://www.crossness.org.uk/sites/20020715PJK/wc.htm.

London Metropolitan Area Population, Demographia, http://www.demographia.com/dm lonarea.htm.

London, Encyclopaedia Britannica, http://www.britannica.com/eb/article?tocId=9016525, http://www.britannica.com/eb/article?tocId=10106.

London Transport Museum, http://www.ltmuseum.co.uk.

Museum of London, Encyclopaedia Britannica, http://www.britannica.com/eb/article?tocId=9105691.

Subterranean Britannica, http://www.subbrit.org.uk. This is a great Web site that looks into the entire country's "man made and man used" underground spaces, including London's.

Thames Water Ring, London Railways, http://www.londonrailways.net/water.htm.

# Moscow

## Interviews

Douglas Birch (Moscow correspondent), *Baltimore Sun.* May 25, 2003.
Liam Pleven (Moscow correspondent), *Newsday,* May 23, 2003.
Vadim Mikhailov (head of Moscow Diggers), May 2003.


## Magazines and Newspapers

Nabi Abdullaev, "Chechen Convicted in Okhotny Ryad Plot," *Moscow Times,* January 18. 2005.

Erin Arvedlund, "Fear Me, Giant Sewer Rodents, for I Am VADIM, Lord of the Underground!," *Outside Magazine,* September 1997.

Denis Baranov, "Moscow's Secret Metro Takes the Party Line," *The Guardian,* Feburary 7, 1996.

Richard Beeston, "Blind Man Has Key to Tsar's Secret Library," *The Times* [London], September 17, 1997.

Douglas Birch, "A Return of the People's Palace Subway: Moscow's Newest Station Recalls the Lavish Designs of Those Built During the Height of Soviet Power," *Baltimore Sun,* May 11, 2003.

Malcolm Browne, "Tunnel Drilling, Old as Babylon, Now Becomes Safer," *New York Times,* December 2, 1990.

Matthew Campbell, "Exposed," *Sunday Times* [London], September 27, 1992. Information about Moscow's secret subway system and other underground relics of the cold war.

_____. "Underground City May Hide Moscow Rebels," *Sunday Times* [London], October 24, 1993.

Clara Germani, "Urban Explorer Digs Underground Moscow," *Chicago Sun-Times,* May 18, 1997. Profile of Vadim Mikhailov, head of the Moscow Diggers.

Fred Hiatt, "Commerce Goes Underground in Moscow: State Rents Out Vast Bomb Shelter System as Fitness Centers, Car Dealerships, Shops," *Washington Post,* November 27, 1992.

"Iconostasis in Archangel Cathedral," Novosti Press Agency.

Andrei Ilnitsky, "Mysteries Under Moscow: The Diggers of the Underground Planet Find Squatters and Corpses as They God Deeper and Deeper into the Labyrinth under the Capital," *Ottawa Citizen,* May 25, 1997. Another profile of Vadim Mikhailov.

Denis Maternovsky, "Paveletskaya Gets $200M Mall," *Moscow Times,* January 25, 2005.

Judith Matloff, "On These Russian Picnics: Take a Flashlight," *Christian Science Monitor,* August 4, 1999.

Peter Reina, "German Boring Machine Digging in Smoother Russian Soils," *Engineering News-Record,* January 13, 2003.

Gabriel Ronay, "Russia's Tunnel Vision in Hunt for Ivan the Terrible's Library," *The Scotsman,* January 18, 1998.

Carey Scott, "Kremlin Refurbishes Nuclear Bunkers as Fear of NATO Grows," *Sunday Times* (London), April 13, 1997.

Ian Traynor, "How Do They Do It?—Moscow," *The Guardian,* August 22, 2001.

Nick Paton Walsh, "CIA Kremlin Bug 'Saved Gorbachev,'" *The Observer,* October 13, 2002.

Olivia Ward, "Plumbing Moscow's Depths: Underground Visionary Wants to Turn City's Legend-Clogged Bowels into a Tourist Adventure," *Toronto Star,* October 11, 1994.

## WEB SITES

The Cathedral of Christ the Savior, Moscow-Taxi.com, http://www.moscow taxi.com/sightseeing/savior.html.

History of Moscow, Moscow-Guide, http://www.moscow-guide.ru/general/history.htm.

Moscow, Encyclopaedia Britannica, http://www.britannica.com/eb/article?eu=115590.

Moscow Subway of Which All Russians Are Proud, Narod.ru, http://www.vorontsova.narod.ru/metro.html.

Park Pobedy, Moscow Metropolitan, http://www.metropoliten.newmail.ru/mtt0603.html.

# CAIRO

## INTERVIEWS

Al Appleton (Senior Fellow at Regional Plan Association, and former commissioner of the Department for Environmental Protection of New York City), interview with the author, March 2003.

Arnd Bruninhaus (Loeb Fellow, Harvard University Graduate School of Design), interview with the author,.

Ezz El Din Fahmy (Consultant, EHAF Consulting Engineers, Cairo), interview with the author, February 3, 2003.

Abdel Halim (architect, Community Design Collaborative,Cairo), interview with the author.

Mona Serageldin (adjunct professor, Harvard University Graduate School of Design, Cambridge), interview with the author, February 18, 2003.

Dr. Maher Stino (a designer of Al Azhar Park, Cairo), interview with the author.

Norris Strawbridge (principal, Sasaki Associates in Watertown, MA), interview with the author, February 2003.

Anthony Tung (author, *Preserving the World's Great Cities*), interview with the author, March 2003.

Nicholas Warner (architect, Cairo), interview with the author, February 2003.

## BOOKS

Anthony Tung, *Preserving the World's Great Cities* (Clarkson Potter, 2002).

*Historic Cities Support Program: The Azhar Park Project in Cairo and the Conservation and Revitalization of Darb Al-Ahmar* (Geneva: Aga Khan Trust for Culture).

## MAGAZINES AND NEWSPAPERS

Robin Allen, "Land Development: Dramatic Gamble with Nature," *Financial Times,* May 13, 1997.

Marda Burton, "The Two Faces of Egypt," *Toronto Star,* December 19, 1987.

"Cairo Pins Hopes on New Subway; Metro: There's a Feeling Among Some Egyptians that If the Subway System Can't Relieve This City's Choking Congestion, Nothing Can," *Baltimore Sun,* January 22, 1999.

Alan Cowell, "Cairo Journal: People Not Ready to Ride in a Hole in the Ground," *New York Times,* November 12, 1987.

John Daniszewski, "Cairo Tries to Reclaim Lost Treasure amid City's Trash," *Los Angeles Times,* July 10, 1998.

"Egypt's Growing Environmental Problems," *Swiss Review of World Affairs,* November 3, 1997.

William Farrell, "For Cairo's Poorest, Home Is Where the Space Is," *New York Times,* June 1, 1982.

Sarah Gauch, "On Egypt's Parched Lands, Farmers Await Their Bounty," *Chicago Tribune,* February 16, 1992.

"Good Progress on Line 2 of the Cairo Metro," *Tunnels & Tunneling International,* July 1997.

Larry Kaplow, "Peace Train-Cairo Residents Escape Traffic Chaos on Subway," *Milwaukee Journal Sentinel,* October 10, 1999.

Herb Lass, "Sewage Threatens Survival of the Sphinx, Experts Say," *Engineering News-Record,* April 20, 1989.

Judith Miller, "Scientists Seek 4,600-Year-Old Air at Egyptian Boat Site," *New York Times,* October 8, 1985.

Susanna Mylly, "Cairo-A Mega-City and Its Water Resources," The Third Nordic Conference on Middle Eastern Studies, Joensuu, Finland, 19-22 June 1995.

Dana Priest and Barton Gellman, "U.S. Decries Abuse but Defends Interrogations 'Stress and Duress' Tactics Used on Terrorism Suspects Held in Secret Overseas Facilities," *Washington Post,* December 26, 2002.

Reuters, "Tomb Found in Cairo Dates Back 2,500 Years," *Chicago Tribune,* November 19, 2001.

Max Rodenbeck, "Chaotic Quilt of Contrasts: The Modern Metropolis," *Financial Times,* May 11, 1999.

Storer H. Rowley, "Humans Do What Time Hasn't: Imperil the Great Pyramids," *Chicago Tribune,* April 20, 1997.

Yigal Schleifer, "Public Concern Increases as Egypt's Environmental Problems Grow," *Jerusalem Post,* June 5, 1992.

Tony Walker, "Contractors Dig Way to Better Days for Cairo," *Financial Times,* November 18, 1986.

Tony Walker, "Egypt Could Tap Desert Water," *Financial Times,* June 16, 1992.

James Whittington, "Trains Move Smoothly Under Cairo Crowds: From Pyramids to Slums, the Arab World's First Metro Serves a Growing City," *Financial Times,* August 1, 1995.

Deborah Wise, "Finance and Economics: Digging Out a Cure for Gippy Tummy-How British Companies Hope That Clean Streets in Cairo Will Lead to Contracts for Building New Sewers in Kuwait," *The Guardian,* April 6, 1991.

## WEB SITES

Egypt, National Trade Data Bank, U.S. Department of Commerce, http://www.stat usa.gov.

Sadat City, http://www.scia.org.eg/index_flash.htm

USAID Sewer Project Brings Ancient Temple into Focus, U.S. Agency for International Development, http://www.usaid-eg.org/detail.asp?id=252

## VISITS TO PHYSICAL SITES IN CAIRO, FEBRUARY 2003

Al Azhar Park

Al-Qahira

Cairo Metro
The Egyptian Museum
The ruins of Fort Babylon around the Coptic Hanging Church
Tahrir Square

# TOKYO

## INTERVIEWS

Robert Fishman (professor of architecture and urban planning, Taubman College of Architecture and Urban Planning, The University of Michigan at Ann Arbor), interview with the author, May 11, 2002.

## BOOKS

Gideon S. Golany, ed., *Japanese Urban Environment* (New York: Pergamon Publishing, 1998).

Edward Seidensticker, *Low City, High City: Tokyo from Edo to the Earthquake.*

William Wheaton, MIT/CRE Newsletter (Boston: MIT Press, 2001).

## MAGAZINES AND NEWSPAPERS

"17th-Century Papers to be Named Treasures," *Daily Yomiuri,* April 22, 2001.

Elizabeth Andoh, "Travel Advisory: 12th Tokyo Subway Line Loops around City," *New York Times,* March 11, 2001.

Masaharu Asaba, "Burying Ugly Cables Requires Digging Up Massive Funding," *Daily Yomiuri,* May 6, 2001.

James Brooke, "Japan Slows Down, but Not Its Road Builders," *New York Times,* January 18, 2002.

Bobby Cuzo, "Security below the Streets," *Newsday,* October 9, 2001.

Roban Cybriwisky, "Shibuya Center, Tokyo." *Geographical Review,* 78 (1), January 1988.

Tracy Dahlby, "Japan 'Molemen' Dig under Waves to Finish World's Longest Tunnel," *Washington Post,* May 16, 1983.

"Developers Blame Restrictive Controls for Poor Housing," *Nihon Keizai Shimbun,* March 7, 1987.

Martin Fackler, "Down the Wrong Tunnel; Building of Tokyo's New Subway Line Is

Years Behind Schedule and Plagued by Billions of Dollars in Cost Overruns," *Hamilton Spectator* (Associated Press), July 26, 1999.

_____. "Japanese Subway Going off Track," *Toronto Star,* July 20, 1999.

_____. "Underground," *Associated Press Worldstream,* July 6, 1998.

Howard French, "Tokyo Journal: The City Isn't Quaking, but Maybe It Should Be," *The New York Times,* October 30, 2000.

Clyde Haberman, "Down in the Subway, It's (Oof!) a Different Japan," *New York Times,* January 22, 1984.

Peter Hadfield, "Rising Water Spells Trouble for Tokyo's Trains," *New Scientist,* March 25, 2000.

Shogo Hagiwara, "Is There A Cure for Tokyo's 'Commuting Hell?'" *Daily Yomiuri,* December 5, 2000.

Susan Hanley, "Urban Sanitation in Pre-War Japan," *Journal of Interdisciplinary History,* 1987. This article was a principal source for how Tokyo (Edo) operated in the 1800s and earlier with a large urban population but without sewers.

"Heavy Trucks Crack Highways," *Daily Yomiuri,* April 28, 2002.

Kakuya Ishida, "Project Aims to Save Rainwater, Money," *Yomiuri Shimbun,* November 23, 1999.

Tim Jackson, "Why Tatsuo Tomioka Can Be Proud of his Station," *The Independent,* January 23, 1991.

Atsuko Kinoshita, "Domestic Train Firms Say Cars Safe," *Yomiuri Shimbun,* February 20, 2003.

Dennis Lim, "Realm of the Senseless," *Village Voice,* June 12, 2001.

Mark Magnier, "Joy-Riding Tokyo's Cattle Cars," *Journal of Commerce,* June 16, 1993.

Hiroshi Masumitsu, "Rising Underground Water Levels Put Urban Areas under Strain," *Yomiuri Shimbun,* February 8, 2000.

Michael Millett, "Trains Brightened Up in Effort to Stem Suicides," *Sydney Morning Herald,* May 11, 2000.

"Ministry, Tokyo Government Agree on Deep Subterranean Expressway," *Kyodo News International,* March 17, 2003.

Colin Nickerson, "Geology: Tokyo—City Sitting on a Time Bomb," *Boston Globe,* November 14, 1988.

Dennis Normile, "Bullet Train Adopts Duck Bill," *Design News,* October 18, 1999.

Toshio Ojima, "Tokyo's Infrastructure, Present and Future," *Japanese Urban Environment.*

Mike Page, "Dial Japan for Exotic TBMs," *Tunnels & Tunneling International,* April 1998.

"Panel Advocates Underground Pipes to Cool City," *Yomiuri Shimbun,* June 28, 2002.

Andrew Pollack, "Japan Questions Its Costly Program to Predict Earthquakes," *New York Times,* January 13, 1998.

"Problem: Sweltering Tokyo; Proposal: Pump in Seawater," *Straits Times,* August 13, 2002.

"Rains Expose WWII Dugouts," *Daily Yomiuri*, August 27, 1999.

George Rosenblatt, "Taming Tokyo: Planning, Patience Keys to Mastering City of 12 Million," *Houston Chronicle*, September 29, 1991.

Christopher Sanford, "On The Verge of Subway Tourist Flip-Out in Tokyo," *Seattle Times*, January 19, 2003.

Margaret Shapiro, "Japan Tunnels to a Cherished Goal; Undersea Rail Link between Honshu, Hokkaido Opens Sunday," *Washington Post*, March 12, 1988.

"Shinkansen Tunnels to be Phone-Friendly," *Daily Yomiuri*, May 8, 1999.

Kevin Short, "Walking Reveals Tokyo's Topography," *Yomiuri Shimbun*, December 7, 1999.

Miki Tanikawa, "The Underground Delights of Japan," *International Herald Tribune*, February 7, 2003.

"Tokai Floods Send Wake-Up Call to Tokyo," *Yomiuri Shimbun*, September 16, 2000.

"Tokyo Bay Link," *Tunnels & Tunneling International*, April 1998.

"Tokyo to Kick-Start Stalled Roadwork Plan: 'MacArthur-doro' to Link Shimbashi, Toranomon Areas," *Daily Yomiuri*, August 15, 2002.

Tokyo Metropolitan Subway Construction Corporation and Kumagai Gumi Co. Ltd., "Triple Face Slurry Shield for Tokyo Metro Stations," *Tunnels & Tunneling International*, July 1998.

Andrew Veitch, "Futures (A Week in Japan): Drill of a Lifetime/Focus on the Seikan Tunnel," *The Guardian*, March 7, 1986.

Jonathan Watts, "Capital Letters: Japanese Flirt with Disaster Waiting for the Big One to Bite," *The Guardian*, November 30, 2002.

_____. "How Do They Do It? Tokyo," *The Guardian*, August 22, 2001.

Kotaro Yazawa, "Historical Sewage System Shows Light at the End of Red-Brick Tunnel," *Daily Yomiuri*, June 23, 2001.

Hiroyuki Yokota, "Hydro Dam Powers Yamanote Line—But at What Cost?" *Daily Yomiuri*, November 18. 2001.

Frank Zeller, "Subway a Mecca for Weird and Wonderful," *Sun Herald*, December 13, 1998.

## Web sites

International Council of Shopping Centers, http://www.icsc.org.

Professor Peter Rowe (former dean of the Harvard Design School), "Tokyo—Inner-City Revitalization," http://www.gsd.harvard.edu/people/faculty/rowe/studios.html#tokyo.

Urban Underground Space Center of Japan, http://www.toshimirai.or.jp/usj/english/mid.html.

# Beijing

## Interviews

Yan Huang (Deputy Director, Beijing Municipal Planning Commission), interview with the author, June 8, 2003.

## Magazines and Newspapers

BBC Monitoring International Reports, "Security Tightened in Beijing's 'Underground City,'" March 23, 2002.

Jasper Becker, "China's Tunnel Vision," *South China Morning Post Ltd,* July 7, 1995.

"Beijing Uses Foreign Funds to Build Burrow," *Beijing Review,* December 1, 1997.

Michael Browning, Knight-Ridder News Service, "Peking Seeks a Use for Mao's Tunnel Network," *Bergen Record,* November 23, 1986.

"Chinese Capital Keeps Sinking," *Malaysia General News,* January 8, 1999.

Henry Chu, "Chinese Treasures Locked Up in Bunker Mentality," *Los Angeles Times,* December 3, 2001.

_____. "Yellow River Giving China New Sorrow; Asia: Overuse, Dry Weather Depletes Waterway Once Known for Flooding," *Los Angeles Times,* February 18, 1999.

Michael Grunwald, "Getting Beyond Beijing's Creepiness," *Boston Globe,* October 26, 1997.

Andrew Lee, "Hidden History Is Unearthed," *Daily Post* (Liverpool), November 30, 2002.

"Mao's Defence Legacy a Commercial Liability," *South China Morning Post,* November 21, 1998.

Damien McElroy, "China's Booming Underworld," *Scotland on Sunday,* March 25, 2001.

Mike Meyer, "Going Underground in Beijing; The Capital's History Is Uncovered in Subterranean Tunnels and Old Districts," *Los Angeles Times,* January 6, 2002.

Marguerite Oliver, "Exploring Beijing's Underground Tunnel Maze," *Los Angeles Times,* February 8, 1987.

Andrew Quinn, "BC-CPE-Travel-Underground," The Canadian Press (CP) February 14, 1992.

Andy Roche, Reuters News Service, "China's Underground Nightclubs and Shops Are Booming," *Toronto Star, January 11, 1987.*

*John Schauble, "In Perilous Times, Beijing Digs Deep," The Age (Melbourne) March 23, 2002. Provided facts on Xicheng District underground areas.*

*Uli Schmetzer, "Underground City Built in Fear of War Now Gives Chinese Room to Work, Play," Chicago Tribune, May 12, 1991.*

Craig S. Smith, "Beijing Journal; Mao's Buried Past: A Strange, Subterranean City," *New York Times*, November 26, 2001.

United Press International, "If You're in Peking and Can't Find a Hotel Room, Look under the Ground," October 18, 1984.

The Xinhua General Overseas News Service, "Beijing's Tunnels Becoming Underground City," October 18, 1984.

_____. "Beijing Makes Use of Geothermal," June 21, 1984

_____. "Underground Hot Water Being Tapped in Beijing," May 24, 1980.

_____. "Underground Buildings under Construction in Peking," November 25, 1978.

# SYDNEY

## INTERVIEWS

Robert Mitchell (chief operating officer, Warren Centre for Advanced Engineering, University of Sydney), interview with the author, June 2003.

Martin Wachs (author of Sustainable Transport Plan for Sydney; visiting fellow, Warren Centre for Advanced Engineering, University of Sydney), interview with the author, June 2003.

## BOOKS

Brian and Barbara Kennedy, *Sydney Tunnels* (Kenhurst: Kangaroo Press, 1993). A short, colorful book about Sydney's tradition of tunneling.

## MAGAZINES AND NEWSPAPERS

Keith Austin, "Convenience Stories," *Sydney Morning Herald*, April 24, 1999.

Keith Austin, "Lost in Spaces," *Sydney Morning Herald*, August 19, 2000.

James Cockington, "Walking the Rails," *Sydney Morning Herald*, April 27, 2002.

Peter Downey, "A Down-to-Earth Idea," *Sydney Morning Herald*, March 27, 2000.

Jaedene Hudson, "Link to Calm the Savage Commuter," *Daily Telegraph*, November 26, 2002.

Nicole Manktelow, "The Bane of Our Streets Could Face Extinction," *The Age*, July 30, 2002.

Charles Miranda, "Harbour Bridge's Secrets Revealed," *Daily Telegraph*, July 5, 2001.

Geraldine O'Brien, "Going to Ground," *Sydney Morning Herald*, November 21, 2001.

Walter Sullivan, "City of Tunnels," *Daily Telegraph*, March 18, 1998.

Jane Burton Taylor, "Urban Space Shortage Forces Planners Underground," *Weekend Australian*, August 31, 1996.

Chris Tinkler, "Melbourne Could Be Sitting on a Network of Military Tunnels," *Sydney Morning Herald*, November 3, 2002.


## WEB SITES

Cross City Tunnel, Roads and Traffic Authority, http://www.rta.nsw.gov.au/construc tionmaintenance/majorconstructionprojectssydney/crosscitytunnel/.

Interview with Robert Hughes, Public Broadcasting Service, http://www.pbs.org/wnet/ australia/qa.html.

New South Wales, Encyclopaedia Britannica, http://www.britannica.com/eb/article?eu= 119627.

Sydney, Encyclopaedia Britannica, http://www.britannica.com:80/eb/article?eu= 115272.

Sydney Subways, Wikipedia, http://en.wikipedia.org/wiki/Sydney_subways.

# PHOTOGRAPH CREDITS

## INTRODUCTION

Bob Sacha / IPN / Aurora Photos

## NEW YORK

p. 14    © David Ball  / Alamy

p. 22    Library of Congress

p. 25    The Granger Collection, NY

p. 27    Copyright © American Map Corporation 1948.  All rights reserved. Reprinted with permission of American Map Corporation.

p. 29    The Granger Collection, NY

p. 30    Courtesy of Con Edison, NY

p. 33    AP Photo/U.S. Coast Guard, P.O. Thomas Sperduto

## CHICAGO

p. 34    © Robert Llewellyn / Imagestate

p. 39    Courtesy Army Corps of Engineers

p. 40    Library of Congress

p. 42    Chicago History Museum

p. 46    The Granger Collection, NY

p. 49    Deep Thoughts (Al Podgorski) © Chicago Sun-Times, Inc.

## SAN FRANCISCO

p. 52    © GOODSHOOT / Alamy

p. 57    USGS

p. 58    Courtesy National Information Service for Earthquake Engineering, University of California, Berkeley

p. 61    USGS

p. 62    Courtesy National Information Service for Earthquake Engineering, University of California, Berkeley

## BEIJING

## SYDNEY

# INDEX